# Creative Activities for Group Therapy

Leading a group is a delicate balancing act of tasks and dynamic group and individual factors, and the group leader's expertise and skill are fundamental to maintaining this balance. However, no matter how competent and well-prepared the group leader is, there can be situations that present challenges that are not easily addressed, defy conventional interventions, or call for a different approach. The material presented in this book is intended to give group leaders evidence-based creative and inspirational tools, techniques, intervention strategies, and the like to address these dilemmas and difficult situations. They can also enhance members' growth and development, stimulate self-exploration, assist to soothe and calm, and deepen and broaden thoughts and feelings. The creative activities included were selected because they do not require specialized training, are easy to implement, do not follow a particular theoretical perspective, and can be effective for both the individual and group as a whole. The major categories of expressive processes presented are fairy tales; drawing; writing; imagery and mindfulness; music; movement, exercise, dance, drama, and role-play; and collage, flats, and scrapbooks. Each chapter will focus on one of these activities and is designed so that they can be completed in one session. The closing chapters will present applications for member's concerns, group level challenges, and case examples of group dilemmas and suggested activities to address them.

**Nina W. Brown**, EdD, LPC, FAGPA, is Professor and Eminent Scholar of Counseling at Old Dominion University. She is a Fellow of the American Group Psychotherapy Association and the author of 21 published books.

# Creative Activities for Group Therapy

NINA W. BROWN

NEW YORK AND LONDON

First published 2013
by Routledge
711 Third Avenue, New York, NY 10017

Simultaneously published in the UK
by Routledge
27 Church Road, Hove, East Sussex BN3 2FA

*Routledge is an imprint of the Taylor & Francis Group, an informa business*



*Library of Congress Cataloging in Publication Data*
Brown, Nina W.
Creative activities for group therapy / Nina W. Brown.
p. cm.
Includes bibliographical references and index.
ISBN 978-0-415-63375-8 (hardback : alk. paper) — ISBN 978-0-415-52706-4 (pbk. : alk. paper) 1. Group psychotherapy. 2. Group counseling. 3. Psychotherapist and patient. I. Title.
RC488.B738 2013
616.89'152--dc23
2012023107

ISBN: 978-0-415-63375-8 (hbk)
ISBN: 978-0-415-52706-4 (pbk)
ISBN: 978-0-203-11913-6 (ebk)

Typeset in Caslon and Copperplate
by EvS Communication Networx, Inc.

Printed and bound in the United States of America
by Edwards Brothers, Inc.

# Contents

# Preface

Ever looked for a creative activity that you could use with a group, but could not find one that met your needs and capabilities? What has frustrated me at times is that there was no resource that presented several types of creative activities so that I could choose among modalities. This lack meant that I had to locate several references which took time, and on many occasions this was not a fruitful search. This book is my response to that need and includes activities using writing, fairy tales, drawing, imagery music, mindfulness, movement such as dance and exercise, role-play, collage, and several other creative and expressive activities. All activities are described and directions provided that can be easily implemented.

The activities are based on the premises that everyone has some creativity and that group members can benefit from them. It is also believed that creative expressions carry real and important messages and insight for the creator; are a rich source of learning, understanding, growing, developing, and healing; and that some form of creative activities can be used in therapy groups. What follows is an evidence based presentation for group leaders who want to use creative activities as a stimulus in their adult or adolescent therapy groups, instructors teaching group leadership courses, and providers of education and training workshops. The activities are not used as well-trained practitioners such as art therapists would use them and it is recommended that these activities be used sparingly and judiciously to meet the needs of the group and its members.

My hope is that readers will find this book to be helpful in guiding them to effectively use the activities. I have used all of the modalities presented here and this hands-on experience has given me a better understanding of my groups' and members' needs, awareness, and self-understanding. I enjoy infusing appropriate creative activities into groups to illustrate concepts, reduce resistance, encourage expression of members' feelings, thoughts, and ideas; and sometimes just to have fun. It is very rewarding to see members gain confidence from expressing and understanding aspects of their selves and their lives, and when an activity helps them realize that possibilities and alternatives exist.

The 100+ activities were developed with the following in mind:

- A group leader may select one or more activities that fit the needs of a particular group and the capabilities of group members.
- The activities can be implemented without requiring the leader to have considerable specialized training in the modality, but it is recommended that some training, such as workshops, be completed before implementing some activities.
- The activities can be easily used by providing sufficient directions.
- The activities have the capability of being used within the time limit of a group session.

I enjoyed creating the book and activities, and hope that they will prove useful to you.

# Acknowledgments and Dedication

I am very appreciative of the many contributions others made to the development of this book. It would not have been possible without the knowledge and skills acquired through the many wonderful presentations at the American Group Psychotherapy Association's conferences, the Mid-Atlantic Group Psychotherapy Association's conferences, and the Society of Group Psychology and Group Psychotherapy (American Psychological Association's Division 49). All of these experiences enriched me and helped me understand the needs of group leaders and members. Finally, I want to thank Dana Bliss, the Senior Acquisitions Editor at Routledge.

This book is dedicated to my family: my husband Will; Toni, Mike, and Linda, my children; their spouses Chris and Jill; and to my grandchildren, Bill, Joe, Samantha, Christopher, Nick, and Emma.

# CHAPTER 1

# CREATIVE ACTIVITIES IN GROUP THERAPY

*Creative activities*
*Alternative paths to understanding*
*Inspiring, challenging, soothing, stimulating, exciting, expanding, enchanting, pleasurable*
*Communications from the internal self*
*New meanings*

This is a cinquain (see chapter 12) that I am using to expand the image for creative activities. It begins with a title, the second line describes what it is, the third line provides adjectives about it, the fourth line provides the relationship, and the last line renames it.

## Benefits and Advantages

Definitions for the term *creative* use words and phrases such as, *to bring into being*, *original*, *new*, and *novel* and this forms the basis for the activities described in this book. Creative activities are defined here as stimuli that can have the following effects and outcomes for both individual group members and for the group as a whole. These stimuli are taken from artistic, performance, and other such endeavors as well as the vast world of crafts. Effects and outcomes include:

- Inspiring and challenging the creator;
- Providing a focus for internal and external chaos, and screening out distractions;
- Distracting from unproductive worrying;
- Expressing complicated thoughts, feelings, and ideas;
- Clarifying perceptions of situations, people, and the like;
- Helping to bring the obvious into focus, and highlighting important aspects;
- A solace when confused, upset, or indecisive;
- Help sorting through complex and conflicting values;
- Can be centering and grounding;
- New meanings can emerge;
- Abstracting essentials from surrounding confusion, barrages;
- Simplifying complexity;
- Can address several levels and planes simultaneously;
- Providing new ways to perceive and relate;
- Reconnecting the parts of self to become balanced and rounded.

Creative activities tap both the internal and external experiencing when used in a group setting. The internal experiencing is made visible by means of the creative activity, and the external experiencing occurs with the communication about the product, what occurred for the person in the production phase, and in the reactions and feedback from other group members and the leader. This process can enhance growth and development, stimulate self-exploration as new awareness emerges, can assist creating an atmosphere of soothing and calm, and deepen and broaden thoughts and feelings. Both the individual members and the group as a whole can benefit from the use of creative activities.

## Address Group Situations

The benefits for the individual group members and for the functioning and progress of the group can be considerable. The group leader's expertise and skill are fundamental to maintaining a delicate balancing act of tasks that include dynamic group and individual factors. The group's goal is important as a guide, members' needs must be identified, and attempts must be made to meet some or all of them, the group as a whole must be attended to, and many other factors and tasks needed for success also play roles. The central and critical figure and component is the group leader, and his or her knowledge, skills, and level of personal development are vital to the members' growth, development, and healing.

However, no matter how competent and well prepared the group leader is, there can be group situations that present challenges that are not easily addressed, defy conventional interventions, and call for a different approach. This book was developed to present one such different approach, the use of creative activities applied to group dilemmas and personal situations. These activities are conceptualized as being nonthreatening means to access material that contributes to the dilemma or situation, express difficult feelings, and allow individual members to better understand their personal responses that are contributing to the dilemmas or situation.

This chapter covers a rationale for using creative activities, descriptions of the activities that are presented in the book, the background evidence for the efficacy of experiential learning, and an overview of the book chapters.

## Group Dilemmas and Situations

Experienced group leaders will have encountered many of the following group dilemmas and situations, and beginning group leaders can expect to encounter them.

- The group is stuck or mired in a situation where the discussion becomes circular, no problem solving or insight occurs, members are exasperated but cannot seem to change the pattern, and therapeutic work is not being accomplished.
- Conflict has emerged in the group and is being ignored, suppressed, or denied. Or, the members fear conflict so much that they will go to extraordinary means to keep it under wraps, and pretend that they are harmonious.
- The group seems over- or underenergized. When overly energized, they skip from topic to topic none of which adds to the work of the group; a lot of squirming and other nonverbal communication of discomfort occurs, but interventions do not seem to help them concentrate or focus. The underenergized group seems depressed or dead, but they resist exploration of their feelings.
- Many or even most group members either cannot or do not express their feelings, or they express them in inappropriate ways. Feelings are considered as dangerous and members avoid expressing them.
- Members exhibit resistance and defensiveness well beyond what is usually expected in the group. They are not making meaningful connections with each other, and are avoiding attempts to promote interactions and involvement.
- Members are extremely tentative and cautious in revealing their selves to the point where they do not disclose anything of importance. While safety and trust need to be established before meaningful connections and disclosures can appear, this wariness has continued to the point where the therapeutic work is thwarted.

Group leaders encountering these dilemmas and situations will intervene as best they can, given their understanding of the group and its needs. However, there are groups where the usual conventions do not work. The material presented in this book is intended to give group leaders other tools, techniques, intervention strategies, and the like not only to address dilemmas and situations, but also to present them with alternatives designed to stimulate exploration and expansion of members' understanding of their personal issues.

## A Rationale

It would be the rare group leader who has not encountered one or more group dilemmas where the group became mired, tense, and unproductive, little therapeutic work was accomplished, and this lasted more than one session. While frustrating for the group leader, these situations can be even more frustrating for group members who probably lack the developed inner resources for coping that the leader may have, all of which leads to a very uncomfortable group situation for all. Adding to the group leader's frustration is when all interventions she or he has tried do not move the group from the uncomfortable place. The leader's analysis does not seem to be effective to produce understanding or for suggested interventions, no matter how experienced or competent the leader is. While these group situations are few and far between, they can occur without warning.

These group dilemmas differ from those presented by a difficult group member. Brown (2006) and Alonso and Rutan (1993, 1996) describe some group dilemmas that can result from the presence of members with unidentified problems and concerns, such as the member with a narcissistic personality disorder or with a destructive narcissistic pattern, a member with a borderline condition, or a quiet but explosive member. They propose that the difficulties and dilemmas in these instances result from the group's effort to manage and contain these members, the members' unconscious sensing of danger and possible destruction for their selves, and their attempts to control their intense emotions that were unconsciously aroused by these members. The leader and members are working in the dark, but nothing constructive can happen until the difficult member is identified and appropriate actions are taken. These difficult group members present their own variations for group dilemmas, but this is not the subject of this book.

Suffice it to say that group leaders encountering these dilemmas look for ways to understand the indirect communication so as to select appropriate interventions. The group members do not have the ability to be clearer in communication because they don't know what it is they want to communicate, can be fearful of consequences for what may emerge, are trying to understand and communicate but are ineffective, and are frustrated at the lack of clarity and understanding from self, other members, and the leader.

This book proposes that the described creative activities can assist the group leader to address the group dilemmas, and provide relevant material for group members' self-exploration. These activities, although group centered and focused, can be personal for each member, bypass defenses, reveal unconscious and hidden material in ways that can be perceived by them as less threatening and dangerous, encourage expression of difficult or complex ideas, thoughts, and feelings, and even may provide guidance for some members in finding solutions to issues. At the very least, these creative activities can provide a release of tension so that group members can think more clearly, be more responsive, and be more willing to engage in self-exploration. Both the group and members can benefit.

## Principles of Experiential Learning

These principles are drawn from the concept of experiential learning proposed by Kurt Lewin (1944) whereby learning is enhanced through group participation. Three basic principles are used here: the contributions of the group environment, active participation, and group membership.

- The social and supportive environment provided by the group promotes intrapersonal and interpersonal learning. This environment encourages experimentation with

new ways of behaving and relating by providing safety and trust, can open new pathways of understanding one's self and others, constructive feedback can be given and received, and self-perceptions are more likely to be changed or become more open to change.
- Learning is facilitated by active participation. When group members are actively involved their different learning styles can be accommodated; the learner can choose to focus on what he or she considers to be personally important; more than one system can be tapped at one time, physical, cognitive, emotional, creative, inspirational; and difficult material can be more easily accepted when personally discovered, thereby reducing resistance and defensiveness.
- Accepting membership in the group encourages behavioral and attitudinal change. Acceptance is facilitated by presenting oneself in a nonthreatening way and receiving positive responses and feedback from other group members.

Additional fundamental assumptions are that the group activities foster the emergence of many group curative factors, promote self-disclosure and member interactions, offer opportunities for members to discover unknown or forgotten parts of the self, and that these can highlight important material for members' exploration. In addition, the activities can strengthen connections among group members, reduce resistance and defensiveness, and teach new ways of understanding, behaving, and relating.

### Theoretical Perspectives

The book does not follow a particular theoretical perspective, and the activities reflect an atheoretical approach. However, there are four main theories that guided the development and selection of the activities: behavioral, cognitive, dialectical behavioral therapy, and object-relations/self-psychology.

Guidance from behavioral therapy includes the use of imagery (Lazarus, 1989), behavioral rehearsal, progressive relaxation, and self-modification (Corey, 2009). The assumptions from behavioral therapy are that clients are expected to assume an active role and that insight is not necessary for behavioral changes; interventions are seen as best targeted to specific behaviors tailored for the individual.

Cognitive theories of Beck (1995), Ellis (1997), and Meichenbaum (1977) provide the perspective that many psychological difficulties stem from faulty or irrational thinking, incorrect inferences or misinformation, and an inability to distinguish between fantasy and reality. The activities in the book address cognitive distortions, such as catastrophizing, inferring the whole from a detail, overgeneralization, magnification and minimization, personalization, labeling and mislabeling, and dichotomous thinking.

Dialectical Behavioral Therapy (DBT; Linenhan, 1993) contributes the integration of mindfulness into therapy, existential factors, and strategies for emotional regulation and control. Although not used in a systematic way as in DBT, the activities capitalize on these strategies and adapt them for use in the group setting.

Object Relations and self-psychology theories contribute to the understanding of what can emerge during the creative activity as well as the outcomes. These theories are more geared to the group leader's understanding, and how to guide members' exploration and enhancement of their products.

Object Relations theories, such as those of Klein (1952), Mahler (1975), Mahler, Pine, and Bergman (1975), and Kernberg (1976), describe how psychological growth and development occur, emphasize the importance of early relationships, and describe how these can continue to affect and impact relationships throughout one's life. As is the case with many other theories, no unified OR theory exists.

Self-psychology incorporates many of the concepts of OR theories and emphasizes the importance of the development of the "self." Kohut (1977) describes psychological development with a focus on narcissism, or self-focus. He proposed that there is age-appropriate narcissism which removes it from always being considered as pathology, and proposes that infantile narcissism, when developed along expected lines, can become transformed into healthy adult narcissism characterized by wisdom, empathy, and an appropriate sense of humor.

## Creative Activities

This presentation is limited to a few creative activities selected from the many activities that are available. They were selected because the described uses do not require specialized training on the part of the group leader, they do not emphasize or focus on therapy. they are easy to implement, and are effective for the group as a whole because they involve the entire group while at the same time they speak of the individual member's personal situation or concern, and they can reveal nonconscious and unconscious material. The major categories of expressive processes presented are fairy tales; drawing; writing; imagery, mindfulness, and music; movement, exercise, dance, drama, simulation, and role-play; collage, flats, and scrapbook. These categories are briefly described with more extensive discussions and presentations provided in their focus chapters.

### *Fairy Tales*

Fairy tales (chapter 8) for adults are described in the literature as having the potential for a rich source of knowledge about the person's developmental lacks and existential concerns (Bettelheim, 1976; Dieckmann, 1997; Holton, 1995). These tales describe parts of a successful individuation process, and the need and rewards for moral development. The tales help reframe existential issues, allow the personal meaning of a story to emerge and be applied, and stimulate the search of the unconscious for greater understanding. Fairy tales are relatively nonthreatening, and present means for exploration of what the individual perceives as dangerous material in a safe way.

### *Drawing*

Drawing exercises (chapters 9–11) are proposed as a means for facilitating expression of difficult, complex, and ambiguous concepts and feelings that could be helpful for members' understanding. These can help moderate the effects of defense mechanisms such as intellectualizing, can provide means for less verbal members to contribute, and reveal nonconscious experiencing. These exercises are not used or interpreted as they would be in art therapy because that requires specialized training. Drawing is used to focus on and facilitate expression.

### *Writing*

Writing (chapters 12–15) is a form of expression that can be used in many ways. Presented here are uses for journals, poems, and personal stories. Writing can aid in recall, expansion of feelings and ideas, provide for the emergence of new perspectives, and tap into the person's creativity. It is a personal and private way to recall, expand, or express oneself, and can then contribute to personal learning and understanding in the group.

### *Imagery*

Imagery (chapter 16) activities provide a way to visualize concepts that are difficult to describe with words, but can be a technique to clarify worries and concerns, hopes and aspirations for the future, current issues and concerns that are just below the level of consciousness, and provide access to past experiences.

### *Mindfulness*

Mindfulness (chapter 17) is a technique to teach concentration and focus for the present, to be aware of oneself and all manner of self-experiencing in the here and now, and as a self-soothing technique. While mindfulness has evidence of its efficacy in alleviating physical and psychological stress and health conditions, it is also valuable for teaching members how to manage and contain uncomfortable feelings.

### *Music*

Music (chapter 18) is presented here to function just as drawing does, as a stimulus but not as the major focus for therapy. Music has the power to evoke emotions, and the use of music can facilitate members' ability to access and express their feelings.

### *Movement*

Movement will be presented as a means to energize, to connect or reconnect to the body, and to become aware of the messages the body may be sending. Simple movement activities are presented that can be performed by people of all ages, and there will be very few who cannot engage in most or all of the activities.

### *Dance*

Dance (chapter 19) like music and art can be the focus and emphasis for therapy, but the activities here again only use this modality as a stimulus to access important material and understanding for group members. The leader does not have to be trained in dance therapy to use these activities.

### *Exercise*

Exercise (chapter 19) is an activity that is also a means for focusing on one's body. What is presented is not intended to be a regime of exercising, but to use some exercise moves as stimuli for expression and discussion. Simple stretching moves, cardiovascular activities, and the like are the focus of these exercises.

### *Drama and Role-Play*

Drama and role-play (chapter 20) are categorized with movement because they call for group members to move and interact, and to be aware of what they are experiencing in the moment. Acting can promote empathy and understanding of oneself and of others as other perspectives are assumed. Simulations can be exciting ways to learn new skills, understand diverse perspectives, and master complexities of situations. Role-play is a specific technique that is similar to drama, but usually is built around real circumstances and personalities. Assuming the role of the other person can produce new learning and a new perspective.

### *Collage*

Collage (chapter 21) is presented because almost anyone can construct a collage, all kinds and sorts of materials can be used, and they are satisfying and fun to do.

### *Mélange*

Mélange (chapter 22) presents artist trading cards (ATCs), flats, and scrapbooking. The ATC is a variation of collage. ATCs are small works of art that cannot be sold, they are to be traded or given away. The small (2½" × 3½") surface is less threatening than larger sheets of paper, but a considerable amount of expression can be constructed on this. Flats are patterned after Flat Stanley and used here as a way to communicate and build relations when people are socially isolated, separated by geography or other means, as well as for group dilemmas. Scrapbooks are a longer term group project and are used here as a means to gather fragmented pieces of self and memories, not as the usual scrapbooks, but are more as a book about oneself.

Chapters 22 and 23 present applications of activities in regard to members' concerns, group level challenges, and cases of group dilemmas and suggested activities.

Some exercises that are described can be completed in the group session, while others will need more time for completion of the product and can be assigned as homework. The group exercises would then be brought back to the group for the expansion and debriefing phase. Group leaders will want to select the kind of exercise to use based on group members' needs, characteristics, and abilities, and to choose particular exercises to fit these, and the time available in a session. It is highly recommended that all exercises, other than the extensive ones assigned as homework, be entirely completed in the particular session, including the expansion phase; but failing that they can be carried over to a subsequent session. Leaders also need to be prepared for homework not to be completed by all group members because this will necessitate their having to deal with those who did the work, and those who did not.

# Chapter 2

# Ethical Considerations

Professionally competent group leaders follow the ethical codes of their professional organizations or licensing boards. This chapter presents an explanation of potentially harmful treatments and group leader practices, and the primary categories of ethical codes to guide their practice.

## Do No Harm

The primary ethical concern when using creative activities is to do no harm. Dimidjian and Hollon (2010) define treatment harm as being caused by the treatment and not an inherent part of the client's original problem. Using this perspective, harm when using creative activities in a group setting would be defined as harm caused by the activity; that is not a part of the presenting problem. There are seven kinds of harm:

- A decelerated rate of improvement: The member showed improvement, but that improvement slowed.

- The cost of unhelpful treatment.
- Member distress from interacting with an unhelpful therapist: While members may experience some temporary distress, the helpful therapist attends to this, but an unhelpful therapist would ignore or minimize the distress.
- The therapist fails to provide helpful treatment.
- Harmful interventions, such as the 61 empirically based potentially harmful treatments (PHT) that are listed by Lilienfeld (2007).
- Treatment that causes the member to experience problems in domains other than the target problem.
- The presenting problem or identified concern becomes worse with treatment.

Lilienfeld (2007) derived the list of PHTs from randomized controlled trials, quasi-experimental studies, meta-analyses, and naturalistic studies. The list was developed where harmful physical or psychological effects were shown for the client or for others, the harmful effects persisted over time and were enduring, and the studies and findings were replicated.

Harmful treatment effects were described by Lilienfeld (2007) and Boisvert and Faust (2006) as follows:

- The treatment procedures and processes produce deterioration.
- The client does not improve with treatment.
- The client's relatives or friends are harmed by his or her responses to treatment.
- Premature termination occurs as the client cannot tolerate the treatment.
- The presenting problem, symptoms, conditions, and the like become worse with treatment.
- New symptoms appear after treatment is begun.
- The client expresses anxiety and concern about the course of treatment, and his or her rate of improvement.
- Physical harm results from treatment.

## Prevention of PHT

Prevention skills that can help reduce or eliminate the possibility of engaging in potentially harmful treatment include the following, with sample studies cited to substantiate their efficacy:

- Enhance the therapeutic relationship (Harvorth & Bedi, 2002; Martin, Garske, & Davis, 2000);
- Understanding of how the therapist contributes to negative interactions, ruptures in the therapeutic alliance, and their influences and impact on improving therapeutic outcomes (Binder & Strupp, 1997; Castonguay et al. 2004);
- Continually monitor and manage countertransference (Gelso, Latts, Gomez, & Fassinger, 2002);
- Identify transference without analyzing it (Crits-Christoph & Gibbons, 2002);
- Restrict interpretations, especially when treating personality disorders (Schut et al. 2005);
- Recognize that the best predictor of outcomes is the level of the therapist's developed self (Wampold, 2006).

## Ethical Considerations and Requirement

Group leaders must be knowledgeable about the ethical requirements for their profession and follow them. The discussion that follows presents the primary ethical considerations that appear to be similar across all mental health professions; American Psychological Association, American Counseling Association, American Psychiatric Association, Marriage and Family Therapists, and the National Association for Social Work. The American Group Psychotherapy Association ethical standards require that members follow the standards for their professions because this is a multidisciplinary organization. The ethics are categorized as the following.

1. The therapeutic relationship;
2. Confidentiality and its limits;

3. Responsibilities and competence;
4. Professional relationships, referral, and consultation;
5. Assessment; and
6. Process for resolving ethical issues.

### *The Therapeutic Relationship*

The therapeutic relationship is a special one that sets the frame for what can be built between the group leader and members. This relationship encompasses more than the leader's personal development, knowledge, and skills; it also includes some professional responsibilities and tasks that are ethical requirements. The group leader who attends to these is helping to promote an atmosphere that can lead to feelings of trust and safety necessary for reduction of ambiguity, mistrust, and resistance; and to promote cooperation, self-disclosure, and reflection.

The tasks and responsibilities for ethically appropriate therapeutic relationships are categorized as the group leaders' personal development and professional preparation, documentation, and client preparation. The personal development and professional preparation of group leaders are central to the therapeutic relationship and group development. Personal development is central in the reduction of possible countertransference to protect members, and in developing the inner states that are critical for developing the therapeutic relationship. Group leaders must constantly stay in touch with their personal needs and values so that these are not imposed on group members.

Professional preparation includes academic knowledge, skills training, and appropriate supervised practice. Another major component in this preparation is cultural sensitivity. Group leaders will most likely have a variety of cultures in every group although, on the surface, members can appear to be homogenous, and it is very necessary that leaders have cultural sensitivity and competence. Further, cultural sensitivity can assist the leader in formulating reasonable treatment plans, and making appropriate interventions. While it may not be possible to fully understand all the cultural differences you may encounter, it is ethically responsible to ensure that you are culturally aware and sensitive, to learn as much as possible about your members' cultures, and to consult about these when you do not have sufficient information about a particular culture.

### *Documentation*

Documentation responsibilities include record keeping, treatment plans, informed consent that includes both forms and presentation of information about the group. Record keeping should have case notes that are timely, accurate, written in clear and unambiguous language, and are secure. Records are generally kept for each member for each session. Agencies, schools, hospitals, and other bodies where groups are conducted will likely have record keeping requirements and guidelines, and group leaders are responsible for knowing and following these regulations. Record keeping is not only an ethical responsibility, it is also a legal responsibility.

Treatment plans are an ethical responsibility, and are generally required by the treatment facility, and by insurers. Your treatment plans can be a guide for working with individual members in the group, and you are encouraged to develop these as a part of your planning for the group. Treatment plans should reflect an integration of treatments; be realistic, objective, and rational; and should be consistent with clients' abilities. It can be very helpful to develop these in collaboration with other treatment professionals associated with members, and with the individual member. The latter may not be possible with some members because of impairment, but even they should be informed and encouraged to try to participate in their treatment planning.

It is important to collect signed consent forms from either the client or from the parent or guardian. These signed forms are your documentation that you provided sufficient information verbally and in writing, to allow members to make a judgment about whether to participate or not. Informed consent means that members understand what is proposed, are able to evaluate the risks to them personally, and are not being forced or coerced into participation without sufficient information. There is always the matter of involuntary participation, such as court-ordered treatment; but even under these circumstances members should be fully informed and provide signed forms to document that you did provide the information.

The information you provide should include the following about the services. It is recommended that the information is available in a brochure or handout as well as being communicated verbally. Be sure to address all of the following:

- Purpose and goal(s) for treatment.
- A description of the techniques you intend to use, such as exercises. This can be especially important if you use exercises that involve movement or touching. You could also include a statement on members' rights of refusal to participate in these.
- A description of procedures, such as if a specific format is to be used.
- Limitations for treatment are important to communicate in order to not raise false hopes.
- Potential risks and benefits. These include psychological risks, especially the uncovering of repressed and denied material that is shameful; and benefits that can be gained from participation.
- Your credentials and relevant experience can help begin to establish safety, trust, and your credibility. Group members will want to know that you are well prepared to lead the group.
- The process set up to continue treatment (i.e., the group), in the event you are unable to continue.

The next set of information to be included focuses on the client's understanding of procedures that will be used and their implications.

- Implications of diagnoses. These are best developed in collaboration with other involved treatment professionals, such as physicians or nurses.
- If testing is conducted, such as personality testing, you should explain how these test results will be used, by whom, and to whom the results will be communicated.
- Describe what reports will be generated, how they will be kept, and who will have access to them.
- The policies and procedures on fees and billing should be described and made clear, such as any charges for phone consultation, missed sessions, and so on.
- There should be written guidelines for clients who wish to obtain information or access to their records.
- It is extremely important to inform members of their right to refuse treatment, and the consequences for doing so. This is important for all clients, and is especially important for involuntary clients who can face severe penalties for refusing to participate.

Client preparation includes screening for group, and determining the level and extent of members' support network. Screening procedures are described in the chapter on planning, and the client's support system can be a part of screening.

## Confidentiality and Its Limits

There are numerous reasons to specifically address confidentiality and group leaders should make special efforts to openly discuss concerns members can have about the leader's responsibility, and the limitations on what can or cannot, be kept confidential. This includes the sharing of information with other treatment professionals, and concerned bodies such as insurance companies. Group leaders should know and attend to the following ethical responsibilities.

- Understand members' cultural context for maintaining confidentiality. Some conditions and illnesses are considered shameful in some cultures, and there is a stigma attached to them. Do not assume that members have the same cultural context as you do.

- Keep a respect for privacy. Just as there are cultural sensitivities, there can be gender related sensitivities and age related ones. What may seem unimportant to you may be very shame inducing for others.
- Proper and planned termination of treatment is expected. It is not ethically responsible to abandon clients, and most codes of ethics strictly prohibit this action.
- If you find that you cannot assist the client for any reason, such as lack of proper training, significant countertransference issues, personal illnesses, or crises, it is your ethical responsibility to provide appropriate referral or other transfer of services.
- Remember that clients have to consent in order for you to share information, even with other treatment professionals, and you must obtain their written consent before sharing any information.
- Clients should be fully informed about the need to share information with other treatment professionals, the limits of your ability to maintain confidentiality with them, and the purpose for sharing information.
- It is essential that security be maintained when sharing or transmitting information about clients. This can mean that you do not share any information in public places, such as hallways and lunch rooms, and that you are aware of the lack of security for phones, fax, e-mail, voice mail, and so on, and that you take proper precautions.
- Court ordered disclosures should be specified in advance, understood by all parties concerned, prevented where possible, and narrowly defined. In all cases, the amount of information should be limited and restricted to essential information.
- The restrictions for court ordered disclosures also apply to third-party payers, and should only take place when the client authorizes release of information.

- Group leaders have an ethical responsibility to report when a client exhibits clear and imminent danger to self or others, and when there is a contagious life-threatening disease. Group leaders are also advised to be aware of and follow state, federal, local, and institutional laws and policies for reporting on these conditions.

## Professional Responsibility

All codes of ethics for mental health professionals have standards for education, training, and supervised experiences. It is your responsibility to secure needed education and so on, and to only practice within the scope of your training.

- Have knowledge of standards of practice guidelines as specified by your licensure and certification, and the ethics for your profession.
- Secure the needed training, education, and other experience specified as basic for professional competence.
- Know, understand, and abide by the state and national professional standards for credentialing.
- When practicing new specialties, techniques, and the like, insure that you receive the proper professional experience.
- Consult when there are ethical issues, concerns, and dilemmas.
- Seek out and obtain appropriate continuing education opportunities.
- Take care to be clear and accurate in presenting your credentials.
- You have the responsibility to report when you are impaired and to obtain treatment.
- It is your responsibility to ensure that your practice is nondiscriminatory.
- Ethical standards require you to seek appropriate consultation and collaboration to benefit clients.

## Assessment

The ethics for assessment include the following:

- All assessment techniques and instruments must have sufficient and appropriate validity and reliability.
- Group leaders must have formal training and supervised practice for the techniques and instrumentation used.
- You must only use those techniques and instruments that are within your limits of competence.
- Use of techniques and instrumentation for assessment require informed consent of clients.
- Clients must be notified if results of assessment are to be shared with others, including other professionals.

## Process for Resolving Ethical Issues

Most processes for resolving ethical issues place considerable responsibility on you to recognize when ethics violations and conflicts exist, to understand when and how to address these, and to be willing to uphold professional standards. You are expected to do all of the following:

- Have a complete knowledge of the ethics of your profession.
- Understand if and when the law conflicts with ethics, and the possible consequences.
- When and how to report suspected violations, and the need for consultation.

# Chapter 3
# The Group Leader's Preparation

Central to the success of using creative activities are the group leader's preparation for developing the therapeutic relationship, attention to process, awareness of the potential for narcissistic injury, and the possible emotional states of group members (Egan, 2006; Yalom & Leszcz, 2005). Most of the activities presented in this book can be best facilitated after safety and trust has been established in the group, and the group leader's ability to form a therapeutic relationship is critical. This relationship allows group members to believe that the group leader will take care of them, that relationships in the group will be constructive, that the possibilities for growth, development, and healing can be realized, and that confidential material will remain confidential.

A significant part of the leader's preparation for establishing a group climate that is conducive to optimum use of creative activities as well as establishing a therapeutic relationship, includes the leader's development of relating attributes, communication skills, and a developed self to provide emotional presence, knowledge, and techniques for facilitating groups, empathic responding, and empathic failure repair. These are basic and fundamental to group leadership regardless of the type of group, but may be even more important when incorporating creative activities into the group.

## Relating Attributes

Relating attributes include warmth, caring, concern, tolerance, acceptance, genuineness, and respect. Rogers (1970) termed much of this as *unconditional positive regard* where the therapist perceives the client as capable, worthwhile, and valued. These attributes are the outcomes for personal development and cannot be taught and learned, the person has to have these as a part of their self.

These characteristics can be extremely important when implementing creative activities as members can be confronted with aspects of self that may trigger guilt and shame. When this occurs, it is vital that the group leader be able to communicate her or his caring and concern, acceptance of the person even with flaws, to be encouraging and supportive of the person's ability to tolerate and benefit from what has emerged, and to be able to do so both nonverbally and verbally. The basic relating attributes are central to conveying this, and cannot be taught because they have to be an integral part of the leader. Techniques and skills can be taught and learned, attributes cannot.

## Communication Skills

Communication skills on the other hand, can be taught and learned. Listening for feelings and content, an ability to express a wide variety of feelings, using in concrete and direct terms that are understood by the other person, understanding the role of questions, and giving verbal encouragement and support are the most basic communication skills that have applications in all kinds of interpersonal relationships, not just in therapy.

The group leader must understand and listen for the underlying feelings because group members may not be aware of these on a conscious level. This is where the skill of the group leader can be helpful in assisting the members in expressing those feelings, or expressing difficult feelings, or even just learning how to express feelings. Activities can and do trigger feelings, other feelings can emerge as members hear about others' reactions and experiences, and a vital part of the group process is the focus on feelings and their expression. Indeed, many of the creative activities have feelings as a central focus and emphasis.

## The Group Leader's Self-Development

There is considerable literature to support the proposal that the developed self of the group leader plays a significant role. This manifests itself in the leader's constructive use of countertransference to understand members' experiencing; in managing and containing intense and difficult emotions; providing an emotional presence where members are heard and understood; and in being empathic (Alonso & Rutan, 1996; Gans & Alonso, 1998; Horwitz, 2000; Yalom & Leszcz, 2005). Constructive use of countertransference refers to the leader's ability to know and understand what he or she is feeling, the roots or antecedents of those feelings, and to be able to use these to better understand the group member(s).

Managing and containing intense and difficult emotions will be a task for the group leader to model for group members. Some group members may be fearful of their own emotions and the emotions of others, fearing that they will become enmeshed or overwhelmed; that is, taken over by others' feelings to the point where they feel out of control. The group can be a good place to learn that difficult and intense emotions can be experienced without loss of control. Group leaders, of course, have to be proficient at expressing their emotions, as well as being able to manage and control them, and this is a part of their self-development.

The self-development of the group leader calls for an understanding of his or her family of origin issues and concerns that are unresolved, past experiences that carry unfinished business, and personal undeveloped narcissism (Brown, 2009; Yalom & Leszcz, 2005). These must be examined and acknowledged because they can be the conscious, nonconscious, and unconscious factors that impact the group and its members.

## A Knowledge Base

A knowledge base about groups and techniques is also basic, and these are covered more fully in chapter 4. Group leaders need a thorough grounding in the fundamentals of group facilitation such as group stages of development, therapeutic factors, and phases of group member development (Brown, 2009; Trotzer, 2010). This is the information that leads to making informed choices and decisions about when and how to use creative activities in a way that promotes group member development.

## Empathic Responding

Empathic responding is essential although it is recognized that the group leader will find it impossible to be empathic with everyone all of the time. However, the group leader has to have the capacity for empathic responding even if she or he cannot *be* empathic at that time. Being empathic means entering the world of the other person to feel what that person is feeling without losing the sense of oneself as a separate and distinct individual. Empathic responding means that the content and feelings of the other person are understood but on a more cognitive level. The leader is not feeling what the other person feels, he or she is able to identify and communicate what that person is feeling. Central to being empathic and responding empathically is that this is conveyed to the other person in words. Nonverbal communication is not sufficient, and can be misunderstood and misleading.

The following can help increase empathic responding:

**FOCUS ON THE SPEAKER**
Orient your body and mind to the speaker
Do not think about personal concerns
Do not anticipate your response
Relax and breathe evenly and deeply
Feel the speaker's presence
**RESTRICT QUESTIONING**
Only ask questions for clarification
Express feelings avoid questions
Do not substitute questions for interest
Eliminate rhetorical questions
**LET THE SPEAKER FINISH**
Become comfortable with silence
Do not interrupt
Do not finish statements for others
**DO NOT GIVE YOUR "ANSWERS"**
You may not fully understand the other person's situation
They may tend to give only the information that makes them look good
You are only hearing one side
Your "answers" are unlikely to fit the other person

## Empathic Failure and Repair

Empathic failure and repair are essential tasks for the group leader. While other group members can and do repair empathic failures, Kohut (1977) feels that this is a primary task for the therapist. What are some indicators that there has been an empathic failure that needs attention?

- A group member self-discloses and no one makes a response.
- Someone expresses a feeling that is not acknowledged, or the discussion changes topics.
- A group member is silently crying and no one says anything.

- Interactions among group members or with the leader become increasingly tense, or circular, or seem stuck.
- A disclosure is minimized, ignored, or a trivial response is given.

These are a few examples, there are many more. What is important to know is that neglecting to repair the empathic failure impacts that person and other group members who can then fear that they too will not be understood or receive an empathic response. A process for repair of empathic failures follows:

The first step is to recognize that the person did not receive a response, received an inappropriate response, but in any event, did not receive an empathic response. Once the failure is recognized, use one of the following four guides.

- Say to the person, "I did not respond when you were expressing (name the feeling[s] the person was expressing or trying to express), and I want you to know that I did hear and understand. It would have been more helpful if I could have told you that I heard you at that time"
- If you tuned out and did not hear what the person said, or only a part of it, say something like the following: "I did not hear or respond to you when you were trying to express something important to you. That was not helpful." Saying what you did hear and understand could be added, if it did not emphasize that you were not listening.
- If you responded inappropriately, for example, by giving advice, you could say the following. "When you were talking about ____ I (whatever the inappropriate response was) instead of letting you know that I heard and understood that you were ___________ (feelings expressed by the person). If I had let you know I did hear your feelings it may have been more helpful than (whatever you did).

- If you failed to report on triggered personal feelings you could say something like the following: "When you were expressing your feelings about ________, I did not let you know that I was feeling ________. I realize that knowing how you affected me could have been useful to you."

## Attention to Process

Although it may be an advanced group leadership skill, attending to process and making process commentary is also facilitative. "Process is the here and now experience in the group that describes how the group is functioning, the quality of relationships between and among group leaders and with the leader, the emotional experiences and reactions of the group, and the group's strongest desires and fears" (Brown, 2003a, p. 228). Yalom and Leszcz (2005) propose that process commentary illuminates what is taking place in the group and may be impacting the group's functioning without members' awareness of what is taking place.

Focusing on and intervening with individuals is productive, but until group members learn how to coat-tail, that is, use what you are doing with one individual to work on their personal issues, the leader is not doing group therapy or group counseling but rather is doing individual therapy in a group setting. Group therapy and group counseling that use the resources of the group to help individuals is very effective and allows all members to work at the same time. Making group level process commentary allows the leader to work with all group members.

Some specific indices that indicate the need for group process commentary are:

- Behaviors of the group, what the group is doing, or is not doing;
- Feelings generated in the leader;
- Feelings noted in members from their nonverbal behavior that seem important but are not verbalized;

- Impact of behaviors on members but they do not respond or acknowledge the impact;
- Links between issues, concerns, and feelings;
- Themes that emerge in group.

When using group as a whole process commentary, a group leader will find it helpful to be able to identify the session's theme, the behaviors the group uses that reflect resistance, how the group manages conflict and difficult member behaviors, feelings that are directly and openly expressed and those that are not, empathic failures and repair, and how the group is using its energy, or not.

## Potential for Narcissistic Injury

Reich (1945/1972) conceptualized narcissistic injury as the hurt or wound that occurs to the developing self and is experienced by the receiver with uncontrollable feelings of helplessness, anxiety, and rage. The person's self-esteem is negatively affected, and these injuries continue to exert their negative influences and can be intensified when additional wounding occurs. Reich isn't clear if the additional wounding is a reinjury of the initial wound or is a collection of different wounds. Kohut (1977) describes narcissistic injuries as disturbances of narcissistic balance that are usually easily recognizable by the painful affect of embarrassment or shame that is experienced, and characterizes the response as one of shame and uncontrollable rage.

Thus, a group leader has to maintain awareness that narcissistic injury can and does occur in groups, that the individual is severely impacted by these and they impact his or her functioning in the group, and to work reduce the incidents, and to repair the wounding.

Narcissistic wounding can occur when others, including the group leader, make insensitive remarks that seem to insult or invalidate the receiver, when microaggressions occur in the group, when the person feels that something shameful has been revealed about him- or herself, when an individual is scapegoated or attacked, and in other such circumstances. All of these cannot be prevented as the narcissistic wounding is unique, personal, and may differ for each group member, but the group leader has to stay aware of the potential for such injuries and intervene. Responses by group members can include withdrawal, silence, becoming combative, premature termination, and other such negative responses.

Repair of narcissistic wounding can be difficult because the receiver may not acknowledge the wounding, may discount the impact on him or her, or become resistant to any attempt to repair it. Kohut (1977) proposes that the repair is accomplished by mirroring and an empathic response by the leader.

## Group Members' Emotional States

A major consideration when using creative activities is the emotional state of members. Tuning into states such as extent of emotional vulnerability, defensiveness, and resistance and how these are manifested, the known and hidden self, the potential for growth and development, and their self-perceptions and self-esteem help leaders to select appropriate creative activities. Careful attention to the emotional vulnerability allows the group leader to select the activities that will be beneficial rather than harmful by producing intense and sometimes overwhelming affect that is difficult to overcome or to control for that person or for several group members. Safety is a prime concern, and not recognizing the emotional vulnerability of one or more group members can make the group not feel safe for many members.

All group members will have and exhibit some defensiveness and resistance, and the group leader can address these with some creative activities that help to bypass them and allow the member to access important information about the self. It is not necessary or helpful to identify members as defensive or resistant, it is much more helpful to allow them to decide when or if to lower their defenses or reduce their resistance. Since it is likely, if there is group level defensiveness and resistance, that each member is displaying these in a different manner and form, the group leader can address all at the same time with an appropriate, well chosen creative activity.

## Judicious Use of Creative Activities

One of the benefits for participating in group therapy is becoming aware of what you do and do not know about yourself. Discovering and rediscovering parts of self can be very rewarding, but is not easy to accomplish. After all, there are many facets to oneself, and some are more visible to the person than are others. Creative activities can point the way and guide the group members to explore, discover, and enhance known and unknown parts of the self, to build or change parts of the self, and to become more fully an aware and authentic person.

Therapy is undertaken with the hope and possibility of growth and development as well as providing avenues for problem solving and decision making. Growth and development of the self, of relationships, of knowing and being are all possible, and are enhanced with the use of creative activities. Considerable growth can and does occur during group participation in creative activities, and because these promote a willingness for self-exploration and self-enhancement, can be stimulating and inspiring.

Essential in choosing and using creative activities is the group leader's knowledge and understanding of group members' self-perceptions and self-esteem (Crits-Christoph et al., 2006). How members perceive and value their selves provide clues as to which creative activities can be used to increase their awareness, to be affirming of the self, to focus on strengths and capitalize on these, and to guide them to explore sensitive areas are part of the growth and change process. Since perceptions and esteem are likely to vary among group members, creative activities allow the exploration and expansion of these to occur for each member wherever they may be in relation to these dimensions.

# Chapter 4
# Group Dynamics, Group Stages, and Therapeutic Factors

## Introduction

There are certain group factors that are fundamental to understanding how and when to intervene in group dilemmas, and are basic to the success of the group. These factors include group dynamics, stages of group development, and therapeutic group factors.

## Group Dynamics

Group leaders can obtain many clues about the group and its members from observing the dynamics of the group. These constantly changing factors are signals about current experiencing for individual members, and for the group as a whole. The observant group leader takes information, analyzes and synthesizes it, ensures its validity from self-contamination of countertransference and projection, and then uses this to decide on an appropriate intervention. This is a process that can be used with individual group members, and with the group as a whole. First, let's define and describe the group dynamics that are the sources of information.

Group dynamics is both a field of study and group processes according to Forsyth (1999), but Lewin (1951) defined group dynamics as the powerful processes that take place in group. Johnson and Johnson (2006) note that the field of group dynamics is a "twentieth-century, North American development" (p.35) that derived from many fields and has evolved into an interdisciplinary field. Contemporary emphases for group dynamics focus on the continuous movement and progression of the group, and on the interacting forces that impact the group and its functioning (Brown, 2009).

As more became known about group dynamics and its complexities, more studies were conducted that produced greater understanding of the helping and restraining forces that comprise the dynamics. Studies included leadership patterns (Lewin, Lippitt, and White, 1939) group decision making processes (Marrow, 1957), response patterns and roles (Bales 1950, 1953), sequential stage theory (Moreland & Levine, 1988), basic themes (Bion, 1961), norms (Sherif, 1936), interaction of personal and environmental factors (Lewin, 1951), communication and cohesion (Thibaut & Kelley, 1959), motives and goals (Zander, 1971/1996), conflict (Deutch, 1949), interpersonal attraction (Newcomb, 1963), and communication networks (Shaw, 1964). Much of the early focus was on the various components and aspects of the group, but as more of the complexities emerged, more attention was given to the interactions of the various dynamics, the importance of group process, and a focus on the group as a whole. The idea of the group as a whole became more prominent through the work of Bion (1961) who applied psychoanalytic theory to groups, and this work added greatly to the understanding of how the whole group functioned.

Bion proposed three basic assumptions for groups: dependency where members feel helpless and look to the leader for support; fight/flight where the group feels in danger and uses one of these actions as a response; and pairing, where members have hopeful fantasies of being saved and of the group being constructive.

Observation and understanding of the group's dynamics reveal the current process for the group, and the identification and understanding of these dynamics allow the group leader to better intervene, and to help the group accomplish its task. The basic group dynamics to observe include: level of participation, communication patterns, feelings expressed, resistance and defenses, and how conflict is managed.

- Level of participation includes the characteristic interaction and changes in interactions, input, and responses for individual members and for the group as a whole.
- Communication patterns include both verbal and nonverbal communication. The verbal communication patterns can demonstrate inclusion or exclusion, deference, where the perceived power and influence rests, group norms, and current emotional state. *Nonverbal behavior* is the major and most important part of communication, and is valuable information about what the group and its members are experiencing at a deep level. Behaviors such as voice tone, body positioning, facial expression, body movements or lack of movement, and clusters of gestures all convey deep and important messages about current emotional states for both individual members and for the group as a whole.
- Feelings expressed can be an important indicator of overt or hidden issues in the group, as well as indicators for individual members' emotional state, sensitivities, and resistance. Hidden, disguised and suppressed feelings are important and significant for group members and for the group as a whole.

- Resistance is an indicator of sensitive material that is threatening and thus, must be defended against, suppressed, or repressed. Acts mobilized as *defenses* include denial, deflection, intellectualization, and displacement.
- Conflict can be revealing of the group's fear, need, or wishes, and the most important signal is how the group manages conflict. Common group conflict management strategies are denial, suppression, ignoring, and working to resolve them.

## Stages of Group Development

There are certain expected member behaviors that usually occur during the group's development, and these are associated with the stage or level of growth that has occurred for the group. Different theorists and authors may use different terms for these stages, but the descriptions for members' behaviors and needs have considerable similarities.

Tuckman (1965) was among the first to propose and document developmental sequences for groups, and this later became known as group stages. These stages are not separate, distinct, or clear cut, but almost all types of groups seem to move through some sequence of development. The literature shows several ways to categorize these stages:

- Forming, storming, norming, and performing (Tuckman, 1965);
- Engagement, differentiate, individuation, intimacy, mutuality, and termination (MacKenzie, 1990)
- Orientation, conflict, cohesion, stability, and termination (Yalom,1995);
- Formation, conflict, rebellion, and termination (Weber, 2000);
- Formative, reactive, maturity, and termination (Rutan & Stone, 2001);

- Defining and structuring procedures, conforming to procedures and getting acquainted, recognizing mutuality and building trust, rebelling and differentiating, committing to and taking ownership, functioning maturely and productively, and terminating (Johnson & Johnson, 2006).

All categorizations include the four stages that are used for this discussion: beginning, conflict, cohesion, and termination.

The group's stage of development can be a rich source of information about what members' needs are at a particular time, can suggest interventions, and can provide clues for difficulties, challenges, and dilemmas that may emerge. This information may be of particular importance for adult therapy groups that are likely to have sufficient time available to experience all the group stages. Below is an overview of a general stage development model with expected member behaviors, needs, and major leader tasks.

### *Stage 1: Beginning*

Stage 1 behaviors are reflective of the behaviors and internal states many experience in new situations where there is ambiguity and uncertainty. Members are usually anxious about acceptance-rejection, the ability of the group to meet their needs, the competence of the group leader to care for them and to guide their changes, what is expected of them, and what will be their role(s) in the group. Their past experiences with relationships and authority figures also factor into their behavior, fears, and expectations. Group leaders must stay aware of the anxiety that the first stage of group engenders in the group members, and focus on establishing trust and safety so that the group becomes a safe place for members' disclosure and self-exploration, and for contributing to each other's growth and development.

Group dilemmas most likely will not occur in stage 1 because the collective need has yet to be developed. Difficulties that generally occur in this stage tend to center around the expected needs for safety and trust. Group leaders understand the expectations for this stage and work to establish trust and safety by acts like the following:

- Openly address members' fears and concerns;
- Identify and highlight similarities among members;
- Collaboratively set goals with group members;
- Seek out members' strengths to build on;
- Provide symptom relief where possible;
- Foster an atmosphere of inclusion;
- Instill realistic hope;
- Model empathic responding.

### *Stage 2: Conflict*

Stage 2 is generally characterized by dissention, discord, and disagreements. Group members are now starting to assert their independence and, just as toddlers do, they want to both hold on for safety and to let go to explore, but don't quite know how to get both needs met at the same time. So, they lash out in confusion and frustration, displacing their conflicting needs on others. These are some of the reasons why this group stage is so uncomfortable and can pose difficulties for members and the leader. Members challenge each other and the leader to be both dependent and independent at the same time.

Group leaders have to stay in touch with both sets of needs, to model how to give and receive constructive feedback to eliminate or moderate negative aspects of the behavior, teach positive confrontation or enlightenment skills, and to monitor their old unresolved parental issues that could emerge as countertransference. The group leader's self and skills are very important for the successful transition of this stage because how the leader reacts to challenges from members shows them how the leader perceives them and their roles. When the leader is not defensive and responds in a positive way, members learn how to be constructive when expressing disagreements, how to use the information from the disagreement to strengthen relationships and not allow the disagreement to be destructive, and they are guided to learn new ways of understanding their reactions and feelings, and new ways to relate and behave. This is a very busy and potentially rich stage even with all of the discomfort.

Dilemmas and difficulties during stage 2 generally arise around conflict and fears of being destroyed because of it. Some members fear conflict so much because of their past experiences that they work hard to suppress any hint of conflict. Unfortunately, there are also some group leaders who meet this description, and unconsciously do everything in their power to ensure that conflict does not emerge in the group, or if it does emerge that it is dealt with swiftly to make it go away rather than using the opportunity to teach constructive or positive conflict resolution.

By far the most difficult situation that usually occurs in stage 2 is when the leader is challenged or attacked. This challenge can come from one or two members, but the challenge also expresses something about what other members are thinking and feeling.

The need to assert independence seems to involve devaluing or demeaning the object that they were dependent on to supply nurturance, safety, and support. How the group leader reacts during these challenges plays the most important role in determining the success of the journey through this stage.

Group dilemmas can arise during this stage. Members have developed some connections to and understanding for each other so that both conscious and unconscious collusion can occur. Further, two members can have the same needs for dependence and the beginning of independence that encourage the challenging behaviors, or the other group level dilemmas. The members are bonded, but not yet cohesive where they are independent and working productively on their own. Any or all of the described group dilemmas could occur in stage 2, and the tension that can exist lends itself to using expressive processes.

The main group leader tasks during this stage include the following:

- Monitor self-reactions and possible countertransference to prevent defensiveness or reactive aggressiveness.
- Model giving constructive feedback.
- Intervene to prevent member to member attacks and other forms of aggression.
- Demonstrate and teach conflict resolution that can strengthen relationships rather than destroy them.
- Use opportunities to provide the corrective emotional experience.
- Accept catharsis but provide guidance to foster intrapersonal and interpersonal learning so that it does not remain as just emotional venting.

### *Stage 3: Cohesion*

Often called the cohesion stage, this level of group development can be very productive for group members. Sufficient trust and safety has been developed so that many of the fears around self-disclosure, acceptance, and positive regard are answered and are of lesser concern. Time and experiences in the group have fostered positive connections, the emergence of many group therapeutic factors, and it is much less scary and threatening to engage in self-exploration of long standing issues and concerns. There is a spirit of cooperation, support, and hope in the group. Members can be more confident in their self-efficacy, and more willing to engage in personal risk taking for disclosure and exploration of issues. There is a deep intimacy for the group.

The group leader is less active during this stage; she or he will let members be more independent and interactive with each other. Members become more willing to explore sensitive issues, support and encourage each other, and considerable therapeutic work is done. Sessions are harmonious, members derive enjoyment and growth, and are able to take charge of much of their development at this point. There are two likely situations that need group leader interventions: when the group starts to value harmony to the point where feelings are suppressed and members are reluctant or avoid confronting each other; and when the group engages in "group think" where no differences among members are tolerated in regard to values, perspectives, opinions, and the like. While the feelings that harmony produces in the group are comforting and supportive, too much harmony stifles expression and growth. Group leaders must stay aware of these possibilities.

### *Stage 4: Termination*

Most all groups have a beginning and ending stage, and the ending stage should be a part of the planning done in advance of the group's beginning (Brown, 2007). The exception for this stage is continuing groups where members may terminate, but the group itself does not end. In this case, the planned closure should be for the terminating member, and for the remaining members who will continue but in a different group because a member has left the group.

Stage 4 member behaviors include some regression to behaviors of earlier stages. The potential loss of the established security, connections, and support can be frightening to some group members, and they can fear being destroyed without the resources to lean on that the group and leader provide. Some groups may even produce dilemmas in an effort to prevent the group from ending. Expected member behaviors can include panic, withdrawal, sadness, and devaluing of the group experience as defenses against feeling the loss of the group.

The major leader tasks are to prepare members for separation and to become independent. This process should begin about halfway through the duration of the group. Preparation includes reminding members of the time boundary, highlighting progress and growth, reviewing personal goals and accomplishments, and affirming members' strengths. It could be helpful for some members to verbalize their fears so as to assess their realism and validity.

The group's ending is a threshold or boundary, just as what is encountered in fairy tales. There will be change, the future is uncertain, and there is concern about one's ability to cope with the changes. A fairy tale at this point could provide group members with awareness of the approach and crossing of the threshold, reassurance that they are not alone with their feelings but that these can be managed, provide a means for them to express their fears and feelings of inadequacy, a reaffirmation that the struggle can be rewarding, and renewal of confidence in their self-efficacy.

## Therapeutic Factors

The importance of factors conducive to promoting therapeutic progress, healing, and change for group members has received attention in the literature (Colijn, Hoencamp, Snijders, Van Der Spek, & Duivenvoorden. 1991; Corsini & Rosenberg, 1955; Crouch, Block, & Wanless, 1994; Dies, 1997; Fuhriman, 1997; Fuhriman & Burlingame, 1994; Kivlighan, Coleman, & Anderson, 2000; Kivlighan & Goldfine, 1991; Kivlighan & Holmes, 2004; Kivlighan & Mulligan, 1988; MacKenzie 1990; MacNair-Semands & Lese, 2000; Tschusckke & Dies, 1994; Yalom 1995). What has emerged from these studies and reviews is confirmation of the impact of behaviors and attitudes that are clustered as categories for therapeutic, curative change; some are common and valued for all types of groups, some differ in their importance and value depending on the type of population; and there are few guidelines for leaders on how to foster and encourage the emergence of these factors.

These factors have been given various titles, but can be generally categorized as Yalom (1995) presented them. These 11 factors are:

- Universality
- Instillation of hope
- Altruism
- Interpersonal learning
- Guidance or imparting of information

- Catharsis
- Corrective recapitulation of the primary family group
- Imitative behavior
- Existential factors
- Socializing techniques
- Cohesion.

*Universality* contributes to therapy by emphasizing commonalties among group members, reducing their feelings of alienation, of being alone in their struggles or misery, or that they are weird or significantly different from others in negative ways.

*Hope* is very valuable in providing motivation to continue the struggle, and provides a feeling that the struggle will pay off in meaningful ways. Hope can increase members' self-perceptions of worth and value to others and to the universe, and is inspiring.

*Imparting information* is *not* advice-giving. Rather, this therapeutic factor decreases ignorance, empowers the receiver to act on his or her behalf, and increases solution development for problems.

*Interpersonal learning* allows members to increase self-knowledge and self-understanding through feedback from others. This feedback provides the person with information that others can see, but that is usually not seen by him or her, but could be important for relating and communicating with others as well as achieving a greater understanding of the person's own thoughts and feelings.

*Existential factors* are usually present in all groups although these may not be visible or prominent. The therapeutic awareness and discussion of these factors are encouraging to members because these discussions promote awareness that these issues do not have solutions (e.g., the indifference and unfairness of the universe); that all human beings struggle with these issues throughout their lives; and that each person has a unique approach and resolution for these factors.

*Catharsis* can bring relief when suppressed or repressed intense feelings are expressed and the individual sees that he or she is not destroyed by this, and neither are others or one's relationships with them. However, in order to be most effective the emotional venting must be accompanied by a greater understanding of oneself through receiving empathic responding, differing perceptions, or other feedback that promotes self-understanding.

*Socializing techniques* are very useful for almost all group members. Teaching members these techniques demonstrates how they can initiate meaningful connections to others, reduce behavior and attitudes that prevent connections, and increase awareness of others-in-the-world as separate and distinct individuals.

*Imitative behavior* is demonstrated by both the leader and members. Members can learn and practice new and more effective ways of behaving to get their needs met, develop more constructive attitudes through seeing the modeling behavior of others that is more effective than their present behavior.

*The corrective emotional recapitulation* or reenactment of the family of origin makes a valuable contribution to therapy by providing a new perspective for old hurts, resentments, and relationships that can promote healing, forgiveness, and changes.

*Cohesion* provides the necessary conditions for the productive or working stage of the group. This is therapeutic because the group has reached a point where members experience feelings of belonging, connectedness, and productivity; they have learned the benefits of cooperation versus individual efforts, and there are increased feelings of satisfaction with self and with others.

# Chapter 5

# Cultural and Diversity Sensitivity

It can be extremely important for the group leader to have an understanding of the need for cultural sensitivity. Culture is a significant influence on everyone's development, and many of its lessons are integrated into the person and acted on unconsciously. In addition, there are different cultures, each with unique characteristics and expectations that were internalized and are now an unconscious component for the various group members (Brinson & Fisher, 1999; Chen & Han, 2001; Colmant & Merta, 1999; Haley-Banez & Walden, 1999; Kim, Omizo, & D'Andrea, 1998; Santiago-Rivera, Arredondo, & Gallardo-Cooper, 2002; Sue & Sue, 2003; Torres-Rivera, Wilbur, Roberts-Wilbur, & Phan, 1999). Thus, counselors and other mental health professionals cannot know all of the cultural influences for every group member, but these influences will have an impact on the interactions with and functioning of clients. Counselors need to have a high level of cultural sensitivity and competence in order to develop the therapeutic relationship, help clients set reasonable goals, understand how ethics will be operationalized, and to build safety and trust (Abernethy, 2002). This is a difficult job even when clients are native-born Americans, and much more difficult when clients are immigrants who continue to practice many of the aspects of their culture of origin.

It is not possible to provide all the information needed for developing awareness, sensitivity, and competence here because the subject is too broad for adequate coverage. Readers are encouraged to consult the many books and articles on the subject, to enroll in courses and workshops, and to consult with experts. The latter will be especially important when you have clients from varying cultures. This discussion is limited to presenting some cultural variables that can be important for many clients. Variables that can be of importance include the following:

- Perceptions of authority figures;
- Source of illnesses or other conditions;
- Gender and gender differences in expressing emotions;
- The role of family;
- Meaning attribution to experiences;
- Language barriers, facility, and understanding.

## Authority Figures

The counselor is generally perceived as an authority figure by almost all clients. Counselors are the holders of knowledge, the guide for information and understanding, the teacher of skills and, if court ordered participation, the determiners or contributors to their fate. However, there can be varying reactions to counselors as authority figures depending on clients' reaction to authority, such as overcompliance or defiance; their perceptions of your authority as moderated by your gender, age, race/ethnicity; and by your attitude toward differences. An example of what is meant:

*Monica is a 28-year-old female leader of a psychoeducational group for patients diagnosed with alcohol abuse problems having been convicted of several driving under the influence violations. The group members are all male, ages 22 to 65, and hold a variety of laboring jobs. Four are new immigrants from Columbia, Nigeria, Russia, and Saudi Arabia, and four are native born Americans. Monica has difficulty from the very first session. Members respond with very short answers when they respond at all, will not interact with each other, deny having any problems with alcohol abuse, do not express any feelings either about the court-ordered group participation or anything else, and appear to her to be very angry.*

Some cultural variables that can be impacting this example are Monica's age and gender as an authority figure. Young women are not perceived as authorities over men in some group members' culture of origin; there is shame around having to be in a subordinate position to a female; and it may be that some members cannot conceive of a female knowing more than they do about anything. There are numerous other possible variables that could impact this group and the leader.

## Source of Illness or Other Conditions

Spierings (2004) provides three perceptions about the source for the illness or condition; medical, magical, or religious. Medical refers to the Western understanding that many illnesses and conditions are caused by viruses, bacteria, genetics, environmental factors, and so on. They tend to look for an empirically derived cause and effect that can be replicated and generalized. There is a considerable emphasis on research and the scientific method.

Some cultures, even some in the United States, believe that illnesses and conditions result from magical outside sources such as the evil eye, an act of a witch doctor, or a curse. They believe that they can only get better and be cured if the person performing the magic can be overcome, or if they can find another source that is more powerful with greater and more effective magic.

Religious sources for illnesses and conditions are seen as punishment for sins, failing the higher power, or as karma or fate. People believe that they must pay the penalty of pain and suffering for being who they are or for what they have done or failed to do. Only the source of the condition or illness can cure them or bring relief.

Faith is a huge factor in healing as has been documented in many studies, and can play a major role for many group members. The term *faith* is used here because the perceptions of the source of the illness or condition relies heavily on faith, whether that faith is in the medical and scientific professions, magic, or religion. Group leaders with members from varying cultures may want to explore what members believe to be the source of their condition or disease.

### Expressing Emotions

I once led a group with a member from Rwanda, and he commented that in his country people did not label or express feelings. They only said that they were ok or not ok. This is a clear example of cultural differences in expressing emotions. Readers are encouraged to learn the cultural expectations for expression of feelings for major countries in the world.

In addition to cultural differences, there can be gender differences within countries/cultures. There can also be unspoken norms about expressing certain emotions such as, shame, guilt, anger, fear, and disgust. Counselors cannot assume that clients are resisting because of personal issues because the resistance to expressing or exploring emotions could have its basis in the culture of origin.

Another issue that merits attention is how feelings are, or are not displayed. In some cultures, even some within the United States, people are not expected to display their feelings and can go to great lengths to keep their nonverbal behavior from reflecting their feelings. Generally, in the United States and some other Western countries, the person's facial expression is thought to be the prime conveyer of feelings. However, this is a fallacy because people learn through their experiences that it is not always appropriate or safe to show one's true feelings on one's face. There are other cultures where subtle nonverbal behavior reveals the person's feelings, and members of that culture become expert at reading those signs. It can be helpful to research how emotions are verbally and nonverbally expressed in the clients' cultures of origin.

### The Role of Family

Cultures that value collectivism (the group) over individualism can also expect that the family and its members are intertwined and that the family makes the decisions for the individual members. Thus, information is freely shared among family members, and actions taken only after consultation among them. Clients from these cultures may not consider sharing information with family members as breaching confidentiality, or may be able to implement an action plan prior to receiving family permission.

When you have clients from collectivism cultures, expect to be educating all the client's family not just the client. Be very specific in an effort to set the limits for confidentiality for these members. For example, it can be permissible to discuss the factual material and the structure for the counseling sessions or group, but not discuss what individual members say and do with people outside the group, including family members. Other things that can be shared are the client's personal thoughts, ideas, and feelings about themselves and their conditions or illnesses, personal action plans, and sources of information. If you have varying cultures represented in your groups, this emphasis and specificity can be extremely important for establishing trust and safety for other (all) group members.

### Meaning Attribution

There are three major systems for attribution of meaning for experiencing; personal responsibility, fate, and unseen forces.

Mainstream U.S. culture places a lot of emphasis on personal responsibility and control of what one experiences. Choices, decisions, and other personal interventions are emphasized, and people are expected to actively participate in their healing and recovery and to take preventative actions. This expectation is the basis for the establishment and wide use of support and therapy-related psychoeducational groups where it is postulated and believed that these groups can help facilitate coping, change, and recovery by providing information, encouragement, and support, and by learning specific skills.

There are some cultures where illnesses and other conditions are perceived as fate or predestination. There was little or nothing the person could have done to escape this experience. This perspective is closely tied to the spiritual/religious bias of the culture, and emphasizes illnesses and conditions as punishment for not being or living in accordance with those principles, either in the person's current life, or in their former life. Clients from cultures that have this perspective are not likely to take an active role in their recovery or healing because they believe that they have no control over or impact on what happens to them.

The cultures that attribute meaning of experiences to unseen forces are those that emphasize spirits in nature or from elsewhere, ancestors, and other people who have magical powers. Counselors cannot assume that members from a particular country or culture will have the unseen forces perspective, as beliefs vary in almost every culture.

There is also a certain amount of fatalism when people believe in the power of unseen forces, and that the person caused the illness or condition by his or her own behavior. The primary way for getting well would be to appease these forces or to overcome them in some way. A counselor can ask them to describe what they feel they must do in addition to the medical or other treatment they are receiving, to address these unseen forces. Do not ignore or dismiss this perspective as being counter to the medical/scientific one as it is important for improvement, healing, recovery, and for building trust and safety in the group that members with these beliefs have some acknowledgment of their perspective, and how it could be incorporated into the more traditional Western medical and other treatments and interventions.

## Group Leader Strategies

There are six basic strategies that can help guide counselors to be more culturally sensitive and competent and be perceived as such by their clients.

- Become open to learning about cultural differences;
- Limit the amount of information given at any one time;
- Check to insure clarity and understanding;
- Use open questions;
- Use simple words and reduce or eliminate jargon;
- Ask for information about respectful interactions and cultural sensitivities and taboos.

The discussion to this point has emphasized the need to learn about other cultures. It is helpful when the counselor demonstrates an openness to learning more about members' culturally determined expectations. Information from consultants, such as college professors from that culture or who have studied the culture; books, the Internet, and other reference materials; and the members themselves can be rich resources for needed information and understanding.

*Limit the amount of information* given at any one time because the language and concepts are foreign and new, and because these clients may need the time to mentally translate the information into their native language and then translate that understanding back to English in order to ask or answer questions.

It is always helpful to have clients *paraphrase* or repeat instructions, information, and so on, to insure clarity and understanding. It can be even more important when clients are culturally different. There can be times when counselors think they are saying one thing, but are perceived as saying something else; that is, clients hear and understand something different from what was actually said. Paraphrasing and asking clients to repeat what they heard, or thought was meant can help prevent errors and misunderstandings.

Use *open questions* that will give clients an opportunity for exploration and elaboration. This approach also prevents being pushed in a particular direction, or to reach a predetermined conclusion or decision that reflects the counselor's rather than clients' perspectives, values, and choices. Do not frame statements as questions because this can be confusing to some people.

*Language* can be a barrier for culturally different clients. Conveying the information so that it is understood is of critical concern, and counselors must pay attention to their choice of words, even if they have to use several simple words instead of one word that incorporates many complexities.

Acuff (1993) presents these rituals and taboos as reducing communication noise. You will want to specifically inquire about the following:

- How to say hello and goodbye;
- Greeting rituals and gestures;
- Correct address, such as Senor, Senora, or Doctor;
- Sequence for names—not all cultures put the family name last;
- Extent of eye contact that is acceptable;
- Acceptability of jokes;
- Unacceptable nonverbal postures, gestures, and body positions;
- Acceptable physical space or proximity;
- Perceptions about authority figures;
- Sensitive topics, such as religion, history, relations with the U.S., and politics;
- How status or "face" is maintained.

There are many culturally determined ways to show respect and regard and conversely, many ways to unintentionally insult or offend.

# CHAPTER 6

# PROCEDURES AND PROCESSES FOR THE USE OF CREATIVE ACTIVITIES

This chapter presents the fundamental principles and assumptions that guide the use of creative and expressive activities, the general procedures for conducting the expressive exercises, and a process for guiding personal exploration and enhancement to facilitate an understanding of what emerges during the experience.

- Each member's personal experience is unique. How members respond to an activity is a combination of many factors such as past experiences, family of origin factors, personality, current physical and emotional states, and so on. Thus, each group member's experiencing will be unique and personally relevant for him or her.
- The meanings for what emerges lies within that person. Although group members have numerous past experiences, the expressive activities described in this book

tend to reflect the person's current inner world. Even past experiences are perceived from a current perspective.

- Elements of the product or outcome are reflective of the inner world of the person at that time. In addition to current experiencing, some of the past cognitive and emotional states for the person can be also reflected in parts of the product. What is helpful is when these can be explored to understand their continuing impact on current experiencing, such as the impact of past relationships on current ones.
- The products or outcomes provide clues to the person's current wishes, desires, and needs. The clues provided and their messages and meaning carry personal implications as to some below conscious awareness or even from the unconscious. These clues are best analyzed and interpreted by that person.
- Defensiveness is reduced with personal versus the group leader's interpretations. There can be a reduction in defensiveness when the interpretation of the product is done by the group member who created it. New pathways of understanding and insight can be opened because the energy goes into understanding rather than to fending off the material or the group leader's interpretation.
- Acceptance of what emerges during the activity in increased and tolerated when the group member provides meaning for the products. Group members can be more accepting of what emerged for them during the activity when they are allowed to derive the meaning. The threat or danger to the self from the material is managed better as the person him- or herself is in control.
- Developmental and existential issues can be tapped to provide guidance. These are issues and concerns that continue throughout life. Many group members may be unaware that this is to be expected and may not understand the impact these can and do have on their functioning. Expressive activities can activate them,

bring them to consciousness, and allow for expression. Finding others in the group who are struggling with the same or similar issues and concerns can be relieving and promote a sense of universality.

- Learning, understanding, and insight can continue after the exercise is completed. The expressive activities stimulate group members to continue to reflect on what they have experienced, and additional learning, understanding, and even repressed memories can emerge after the activity is completed, and between group sessions. The continued processing of the experience can contribute to their growth, development, and healing.
- Intense and unexpected emotions may arise during an exercise, and these must be contained and managed during the session. The group leader must be mentally and emotionally prepared to cope with members' intense emotions as these can be an outcome of an activity. In this event, it is necessary to ensure that the member(s) do not become mired or overwhelmed with the intensity of feeling, and that they do not leave the session while still experiencing more emotional intensity than they can tolerate.
- Ethical principles guide the use of expressive exercises. A variety of expressive activities are presented in the book and these were chosen as examples that do not require specialized training. However, it is suggested that readers do get some training before implementing these in the groups that they lead. It is not sufficient to have experienced these in their training or therapy and found them valuable; some more formal instruction is generally helpful. Workshops, conference institutes, and other means of training could be used.

## General Guiding Assumptions

Six major general assumptions guide this presentation.

- The focus is on the group as a whole.
- Clinically focused groups are the target groups.
- The leader has tried to intervene without success.
- Members may vary in the reasons for the dilemma.
- The group leader can mirror and contain the dilemma.
- The dilemma reflects resistance, confusion, fear, or uncertainty.

### *Group as a Whole Focus*

One or more members may be reflecting the dilemma and there is a tendency to focus on these members. Attending to the group as a whole allows the leader to address each member's concern, to be inclusive, lessens the potential for scapegoating, and demonstrates understanding and empathy at a deep level for all members.

### *Clinical Groups*

Dilemmas can be reflections of deep seated issues, concerns, and problems that are usually the focus for clinical groups. Other types of groups, such as educational and task groups, have a more cognitive focus, and are usually of short term duration that will not have a sufficient number of sessions to adequately deal with the sensitive material that can emerge. Expressive processes could be used to relieve tension for these groups, but may not be as helpful as they would be for clinically focused groups.

### *Interventions Were Ineffective*

Group leaders are likely to have tried several interventions that were not successful since the dilemmas continue to exist. Interventions may have focused on individual members, exploration of feelings, group process commentary, and other such usual interventions that worked for the leader in the past. Individual interventions don't work because the dilemma is a shared group member concern, although it is usually expressed differently for each member. Exploration of feelings don't seem to be effective because no understanding occurs and venting alone isn't sufficient; or some members may be suppressing, repressing, or denying feelings and these are not being expressed; or members may be confused about their feelings and unable to sort through them.

### *Reasons Vary*

Most often, members will have different reasons and sources for their reactions. For example, some could be experiencing transference, some are projecting, some fear destruction of the self, and others could be so fearful of what could emerge that they shut down. The group leader may not know or be aware of all of the individual reasons, and each may need a different intervention, but the entire group is still impacted and reacting.

### *The Leader Mirrors and Contains*

The group leader's inner experiencing can be a rich source of information about what the group is experiencing. Leaders mirror and contain affect for the group, and this is what the leader's inner experiencing can be reflecting. The leader's level of personal development to reduce countertransference (Gelso & Hays, 2007), self-understanding to reduce projecting, and the ability to be aware of here-and-now experiencing, monitoring of his or her possible countertransference and projecting, permits the leader to judge the validity of his or her inner experiencing as mirroring and containing something for the group.

### *Reflects Resistance, Confusion, Fear, or Uncertainty*

The group members' reactions will usually be resistance, confusion, fear, or uncertainty. Resistance to what can emerge about oneself, confusion about what is being felt but not understanding one's feelings, confusion about the dissonance in the group and its source(s), fear of destruction or abandonment of the self, or uncertainty with all of its accompanying terror.

## Guiding Assumptions about Group Members

Eight assumptions are made about the group members.

- Each group member has a unique contribution to the dilemma or difficult situation.
- Each member's history and personality is different.
- Members are unaware of the fantasies and fears that may be influencing their responses.
- Some group members may be  or are at a crossroads, threshold, or boundary that produces fear and anxiety.
- Developmental tasks such as separation, individuation, and line of narcissistic development, may be incomplete.
- Existential concerns may be influential, acute, or dormant.
- Group members have (use) various means to make sense of their experiencing, and to understand and integrate external and internal forces.
- Dilemmas are introduced as defenses, and the mechanisms used can vary among members.

### *Members' Unique Contributions*

All members contribute to the group's dilemma, and each member makes a unique contribution. Some members can opt for deflecting tactics; some withdraw and are not emotionally present; some may become more active but the activity lacks meaning or purpose; members may engage in conflict that does not get resolved; there can be sniping and unflattering remarks made to and about each other; refusal to explore feelings; and other actions that bring the group to the dilemma. No one person institutes or maintains the dilemma and it is the group leader's responsibility to recognize each contribution to its maintenance.

### *Members' Histories and Personalities Differ*

This may seem obvious, but it bears repeating. Each member brings a different personality and history to the group, and these too contribute to the dilemma and to their specific reactions. Selecting an intervention under these circumstances can be a challenging endeavor because what might be useful for one member could be so threatening for another member that he or she would retreat even further, or worse. Further, there are family of origin and other past experiences that are influential, but these may not have been revealed leaving the group leader in ignorance, or the member could have repressed them, but they still continue to exert influence.

### *Unawareness*

Members may be unaware of their fears and fantasies that are influencing their reactions. Thus, when asked about their reactions, their responses are not meaningful or helpful. They are unaware and cannot articulate their inner experiencing in ways that others can understand. They resort to noncommittal responses, to telling stories, or not responding, none of which provide the leader with clues to their real concerns.

### *At a Crossroads*

It would not be unusual for some or all group members to be at a psychological crossroads, threshold, or boundary that produces fear and anxiety. These members can dimly sense impending changes, or even be acutely aware that change is inevitable, but still be fearful and anxious about the uncertainty and unknown personal future. Members will also vary in how they accept and use their inner resources to cope, and will display these in varying ways.

### *Incomplete Development*

Members can display indices of incomplete development, such as separation, individuation, and narcissistic development. Since each member is unique and different, each will be at a different point for each of these lines of development. The expressive processes take these incomplete development statuses into account, and work with each member at his or her particular point of development.

### *Existential Concerns*

Yalom and Leszcz (2005) propose that existential concerns are present in every group regardless of the group's focus, but that these concerns are not always addressed, and some may never be mentioned in some groups. However, there are also groups where some of these concerns, such as death and existential despair, are acute and prominent in the group's discussion. Even when existential concerns are not emphasized, they can still be influential on group members.

### *Varying Means of Making Sense*

Group members will use varying means to try and make sense of their worlds. There are their internal forces that are not completely understood or fully integrated. In addition, there are external forces that impact them over which they have little or no control. For some members this seems chaotic and directionless, and they have trouble sorting through and making sense of them. Others can feel competent to handle one set of forces, but not both at the same time. Others can feel overwhelmed and just shut down. Each member responds in a unique way.

### *Dilemmas as Defenses*

Think of the group's dilemma as a defense mechanism, but what it is defending against is unknown, may be different for each group member, and each uses a different defense mechanism although they collectively share in producing the dilemma. These variations can make it difficult for a group leader to zero in on the commonality because all he or she is presented with are the differences.

## Basic Conditions

There are several basic group conditions that guide the use of creative activities; sufficient safety and trust has been developed, there are rules and guidelines for participation and for giving and receiving feedback, the group needs assistance to further its functioning, and a problem solving strategy is needed.

It is critical to develop sufficient safety and trust before conducting most of the described activity. The only exceptions may be when an activity is used to facilitate introduction of members where the activity is nonthreatening and does not call for disclosure of sensitive personal material; or using an activity to just play and have fun. Safety and trust will facilitate self-disclosure by members, and the level to which they are willing to reveal the real self.

Group leaders will usually have collaboratively established rules and guidelines for participation, reviewed these with members to get their commitment, and members will generally know what is expected for communication, disclosure, and providing feedback to each other. It is recommended that members be put in charge of their disclosure to decide when and how much to disclose, and that neither the leader nor other members push for a deeper level of disclosure. It is also helpful if members know that courtesy and civility are expected in their relations and communications with each other, but not to the extent where nothing significant is communicated. Labeling, calling names, being disrespectful, and similar behaviors are to be prohibited and blocked.

Relationships are enhanced when members can be open and direct with each other, but that also carries the responsibility of being tolerant, respectful, and mindful when giving and receiving feedback. It is helpful for the group leader to teach group members constructive ways to provide feedback, and to help members learn how to receive and accept feedback. These competencies will facilitate personal learning from the creative activities.

There are times when the group members need assistance to express their thoughts, ideas, and feelings in appropriate ways. One of the reasons that some difficult situations or group dilemmas occur is that members are reluctant to express negative feelings because they fear the fantasized outcomes to be destructive, either to them, to the leader, or to the group. The leader's expertise and use of creative activities can facilitate expression and demonstrate how to do so appropriately. Most of all, members can learn that feedback need not be negative or destructive.

Group members can also learn problem solving through participation in creative activities, especially when things are complex, ambiguous, and uncertain because these occur in the group setting. Demonstrating that there are alternative perspectives, different means to approach a problem or dilemma, and even just the use of creativity can suggest to members that problems need not be overwhelming and frustrating to the point where nothing constructive is accomplished.

## Other Assumptions

- The stage of the group is influential, especially when choosing an intervention.
- The group leader's inner experiencing and clinical judgment are critical to resolving difficult situations and dilemmas.
- The therapeutic relationship is also a critical component; the extent of development for the relationship, and the level of trust and safety established in the group.

# CHAPTER 7

# GENERAL GUIDELINES FOR THE USE OF CREATIVE ACTIVITIES

Each set or category of creative activity is unique, and specific instructions for the use of each category are presented in the specific chapter. This chapter presents some general guidelines that apply to all categories. One of the major premises for this book is that these activities should have purposeful intent. The group leader should understand the group and its members' needs before implementing creative activities. This chapter presents the process for planning that also describes a decision making process for selecting a suitable activity; and the following processes:

- *Implementation*: This includes procedures and directions for when and how to introduce the activity, and what to do while members are creating projects.
- *Reporting*: How to facilitate member sharing of the products of their creative activities.

- *Expansion*: Procedures to guide group members to understand their products, and the feelings they had while constructing them, and feelings they had during the reporting phase.
- *Enhancement*: Guiding members' meanings and associations that derive from the creative activity.

We begin by describing general guidelines for the use of expressive exercises, divided into phases. The phases are planning, a decision making process for selecting an activity, a process for implementation, reporting, exploration, and enhancement.

## Planning

Even experienced group leaders are encouraged to use the planning process to gain optimum outcomes. Expressive exercises should be planned in advance and not impulsively used during the group session. Planning involves determining the purpose of and goal(s) for the exercise, selecting an activity and a decision making process for selections, materials and supplies, and developing the questions used to guide exploration and enhancement.

When you first begin to use expressive exercises, you will find it helpful to write your plan. That way you can ensure that you've covered all the major requirements, and do not have any lapses when using the exercise in the group. As you become more familiar with these and develop your personal favorites, you may not need the security of writing a plan.

### *Purpose and Goals*

The first step is to establish the purpose and goals for the exercise. What are you intending to accomplish? How would the exercise meet the group's need? Have you identified a group need? There are numerous purposes for exercises such as the following:

- Group members seem skittish and fearful of conflict emerging in the group, and an exercise focused on conflict or the fear of conflict could reduce some of their apprehension.
- There is considerable intellectualizing and talking about feelings rather than expressing feelings. An exercise could provide a means for getting around these defenses to allow members better access to them, or facilitate expression of feelings.
- Group members have low verbal skills, and have difficulty expressing personal thoughts, feelings, and ideas because of vocabulary deficits. An exercise could facilitate their expression for these.
- There is suppressed conflict in the group that is causing considerable tension and discomfort. An exercise could relieve tension and facilitate the expression of the suppressed intense feelings.
- The group seems stuck and discussions are circular.
- Several members engage in continual emotional venting over several sessions about the same concern indicating that little or no understanding or problem solving is occurring.
- The group is avoiding or resisting a major concern, such as developing intimacy, fear of not being safe in the group, and so on.
- To relieve tension, play, have fun.

The initial purpose for using an exercise is revisited during the decision-making process (step 2) to select the exercise that best fits the purpose and group members.

## A Decision-Making Procedure

It is more helpful to work through the decision-making procedure rather than just using an activity. The procedure is used to determine if an expressive process could be beneficial for the group and its members, and which expressive process to use. This procedure has the following steps:

1. *Identification of the concern, barrier, or dilemma*. The decision making begins with specifying the concern, issue, or dilemma where a creative activity could be used as an intervention. These activities should be used to tackle something that is affecting the group as a whole, and is not focused on one or two members' individual concerns. Try to be as specific as possible in this identification and use both observable behavior and your (the group leader's) inner experiencing.
2. *Exploration of possible creative activities as intervention alternatives*. Review the kind of possible creative activity that could be used, such as examining the various kinds of activities presented in this book. If you have used exercises and activities, you could look at the list of these or consult references for suggestions. Select an expressive process that can be fully completed in the session.
3. *The possible positive and negative outcomes*. These should be explored for each possible creative activity. Think about what you are trying to accomplish, your group members' vulnerabilities and emotional states, and the purposes and goals for the various creative activities.

   Think of the positive and negative aspects for each possible alternative, the known characteristics of each group member, and if there could be a negative impact or not for any member, the possible benefit for the group as a whole, and if any suggested activity could be eliminated because of members' capacities and ability to participate. You will be able to narrow your choices with this process.
4. *Consider the possible impact on each group member*. Reflect on what you have already gathered about the group members, such as their defenses, arousal, and handling of difficult feelings, uncomfortable memories that can

be triggered, and so on. Consider the possible impact on each group member. Examples include the following:

- Fairy tale: May tap unconscious material.
- Drawing: Members may be resistant and self-conscious about their products.
- Writing: Some members may fear being judged on the technical aspect of their writing, some people do not like to write, the time may not be sufficient if they need to think it through before writing.
- Movement: This may arouse memories of old traumas, fears, or abuse.

5. *Benefits for the group as a whole.* How will the group's functioning, progress, and process be facilitated by using the creative activity? Benefits for the group can include increased energy and interest, assistance with expression of some feelings, and reduction of tension, which may help produce a group atmosphere more conducive to growth and development. New material can emerge that promotes therapeutic group factors such as universality and interpersonal learning.
6. *Members' abilities to participate.* When selecting an activity, group leaders need to be concerned about group members' abilities and competencies to participate and gain from the activity. There can be cognitive impairment, motor dexterity, and other disabilities that would interfere with their being able to fully participate. It is recommended that no activity be used unless all group members can participate.
7. *Group factors.* Estimate the time needed to introduce the exercise and distribute the materials, working time to complete the product, the time needed for members to present their products and share feelings in the group, and time needed to complete the enhancing phase.

Another important consideration is the stage of the group's development. For example, an exercise that focused on a deep level of self-disclosure in the first stage of group development where trust and safety may not be firmly or completely established is not a good idea. Group members may feel threatened and that makes trust and a feeling of safety harder to develop.

Ethical considerations should also be reviewed. Questions such as the following should be explored and answered.

Is there potential harm for any group member?

Am I, the group leader, qualified to conduct this exercise, and able to handle intense emotions that may emerge?

Is any part of the exercise forced self-disclosure?

Do I provide for informed consent?

Are members free to choose not to participate, and are there penalties for not participating?

8. *Tentative selection.* By this time you have narrowed your choices to a very few, or to one creative activity. If you still have more than one as a possibility, review both for suitability for your group. Each group has its own unique set of characteristics and you can now select the one that seems to best fit the group and its need at this time.

## Example of a Decision-Making Procedure

Following is an example of working through the decision-making procedure for a group of adults who have no known disabilities, and after the group has met for several sessions.

### *Identification*

The group has no energy, members are listless, feelings are not being expressed, and the atmosphere is heavy.

*Possible Alternatives*

- Fairy tale: **Positive aspects**—relieve tension and focus thoughts. **Negative aspects**—Completion may take more time than is available in a session.
- Drawing: **Positive aspects**—provides a nonverbal way to express feelings. **Negative aspects**—members may feel judged on artistic ability, sufficient materials may not be available.
- Writing: **Positive aspects**—can be private, and provide an alternative for expressing feelings. **Negative aspects**—lack of member to member interaction, members could become more withdrawn, time constraints.
- Movement: **Positive aspects**—tend to be energizing. **Negative aspects**—promotes members' self-consciousness.

*Benefits for the Group*

Members can be taught how to express feelings and encouraged to express these through use of a creative activity, members will become actively engaged in creating a product, energy is introduced, and the group can move forward.

*Ability to Participate*

This was noted earlier in the description of the group. All members have the capacity to participate.

*Group Factors*

The group seems to have moved beyond the beginning stage so that many creative activities could be less threatening. Thus, it is likely that sufficient trust and safety have been established so that members can trust the group leader to protect them, and this will increase their willingness to participate.

### *Tentative Selection*

Narrow your choices to a very few, or to one. If you still have more than one possible exercise, review both for suitability for your group.

### *Questions for Exploring and Expansion*

Develop a set of three to four questions you could pose that would keep the exercise focused on the goal and purpose, and that would guide members' personal exploration of their experiences or outcomes. General questions that are almost always appropriate are as follows. These are in addition to the focused ones.

- What feelings, thoughts, or ideas emerged as you completed the exercise?
- What feelings are you experiencing as you talk about the exercise?
- What associations to your current or past life can you identify?
- Was any part of the exercise a surprise or troubling for you?
- How would you summarize this experience for yourself?

The use of the described creative activities relies on the group member's personal understanding and associations, and does not expect that the leader and other group members have special knowledge that would provide an interpretation that the member must accept. In other words, the leader does not interpret the symbols for members, but rather allows the individual member to suggest his or her own interpretations, associations, and meanings. The assumptions that guide this perspective are described in chapter 6 and are briefly listed here.

- Symbols can have personal meanings and associations for members.

- Group members will be more open and accepting and less defensive when they can provide their own interpretations.
- It is much less threatening to the person when personal associations are accepted as valid.
- The understandings can emerge in a form that the person finds useful and accurate.
- Members are in charge of their own self-disclosure.
- Shame and guilt feelings can become more manageable for the group and its members.

### *Materials and Supplies*

If you decide to incorporate expressive activities into your groups, it is helpful to have appropriate and sufficient materials readily available. Each activity in this book has a list of needed materials, but you may want to have a "toolbox" always available. Suggested materials for a toolbox, or to always have available include the following.

1. A variety of paper in several sizes such as newsprint, copy paper, and construction paper. The paper does not have to be expensive, but should be available in sufficient amounts.
2. Glue sticks or paper glue.
3. A set of crayons, or colored pencils, or felt markers for each group member. When you compile your toolbox you may not know how many members are in the group, and it is suggested that you plan for at least 10 members.
4. Scissors for each member if the group members are able to use these. Some group members may have difficulty using scissors, or it may not be advisable to let them have scissors and in these cases, the group leader needs to adjust the exercise to eliminate their use.

However, if it is appropriate and the activity calls for their use, try to have at least one pair of scissors for every two group members.
5. Unlined index cards in a variety of sizes. These can be used instead of paper for some activities, and are sturdy for drawing and pasting.
6. Masking tape for posting directions or products.
7. Collect a variety of catalogues and magazines that can be used for images and collages.

Once you have selected the kind of exercise, or the specific exercise you intend to use, the next task is to gather needed materials, such as paper and glue. Try to have sufficient materials so that each person has a separate set. The exercises presented in this book call for relatively inexpensive materials so that having separate sets for group members should not be overly expensive. The only kind of exercise presented here that would be the exception to the group leader's supplying the materials is for scrapbooks. These are so personal that it is probably best to have group members secure these for themselves. If cost is a concern for group members, there are alternatives presented in the discussion on using scrapbooks in chapter 20.

## Generation of a Formal Plan for Implementation

A formal plan for implementation can begin now that you have an exercise to use. Up to now the planning has been primarily cognitive; that is, thinking about what to do. It could be helpful to write an outline for the information such as the following:

## Example of a Formal Plan

*Exercise: Emotions*
*Goal and objectives:* To energize the group, and provide a means for expressing difficult feelings.
*Materials:* A set of crayons, felt markers, or colored pencils for each participant, and sheets of paper for drawing.

Procedure

1. Introduction: 3 minutes
   (More time may be needed if there are numerous questions.)
2. Distribution of materials: 2 minutes
3. Instructions and production: 10 minutes
   (Read these one at a time allowing time to finish the symbol before moving to the next one.)
   a. Select one color and draw a symbol for happy.
   b. Select one color and draw a symbol for sad.
   c. Select one color and draw a symbol for frustrated.
   d. Select one color and draw a symbol for contented (peaceful).
4. Reporting and expansion: (Sharing products) 10 minutes
5. Enhancement: 15 minutes
   Explore the following questions:
   What personal associations, thoughts, and feelings emerged as you completed the exercise?
   Which symbol was easiest to think of, and draw? Which was most difficult?
   What similarities do you see among group members? Differences?
   What is the most intense or focal feeling for you now?
6. Review and evaluation: Take time to mentally review the session and reflect on what went well, what didn't go as planned or presented difficulties, what needs to be changed, and if the goal and objectives were accomplished. It can be helpful to reflect on what emerged for the group and its members as material for further consideration and exploration. Some exercises can be very meaningful for some group members, they will continue to reflect and explore their personal material, and this can reemerge in future sessions.

## The Process for the Implementation Phase

The process for implementation discusses introduction of the activity, how and what to observe as members work, handling questions, and providing encouragement.

### *Introduction of Activity*

It is very important to introduce the exercise in a way that allows members to assess their personal psychological risk(s), and make an informed choice about participation. It is also ethically responsible to give members the option not to do the exercise, and if even one member objects, it is best to relinquish the exercise and to use the time to explore the resistance. The group does not benefit when one or more members are openly resistant about completing an exercise. There is probably a shared reason for the resistance that could be a reflection of unspoken resistance from other members. Do not force or push an exercise. Take that time to try to better understand what the resistance is about, such as the following possibilities:

- Fear of unleashing uncontrollable conflict;
- Fear of intimacy;
- Fear of finding out something about oneself that could be upsetting;
- A disguised way of challenging the leader;
- Feelings of danger in the group such as an unidentified narcissist, borderline, or quietly explosive member (Brown, 2007);
- An unrevealed urgent and important problem someone is experiencing.

There are numerous valid reasons for the resistance and these should be respected.

Let's assume that group members are cooperative and are willing to try the exercise. Don't skimp on the information provided in the introduction, but don't overexplain either. Too much information could affect spontaneity and creativity. Members may be inclined to want to give you what they think you expect instead of their personal experiencing when you overexplain. Introduce the exercise with an explanation of the general purpose, what members will be asked to do, such as draw or write, and an overview of what to expect will emerge for them such as their feelings. Stay vague and general for the last item as you don't want to direct their personal experience. Give them the option to stop participating at any time during the exercise if they should become upset, or feel overwhelmed. Note: If a member should stop participating after beginning the exercise, it would be helpful to guide them in understanding what was emerging for him or her, and what was producing the upset or feelings of being overwhelmed.

A sample script for an introduction follows. The script is based on a perceived group constraint around expressing feelings.

### *Sample Introduction of Activity Script*

*Some group members have identified one of their relationship difficulties as an inability to express feelings, and all members seem to agree that it is difficult or impossible for them to express negative thoughts and feelings.* ***(Problem identified)*** *I would like to try an exercise that could begin to help make it easier to express all types of feelings, and I need your permission to continue.* ***(Giving members control)***

*The exercise consists of having you think of symbols for four emotions I'll name, then select a color that you related or associate with the symbol, and draw the symbol on a card. We'll then talk about the symbols and their associations for you.* ***(Description of the procedure)*** *You can stop at any point along the way if you choose.* ***(Permission to opt out)*** *Are there any questions?* ***(Pause and answer questions)*** *Does anyone object to doing this exercise?* ***(This is where objections and resistance could be explored)*** *Are we ready to begin?* ***(One last chance to opt out)***

### *Observing Members as They Work*

Important information can be gained through observing the individual group members as the exercise is introduced and as they work. Notice their facial expressions, body postures, the pace at which they work to complete the exercise, pauses, and the need for clarification. At different points during the exercise, walk around while they are working to observe each member from the best angle.

*Facial expressions* can signal distress, confusion, impatience, delight, and involvement, and other such feelings that can arise during an exercise. Don't do anything unless it seems as if the member is becoming flooded or overwhelmed with negative emotions. If this should occur, go to that member and quietly ask if you can help as you noticed his or her distress. Give the distressed member permission to stop participating at this point, and ask if he or she will be willing to talk about their experience during the reporting phase.

*Body posture*, like facial expression can also provide clues. Look for tense body positions; if the member is protective or hiding their product, such as an arm positioned as if they were shielding their product from sight; legs moving restlessly or entwined tightly; or other postures that signal excitement, pleasure, and so on.

*Notice the pace* used by each member when working. Do they work effortlessly at a quick or measured pace, or are there starts and stops? Do they seem decisive, at a loss, pensive, and so on? Interruptions of working could signal thinking, unpleasant associations emerging, pleasant memories and associations, and other such feelings.

Observing also extends to the other phases; reporting, exploration, and expansion. Observe members and the group as a whole because there is much information that can be gathered other than the content that is verbally expressed. Group leaders can find the following observations to be helpful.

- Similarities among members can be identified and remarked on even when the similarities are not readily apparent to those members.
- Areas of sensitivity for members can be noted for exploration in subsequent sessions.
- Intense emotions can be observed and steps can be taken to reduce these before the session comes to a close.
- Member to member empathic responses can be indicative of unrevealed or unaware similarities that could be the basis for strengthening connections, and for fruitful exploration.
- The strength of defenses mounted against knowing sensitive information about oneself can help to understand that member.
- Validation of hypothesized issues, concerns, or unfinished business for various group members.
- Any shared resistance among members as well as that for individual members.
- The atmosphere and feeling tone during and about the exercise.

### *Questions*

Questions after the introduction can signal resistance, a need for clarification, or uncertainty. Some members can be resistant either consciously or unconsciously and this is expressed in questions about the instructions, purpose, what the leader expects, and so on. Indeed, some may not hear the instructions and ask that they be repeated again. This is one reason why it can be helpful to post the instructions on a chalkboard or newsprint so that members do not have to remember what to do. Others may express their resistance by misunderstanding instructions, and later ask for clarification. Another possible reason for requests for clarification is that the instructions were not as clear as needed. The group leader should note this need to revise the instructions to be clearer. There is no need to address the resistance, just note it, and provide the needed answers to the questions.

### *Encouragement*

Some members may need encouragement. They may want to be perfect in what they do (e.g., write or draw), and past experiences have led them to be very insecure about their ability. The group leader can provide the needed encouragement and support by being very clear that talent and ability take a back seat to expression, and by being very accepting of whatever is produced.

## The Reporting Phase

Each member should have an opportunity to present and share his or her experience and product. The exercise loses its power to promote understanding or insight when carried over to another session and much valuable information for and about the members can be lost as a result of the delay. The group leader must manage this part of the exercise experience to ensure that every member speaks about his or her experience and product. This management of reporting can be a challenge because some members will reveal material that could be very fruitful for exploration, some members can be so excited about their experience or product that they want to do more self-exploration immediately, and the group leader wants to seize the opportunity to deepen the self-exploration and feeling experience as members could benefit from this. All these reasons are valid and enticing, but must be resisted for the moment as it is more important at this point to have enough time for every member to report. Further exploration and deepening can be accomplished during the expansion phase which can be delayed to another session when adequate time does not remain in this session. Group leaders can note what could be returned to and explored further.

Why this insistence on having every member report?

- Each member feels validated and that he or she is not being ignored, overlooked, or minimized.
- Old feelings around sibling rivalry are less likely to be triggered.
- The group leader would not be perceived as playing favorites.
- Members would not run the risk of being perceived as more worthy, or more needy.
- Any hidden intense feeling could be revealed or observed, and taken care of before the session ends.
- It becomes easier to identify commonalities.
- The group leader gets a better understanding of what the experience was like for the entire group, and this provides information for group as a whole interventions.

Initiate the reporting phase with clear directions about what members are supposed to do, such as the following. Gather members back into the circle and tell them that this phase involves having each member briefly present his or her experiencing or product, and that there will be limited comments, questions, or explanations because it is important that everyone have an opportunity to present. Tell them that exploration will continue during the expansion phase where the leader's previously developed questions can be used as a guide. Tell members that they are being asked to give reflective or empathic responses to each other at this time when they are reporting, and to save other responses for later. The group leader should also follow these directions, but can vary when it is therapeutically needed, such as when a member becomes overwhelmed by intense emotions. That situation calls for immediate intervention, but even then the leader should resist deepening the experience or going too far with exploration.

It is probably best that the leader not give each member a time limit for presentation, such as saying that each member has 2 minutes for presenting. Giving a time limit could make some members rush, or feel rushed, and they then can leave out what could be important information. What could work better is to ask members to briefly present what seems important for them to report at this time, they can have more time later for expansion and exploration either in this session or in later sessions, and to mentally set a time limit for each presentation. This will enable the leader to restrict his or her tendencies to deepen the experience at this point, and to move on to the next member's reporting.

If there seems to be something urgent and important for a member when reporting, the group leader can respond empathically, and say that it will be explored after all members have reported. The same script can be followed when something is not urgent and important, but seems to be sensitive or has the potential for fruitful exploration. Most exercises, especially those presented in this book, are unlikely to arouse deep-seated issues or uncontrollable intense emotions, but the potential for these continue to exist, and a leader must be prepared to manage these for the therapeutic benefit of group members.

## The Expansion and Enhancement Phases

After each member reports on personal experiencing for their products, the group can move to the expansion and enhancement phase where the emerged material can be explored for additional meaning and insight. This can be done verbally, or through guided writing together with verbal reporting. The previously developed list of questions can be used for both.

When verbal expansion is used, the leader and other members have an opportunity to give empathic responses, and to ask for clarification. I would recommend that the group leader set the direction and tone for this phase by telling the group that it will be helpful to the speaker to give empathic responses, and to restrict questions for clarification only. This will prevent any member from facing a barrage of questions that could be potentially upsetting if he or she is in a sensitive state with memories, associations, and the like, that were aroused by the exercise. The leader should block digressions, questions, and other inappropriate comments so as to stay focused and to allow sufficient time for exploration by this and other members.

One disadvantage of verbal expansion is that members, other than the speaker, can consciously or unconsciously incorporate other members' reactions and feelings into their own presentation and thereby become contaminated and not entirely focused on their own personal experiencing. Some members may be more open as a result of the exercise, and this openness facilitates catching other's feelings. The similarities of experiencing can also contribute to emotional susceptibility. Another disadvantage is that more time may be taken per member to facilitate his or her personal exploration so that there is not sufficient time remaining to take all group members through the process.

Guiding personal expansion and enhancement through writing prevents the two disadvantages seen for verbal expansion and enhancement. Every member facilitates his or her own exploration. The procedure would be as follows:

1. After the reporting phase is completed, distribute paper and writing instruments.
2. Ask group members to reflect on their experience and products, and to write responses to your questions.
3. Present the questions developed during the planning phase one at a time, allowing sufficient time between questions for members to write their responses. If someone does not seem finished, tell the person that he or she can return to the question later.
4. Have a mentally set time frame for writing, stay on task, and move it along without wasting time.
5. Regroup and have members report as much or as little of what they wrote as they choose.
6. Give empathic responses, restrict questioning, and ask group members to do the same.

Additional expansion and enhancement can continue at a later time.

Group members can be less resistant and defensive when they are the ones to decide what material to focus on, and this leads to more fruitful self-exploration. Group leaders can note what emerged that can be returned to at subsequent sessions, deeper and more meaningful similarities among members, and possible areas of sensitivity.

Other procedures for exploration and expansion of products and experiencing are presented in the chapters that describe the particular activity, such as chapter 8 on fairy tales.

# Chapter 8
# Fairy Tales

## Introduction

Bettelheim (1976) writes, "In child or adult, the unconscious is a powerful determinant of behavior" (p. 7) and as such, is a rich source of information about anxieties, fantasies, fears, hopes, and wishes as well as material for creative and inspirational pursuits. It is through this material that some of the psychological growth concerns are addressed: adjusting to narcissistic disappointments, resolving sibling or parental rivalries, becoming independent and separate from the family of origin, and developing healthy self-esteem. But, when the unconscious material is either kept rigidly under control, or emerges in consciousness as overwhelming derivations of the constructs, rather than being integrated in a rational way, the person cannot make constructive use of the material. When this is the pattern from childhood on, the adult can become severely hampered in functioning, fearing the material instead of knowing how to make positive use of it.

The fearful, threatening, and potentially shameful nature of the material in the unconscious can lead to the use of defenses; both to keep from knowing and to prevent others from seeing. Adults in therapy have had numerous years of employing their defenses, and are afraid to let go of these as they fear the material that will be revealed to self or to others will be extremely shaming. This is only one reason why therapy is an uncovering process that helps peel away layers to correct misperceptions, integrate polarities, rediscover parts of self, reclaim disowned parts of self, and to develop a more cohesive, grounded, and centered self. These defenses are generally strong, of long standing, and effective so that it is difficult for the person to relinquish them. This may be especially so in groups where there are strangers who would see the shame. Group leaders must be understanding, tolerant, and patient and not expect group members to lower their defenses any time soon.

While there are numerous paths to encourage the lowering of defenses, to uncovering repressed and denied material, and to the unconscious, one relatively nonthreatening approach is through the use of fairy tales. Bettelheim (1975) proposes that fairy tales are a unique art form that enlightens and fosters personality development. These tales offer meaning on several different levels, present the process of healthy psychological development in metaphors and symbols, and help to reduce some of the anxiety and fear about the unknowns of human existence. These characteristics of fairy tales may be especially helpful for the group setting where members are most likely to be on differing levels of psychological development, and are at different points in dealing with existential concerns.

## Applications and Uses from the Literature

Literature reviews will reveal much more information on uses of fairy tales with children than with adults. However, there are articles that describe uses with a wide variety of adult conditions, and proposals for further uses with adults in therapy. Adult conditions incorporating fairy tales include the following:

- Chronically mentally ill patients in a maximum security hospital setting (Diana, 1998);
- Caregivers (Golden, 1999);
- Mother–daughter relationship (Whitaker, 1992);
- Depression and isolation (Dieckmann, 1997);
- Midlife depression (Zed, 2003).

Proposed therapeutic uses include the following:

- Reframe existential issues (Biechonski, 2005; Stevens-Guille & Boersma, 1992);
- Maturation concerns (Shee, 1976);
- Corrections environment (Holton, 1995);
- Ego development (Schapiro & Katz, 1978);
- Cognitive development (Chinen, 1996);
- Moral and spiritual development (Brun, Pedersen, & Runberg, 1993, Chinen, 1996);
- Social and emotional competence (Hohr, 2000);
- Human services training (Brown, 2007).

This chapter presents a discussion about the contrasts of fairy tales with myths, legends, folk tales and the like, and some meanings for metaphors and symbols that appear in fairy tales.

## The Psychological Importance of Fairy Tales

Fairy tales begin with an existential/developmental dilemma that is briefly stated. The central figure or figures are at a threshold where their world is changing (usually their internal world), the future is uncertain, the self is in danger or in a state of confusion, and old answers do not fit the new situation. Sometimes there is a period of wandering where new events, challenges, and enchanted characters are encountered. But, central premises are that everyone has difficulties in life, these are unavoidable, and they are a part of the human condition. The struggles, metaphors, and ultimate triumph for the central characters show that it is possible to attain a higher level of self and moral development when one's inner resources are used in a constructive way, and that problems can be solved if only for the present.

Bettelheim (1975) proposes the following characteristics for fairy tales, and these also apply to adults who may not have fully completed some developmental tasks, and those who are confused and unaware of existential issues that have emerged for them. These tales do the following:

- Direct the individual to discover his or her personal identity.
- Present experiences that show a potential for developing character.
- Suggest that a rewarding and good life can be attained if you are willing to work through adversity and other struggles.
- Demonstrate the universality of internal processes and make them visible and external.
- Personal problems, dilemmas, and concerns are shown to be capable of personal solution.
- Provide reassurance and encouragement, but do not demand that one do or be something.

### *Personal Identity*

Fairy tale characters seldom have proper names. They are usually identified by their position in the family such as Simpleton in *Queen Bee* and Cinderella who lived among the cinders; by clothing such as Red Riding Hood; by their role such as mother/stepmother; or by their occupation such as *The Shoemaker and the Elves*. Some tales do have characters with proper names such as Jack in *Jack and the Beanstalk*, and Hansel and Gretel. But, most tales are built around a character or characters who can be anyone, thus making it easier to identify with him or her regardless of age or gender. Readers and listeners can identify with the central character or characters, connect with them in their challenges and struggles, hope for their success and survival, and celebrate their achievements. Just as these ordinary people in the story were able to overcome adversity, so too can others overcome theirs. The question, "Who am I?" is eternal, ever changing, and is worthy of exploration at any age.

### *Developing Character*

Character and moral development are human challenges that present struggles to tame and overcome what Bettelheim calls id impulses, where self-centered attitudes and selfishness dominate the person's thoughts, ideas, and feelings; others are not respected as worthwhile, separate, and distinct individuals; and where thoughtless and insensitive acts are fueled. Fairy tales metaphorically recognize the id impulses, and show the value and rewards for taming these, and for developing an appreciation and awareness of greater humanity that is altruistic and affirming of others. A shift from self-centeredness to self and others in the world is an inner developmental process that cannot be mandated or demanded by external forces. The shift can be facilitated by the tale which shows that id impulses can be tamed, and that the person can act morally.

### *Work through Adversity*

Fairy tales have been criticized for happy endings as some people assert that this sets up unrealistic expectations. However, what Bettelheim and others propose is that these tales show that one's life can be rewarding when one is willing to face whatever life brings, and that the rewards are life enhancing whether or not things work out as one wishes or fantasizes that they would. The struggle is worth the effort, you can prevail in some way, and your self-efficacy can become stronger. How you live your life is as important, or more so, in determining the person you become.

The rewards in fairy tales are metaphors for:

- Enduring and satisfying relationships;
- Meaning and purpose for one's life;
- Hope for the future;
- Strong inner resources for coping with life's challenges;
- An integrated, centered, and grounded self;
- Respect, positive regard, and love for self and for others.

These tales assert that life is a journey and that you have considerable say in what the journey holds for you.

### *Make Inner Processes Visible*

Bettelheim (1975), Cashdan (1999), Dieckmann (1997), and others propose that fairy tales tap into unconscious conflicts, frustrations, fantasies, and wishes that the person is struggling with, developmental tasks that are not yet fully completed, and existential concerns. The characters and events in the tales are metaphors for these and for the personal feelings of the reader or listener. The tale is an indirect and nonthreatening way of allowing the person to recognize and address what is hidden, and can be threatening to their self if approached directly.

Further, these tales demonstrate the universality of these internal processes, developmental tasks, and existential concerns and make them visible and less anxiety producing. The suggestions that these are common across people, are capable of being resolved if only for the present, and that everyone has internal resources that can be tapped to work through the challenges can be affirming and encouraging, and can help reduce feelings of isolation and alienation.

Prominent in many fairy tales are the themes of taming id impulses, and achieving separation and individuation. These are two developmental tasks for everyone, and these tales suggest that the struggle is worth the effort, and can produce positive outcomes; that is, the struggle is rewarding. Also embedded are existential themes that speak of their connections and universality for everyone regardless of country, age, or gender. The reader or listener can become less anxious because they understand that they are not alone in having to struggle with these issues, concerns, and developmental tasks, and they begin to understand that the answers they achieve today will not always be sufficient, and these concerns and dilemmas will reemerge throughout one's life.

### *Personal Solutions*

Each person's situation is unique in many ways, and his or her struggles to resolve life's dilemmas and problems call for uniquely personal solutions. There are times when these can appear to be overwhelming, confusing, incomprehensible, and unsolvable. It is during those times that many people search for answers from external sources, but cannot find what is needed or seems right for them. Some will search inwardly, but will overlook or ignore possible inner resources that can be used for help with solutions. Fairy tales encourage self-reflection and can reveal for the person, personal internal resources that can be used to address the issue, problem, or concern. For example, in a class exercise a student reported that she knew she had been overspending on unneeded items, and the fairy tale for her revealed her real underlying concern which was about a current intimate relationship. She said that she had not realized until that moment that she was concerned about the relationship, and although she was conscious of overspending, she felt unable to stop doing so. She said that she could now explore what the real concern was about the relationship, and felt that she could better control her spending.

### *Reassures*

Fairy tales can reassure readers or listeners that they are not alone in their struggles that the struggles and adversity are worth the effort, that the reader or listener need not become mired in their concerns, and that helpful internal resources do exist if they will open themselves up to searching for these. The sense of safety and security they receive encourages them to persist.

How do fairy tales reassure and encourage? First, the metaphors used in fairy tales demonstrate understanding of what the characters are facing in a way that allows group members to recognize the threatening material in their own lives, but not have to fear that they will become mired in it, overwhelmed and unable to cope, or will be destroyed if they explore it. Any and all of these states are to be resisted. The reader or listener is reassured that he or she does not have to be superhuman to overcome adversity, that problems can be solved even if only for the present, that it is possible to have some influence and control if you can find and use the resources you already possess, and that you don't have to be at the mercy of your inner factors that appear to be threatening and powerful, and are feared as potentially destructive.

Thus, readers and listeners can be encouraged and become hopeful that they too can work through their problems. They realize that they are not alone in these struggles, and that their inner conflicts are not unique to them, but are an expected part of growth and development, and that moral development leads to greater feelings of belonging and connection. Feeling encouraged and hopeful, they can be less discouraged when things don't work out as planned, when their attempts at solving problems are not entirely successful, or when other concerns emerge. They now have more confidence in their ability to cope and manage their emotions, and to seek guidance from within themselves. They can become more independent.

## Fairy Tales and Other Forms of Stories

Folk tales, legends, myths, and fables are not fairy tales as the term is used in this discussion. These other story forms can have some therapeutic value, but this discussion is limited to fairy tales as generally recognized in Western literature, and these have some significant differences from the other story forms.

Coulacoglu (2000) describes fairy tales as reflecting universal human conditions, development, and values. The existential issues of isolation, alienation, fear of abandonment and ultimately death, existential anxieties, freedom, responsibility, and will are major theses and components of fairy tales. (Bettelheim, 1975). Developmental issues and concerns such as, separation and individuation, achieving independence, integration of polarities for self and for others, and mastering primitive affect such as anger and jealousy are also frequent components of fairy tales. The central components for these tales could be seen as recognizing inner resources and achieving a higher level of humanity that incorporates tolerance, forgiveness, mercy, and sharing. Other story forms share some characteristics with fairy tales, but none has all these characteristics.

*Folk tales* tend to be universal because, although the characters have different names, and some details vary, the essential story remains the same in many countries. For example, DeVos and Altman (1999) term Cinderella a folk tale that with different names and details appears in stories told in China and Africa and elsewhere. Many folk tales differ from fairy tales in several ways; characters have names, the stories are designed to teach a specific lesson valued by that culture, they suggest what one should or ought to do, and there is punishment for failure to do what is needed or expected.

*Legends* are stories about heroic and romanticized events that are handed down from previous generations. These stories usually have a kernel of truth, but the events, people, and actions have become magnified and exaggerated to a great extent. Because of their historical nature, legends are usually verifiable. Legends differ from fairy tales in that many legends are about real people, the events happened in some form, and they are designed to entertain and provide role models for the listeners. Legends are more real world than are fairy tales.

For example, look at the legend of Johnny Appleseed, who was a real person named John Chapman. In 1797 Chapman appeared in northwestern Pennsylvania and began his journey between there and Indiana planting apple seeds and preaching Swedenborgianism, a very complex Christian theology. He began to call himself Johnny Appleseed, and gave away or bartered his seeds and plants.

*Myths* deal with supernatural beings, ancestors, or heroes that embody a culture's ideals or deeply held emotions, and who serve as fundamental primordial types (Hohr, 2000). Bettelheim (1976) notes: "The myth presents its theme in a majestic way; it carries spiritual force; and the divine is present and is experienced in the form of superhuman heroes who make constant demands on mere mortals" (p. 26). The mortals cannot hope to emulate the superhuman heroes, and will always be inferior. Fairy tales are about ordinary people who meet the challenges that everyone faces, and the listener can learn from this, and can aspire to achieve the same tasks or goals. In myths, heroes have names, do extraordinary things, and are grander than humans can become.

*Fables* are designed to teach cultural values and morals. These stories have a specific point to convey and the listener is supposed to learn that particular lesson. While magic and improbable events are used in fables as they are in fairy tales, these do not stand as metaphors or symbols for the listener's inner states, they are used as vehicles to get attention and transmit a particular message.

An example of a fable and lesson is seen in the story of "The Fox and the Grapes" (*Aesop's Tales*, 1993). A fox set out to steal some grapes from a farmer. He ran and jumped over and over again trying to reach the grapes growing on a vine, but was unsuccessful. He gave up and rationalized that the grapes were probably sour anyway. The moral of the story was "Sometimes when we cannot get what we want, we pretend that we did not want it at all really" (p. 8).

## Fairy Tales in the Group

Judicious use of fairy tales in groups can address both individual and group concerns and issues. Individual concerns and issues include the following:

- Clarify developmental tasks that are uncompleted.
- Highlight causes and sources for resistance.
- Point out the value of integrating polarities so that the self and others are not seen as all good or all bad.
- Clarify current personal concerns and the need for decisions.
- Identify internal resources that may be ignored or overlooked.
- Promote self-exploration.
- Reduce anxiety.
- Reveal hidden and unknown parts of self.
- An individual group member can derive considerable benefit from the appropriate use of a fairy tale.

The group as a whole can also have its concerns and issues addressed at the same time as are the individual ones. These include:

- Group challenges, such as collective resistance.
- Encouragement of awareness of universality for deeper issues, values, thoughts, and ideas.
- Fostering the emergence of hope and altruism.
- Highlight unspoken existential issues.
- Reducing defensive behaviors, such as intellectualizing.
- Reducing anxiety and tension.

Each group member has a unique collection of personality characteristics, past experiences and their resulting impacts, completion of developmental tasks and the lack, current issues and concerns, self-awareness and other self-factors, and a unique perspective of self and others in the world. Even when the focus and theme for the group is around a common concern, such as in substance abuse treatment, each group member differs on several of these factors. Adding to the complexity is the usual situation where group members are unaware and ignorant of some important and major parts of their selves, and some parts that they do know about they want to keep hidden for fear of being shamed and ejected. The group leader has the difficult task of balancing all this with the need to promote change and growth.

Fairy tales provide an indirect and nonthreatening way to accomplish some individual and group tasks and needs. Individual members can discover something about self, learn that there are many universal concerns and issues and thereby reduce isolation and feelings of alienation, and can gain new perspectives for old issues and concerns. The group as a whole benefits when individual members do, and members benefit when the group does.

### Provide Assets for the Group

There are other positive outcomes for using fairy tale exercises in the group, such as the following.

- Members with low verbal skills are encouraged to talk.
- Thoughts and ideas can be expressed that would not be expressed in other circumstances.
- Insight can be gained about dimly understood self factors and states.
- The symbolic and metaphorical nature of the tales allows threatening material to become less dangerous for exploration.
- Ideas for resolving problems and dilemmas can emerge.
- Awareness of the universality of existential issues and the inability to have permanent solutions as these persist and reemerge throughout life.
- Hope is highlighted.

Group progress and process can be enhanced as group members continue to reflect on the material that was personally relevant for them. They can see each other in new ways, forge new connections around similarities at a deeper level, become more willing to explore personal issues, and feel safer in the group.

Fairy tales acknowledge their inner conflicts and confusion, validate them, and reveal their universality.

Since the focus for this discussion is on the group, let's look at some possibilities for how using a fairy tale can be helpful for the previously described group dilemmas. The next section presents descriptions of groups, possible reasons for the dilemma, and suggested fairy tale applications.

## Guidelines for Using Fairy Tales, and Understanding the Outcomes

The basic procedures for using fairy tales with adults in therapy are presented in this section. Guidelines are also presented for the exploration and enhancement phase that will facilitate members' understanding of their products. The basic procedures involve planning, implementation, and association.

### *Planning*

1. Identify a rationale, problem, or dilemma where using a fairy tale exercise could benefit several members or the group as a whole.
2. Use the decision-making model described in chapter 5 to reinforce the decision.
3. Select several fairy tales for consideration:
   a. Identify the major themes for each fairy tale.
   b. Identify the developmental issues addressed by each.
   c. Identify the existential issues addressed by each.
   d. Associate the themes, developmental issues, and existential issues for each fairy tale with the needs and characteristics of the group as a whole or individual group members.

Some themes, developmental issues, and existential issues are provided in Tables 8.1, 8.2, and 8.3 for a sample of fairy tales. An example for matching as described in step 3 is provided later in this chapter.

1. Decide which method of exploration and expansion you will use. These are also described later in the chapter.
2. Make a list and gather any needed materials.

***Rationale, Problems or Dilemma***

Several rationales for using a fairy-tale exercise were identified earlier in this chapter. In addition, the following also can apply.

1. A fairy tale exercise can make some unconscious or non-conscious material available to consciousness in a non-threatening way.
2. Meanings are provided on several levels.
3. Resistance and defensiveness to self-exploration can be reduced.
4. Universality and hope can be fostered.
5. Potentially shaming material is presented in metaphors and symbols where it is more likely to be tolerated and accepted by the individual.

Any or all of these are beneficial to the group and to individual members. Problems that several members or the group are having that can be addressed include the following:

- The group is stuck or mired in circular discursions.
- The group fears challenging the leaders.
- There is suppressed conflict among members.
- Group members stay focused on surface similarities and concerns.
- Difficult member behaviors are emerging and negatively affecting the group's progress.
- Difficult behaviors are those such as story-telling, advice giving, monopolizing, and yes-but responses.
- Members seem overwhelmed by the complexity of their problems and concerns.
- Difficult decisions and actions are avoided.
- There is refusal on the part of members to admit or experience negative emotions.

Group dilemmas are those that are shared by all or almost all group members, and are contributing to a group atmosphere where little or no therapeutic work is being done. The group is at a standstill and is in danger of disintegrating. A fairy-tale exercise could highlight the shared unspoken concern; relieve tension so that members could engage in self-exploration instead of working so hard to defend themselves, as well as addressing their individual concerns.

### *The Decision-Making Process*

Let's assume that you have reached the point where you are selecting the fairy tale to be used in the exercise. You don't have to be overly concerned about age, educational level, or even developmental level because although these fairy tales were developed for children, they are suitable for all age groups. You will have to take into consideration the following group member characteristics:

- Ability to hear the story when read aloud;
- Physical disabilities that would prevent drawing or writing if you use these as the means for producing a product for exploration and expansion.

The most important variables for selection would be matching the group's need to the fairy tale theme for optimum results. It seems that almost every fairy tale could produce some positive outcomes and learning, but some could be more appropriate for what a particular group needs at that point. One important constraint when selecting a fairy tale is to not use one that has been featured in film or television as the images members see could be unduly influenced by the translation to media. There are so many other tales that selection of one that has not appeared in the media should not present a problem.

## General Fairy Tale Themes and Symbols

Table 8.1 presents some developmental and existential themes for a sample of fairy tales as suggestions for matching with group and/or individual needs. Tables 8.2 and 8.3 present the possible developmental and existential issues that can be addressed in fairy tales. Some general symbols and themes derived from Bettelheim (1975), Brown (1992), and Brun et al. (1993) include the following:

- Wandering—Latency, becoming ready for the next level of development;
- Forest—Search for meaning, purpose, or direction;
- Helpful animals, nonhostile dwarfs and other people—Unrecognized strengths and other inner resources;
- Wild animals, birds of prey, and destructive acts by others—Immature parts of self;
- Leaving home—Becoming separated, achieving independence;

**Table 8.1** Fairy Tales and Example Developmental and Existential Themes

| Tale | Developmental | Existential |
|---|---|---|
| Queen Bee | Controlling id impulses Integrating self | Achieving a level of self-actualization |
| The Pink | Becoming self-sufficient as a process | Loneliness, death |
| Jardina and Joringle | Integrating and freeing parts of self | Living fully |
| The Three Children of Fortune | Constructive use of personal resources | Freedom and responsibility |
| Fundevogel | Becoming independent, master development issues | Search for meaning |
| Twelve Dancing Princesses | Curbing id impulses and destructive aspects of self | Accepting responsibility |
| Karl Katz | Latency, slow growth not yet ready | Death |
| The Water of Life | Overcoming destructive narcissism | Search for meaning |

- Flowers—The idealized self;
- Water, ponds—Emotional life;
- Church—Sanctuary, safety;
- Keys—Untapped knowledge, resources;
- Turned to stone, stone animals or people—Lack of humanity and connection to others;
- Food—Need for nurturance; overabundance or feasts—oral greediness;
- Simpleton, witling, and so on—Simply childlike, the reality based part of self;
- Hostile attacks and hostile people—Ineffective, aggressive, and destructive parts of self;
- that are not yet understood or controlled;
- Sleeping—suspended animation, latency, waiting;
- Completing Tasks—Achieving self-actualization;
- Jewels—Rewards, success;
- Forester, Hunter—Protector.

### *Reading Instructions*

The preferred procedure is to read the fairy tale to the group. However, you could also tape yourself reading the tale, or get

**Table 8.2** Existential Issues in Fairy Tales

Death
Freedom
Will, the trigger of effort, responsible mover, mainspring of action, seat of volition
Indifference of the universe
Struggle and suffering
Existential isolation
Meaninglessness
  Crisis of life
  Senselessness
  Aimlessness
Responsibility, taking authorship and not blaming others
  Creating one's self
  Destiny
  Life predicament
  Feelings

**Table 8.3** Developmental Issues in Fairy Tales

| |
|---|
| Achieving independence |
| Developing moral values |
| Separation and individuation, development of self |
| Line of healthy narcissism development |
| Psychological boundary strength |
| Emotional regulation and control |
| Fear of abandonment , inadequate to care for self |
| Fear of destruction, safety – protection |
| Helplessness – self efficacy |
| Hopelessness |
| Despair |
| Longing and yearning for love and acceptance |

someone with a pleasant voice to do the reading. The tale should be read at a modest pace, with as much inflection as would make the story interesting. Try not to rush through the tale or to go too slow as neither will produce the material that is looked for.

## Methods for Exploration and Expansion

There are numerous methods for exploration and expansion, but the ones proposed here rely on self-interpretation by group members where the role of the group leader is limited to facilitating the exploration and expansion. This step is presented as part of planning as almost all of the methods suggested here require materials that should be gathered in advance. Four possible methods are presented; read and discuss, read and draw, read and write, and read, draw, and write. All are designed for every member's participation and exploration so that each member derives some personal benefit from the exercise.

### *Read and Discuss*

Read and discuss is the method where the leader reads the chosen fairy tale, and afterwards asks group members to discuss their thoughts, feelings, ideas, and personal associations as these emerged while they listened. This method requires no materials, which is an advantage but does have some disadvantages. The major disadvantages are that time may not be sufficient for the presentation and the exploration and expansion for every group member; and members can lose parts of their experience because it can become confounded with listening to others, or they make changes to appear different, or they can follow group members and the leader.

### *Read and Draw*

Read and draw is another method that has members draw one or more scenes from the fairy tale after hearing a story read by the leader. The members then present their drawings and make personal associations for the symbols in the pictures. The procedure would be as follows:

1. Let all members present their pictures with only empathic responses from the leader and other members. Do not elaborate or let the speaker story-tell or ramble unless something of concern that is urgent and important emerged for that member that calls for immediate attention.
2. Ask members to make personal associations with the symbols in their drawings as the list is read to the group. Every member will have some of the symbols, but not all of them. Focus on the ones in their drawings. The leader then slowly reads a previously prepared list of major symbols. An example for a list of symbols, would be the following for the fairy tale, The Pink:
   Flower
   King
   Queen
   Doves
   The hunt
   Wild animals in the garden
   The tower
      Poodle with gold chain
      Eating coals of fire

Pink (The color)

3. Open the expansion and enhancing phase by asking members to tell what associations they have for the symbols, and whether there are symbols that have associations for them that are in their pictures but not on the list. Make sure there is sufficient time for every member to report his or her associations by not deepening the experience at this point, but simply noting what to return to and telling the member that this could be a fruitful area for exploration at a later group session.

The advantages for reading and drawing are that each member gets an opportunity to depict several symbols that will have personal meaning and associations, it takes less time to draw than to talk about scenes, and there is less opportunity that personal experience will be forgotten or confounded. The disadvantage is that this remains an individual not a group- related interaction experience.

### *Read and Write*

Reading and writing is similar in some respect to reading and drawing in that, in method 1, focus on one or two scenes and visualize these while the leader guides their writing about the experience. In method 2 members write about the scenes without guidance from the leader, but the exploration and expansion is guided. The procedure for method one is as follows.

*Reading and Writing—Method 1*

1. Prepare a list of questions and symbols in advance. These will be used to guide the writing exploration.
2. After reading the story, ask members to visualize one scene from the fairy tale and write the following:
   a. A list of characters in the visualized scene.
   b. A description of the action(s).
   c. Other elements in the visualized scene, such as towers, castles, jewels, etc.

3. Once these lists are complete use the questions and symbols to guide exploration and enhancement.
4. Ask members to list feelings they experienced while listening, visualizing, and writing.
5. Regroup and ask members to share their lists and thoughts.
6. After step 5 is completed, ask members to write any associations they have realized after steps 1 through 5 that relate to their current life, and issues and concerns they have. These are shared in the group.
7. The final step would be to write a summary statement about the experience that is a personal statement about them, not just an overview of the experience.

*Reading and Writing—Method 2*

1. Same as method 1.
2. After reading the fairy tale, ask group members to write a description of one or two scenes from the tale.
3. After writing is complete, read the list of focal symbols for the particular fairy tale and have members note if the symbols appear in their descriptions. If so, make a list of these.
4. When the lists are complete, ask members to think about each item separately and write down the first association that comes to mind without editing or judging the association.
5. Regroup and share descriptions, lists, and associations.
6. After step 5, ask members to review the associations and make further associations for their current lives, past issues and concerns, and present-day issues and concerns.
7. Regroup and share some or all of what emerged in step 6.
8. Write a summary statement about feelings, thoughts, and ideas members experienced, and what seems focal or important to them.

The advantages of reading and writing are that each member can be guided in personal exploration at the same time, there is less opportunity for confounding the experience, and members can be less resistant to personal exploration because they are working alone, and they can choose what and how much to share with the group. The disadvantages are that members write at different speeds so that the group is held up or a member doesn't have time to fully complete his or her exploration; and the leader has less opportunity to empathically respond and to identify issues and concerns for further exploration.

### *Read, Draw, and Write*

The advantages of this approach are many as it provides opportunities for personal exploration of connections to past unresolved issues and concerns, unfinished business, and emotional content. The procedure(s) described will take more time for individual work, but can produce more understanding and insight. Considerable material for exploration in subsequent sessions can be revealed. Two methods are described; one that focuses and guides the writing.

*Read, Draw and Write—Method 1*

1. Gather materials needed for drawing and for writing.
2. Read the fairy tale, and ask group members to draw two scenes from the tale and title each.
3. Regroup and report on experiences and drawings.
4. Distribute paper for writing and provide the following instructions:
    a. Examine your drawings and list all elements, people, and actions in both drawings in one column.
    b. Beside each listing, write a word or phrase about you that comes to mind as you think about the particular item. For example, if you listed flower, your personal association might be growing and thriving.

c. Write the titles for your drawings below the list and associations, and make an association of the titles with your present life as it is for you today.
d. Read what you wrote, and now write a summary of the lists and its associations with your current life.
e. Identify one or two themes you see in what you wrote.

5. Regroup and have members share what they wrote. If time permits, all material can be shared, but if there are time constraints, only share items d and e.

*Read, Draw, Write—Method 2*

1. Follow the directions for method 1, steps 1 through 3.
2. Distribute the paper for writing and proceed through the following sequence:
   a. Ask members to list all of the following that are in their drawings. Space should permit three columns:
      Material elements; for example, castles, trees, and the like;
      Actions or implied actions; for example, weeping, fighting;
      People; for example, kings, witches, sons, princesses;
      Animals and insects; for example, ants and birds;
      Immaterial beings; for example, fairies, trolls;
      Feeling tone; for example, danger, relief, happiness.
   b. Beside each item on the list, write an association without thinking carefully, editing, or evaluating the association.
   c. Ask members to review the two lists and write a summary paragraph about the list of elements and associations that reflects their current life—situation, concerns, struggles, celebrations and so on.
3. Regroup and share at least one portion of what they wrote for a, b, and c, or all of what was written.

4. Ask members to do one of the following:
   a. Write the feelings experienced while listening to the fairy tale, and when they were drawing, writing, and reporting; and relate these feelings to their current life.
   b. Verbally report on the feelings as described in *a*.
5. The final step is to have members integrate or relate the titles of their drawings to what was written and reported about their current life.
6. Regroup and share awareness, surprises, and feelings about the exercise.

### Other Procedures

There are other procedures that could be used that could produce personal material for further exploration, but these tend to lack the guidance that is used in the methods described in this chapter. Without some guidance for meaning, exploration, and enhancement, group members can lose the focus, overlook important material, and move away from intense feelings. The group leader's guidance and presence provides safety for attending to potentially sensitive material. Some other methods include the following.

1. Group members read the assigned fairy tale outside the group, and report their reactions in the next session.
2. The assigned tale is read outside the group and the members write responses to a prepared list of questions. These are discussed in the next session.
3. Each group member reads whatever tale he or she chooses, and reports on reactions in a subsequent group session.
4. Members read a self-chosen or assigned tale and exploration takes place in the here and now, but other approaches could be used. A self-contained experience is the one recommended here.

### *A Deeper Exploration*

The final method presents a procedure for a deeper exploration of the written or drawn products. It would probably be best to use this procedure with relatively well-functioning adults who have established safety and trust in the group, or even cohesion. Time available would also be a consideration as the group leader would want to provide for frequent checks on members' aroused emotions. These checks are suggested in the procedure, but group leaders should be guided by their observations, knowledge, and intuition to suggest that members pause and report on aroused feelings, thoughts, and the like.

*Deepening the Experience*

1. After reading and drawing or writing, ask group members to identify and list one or more developmental issues they see in their products. The leader can refer to Table 8.3 for suggestions.
2. Repeat the directions for step 1, using existential issues listed in Table 8.2 for guidance.
3. Tell members to review the identified issues and write the personal feelings they experience about themselves as they read their lists and reflect on their life situations. Pay special attention to feelings that are associated with self-adequacy, self-efficacy, self-acceptance, and so on.
4. Using a separate sheet of paper, ask members to write a list of the objects, persons, actions, animals, and immaterial beings such as fairies, that appear in the drawings and writing. After completion, put the list aside to use later.
5. Using another sheet of paper, list the following:
    a. A short description about a current life situation, such as a relationship, financial concerns, work problems, and the like.
    b. List the feelings associated with the situations, feelings about self, and feelings about the people involved with you.

   c. List the thoughts you have about the situation and people involved.
   d. List your wishes, desires, and longings associated with the situation.
6. Retrieve the list of elements developed in step 5, and associate each symbol with a possible meaning. Try first to do this independently, and if there are blank spots, suggest the meanings found in Table 8.3.
7. The next task is to match the lists and symbols developed in steps 5 and 6 to determine how the drawings or writings mirror the current situation.
8. Write sentences, phrases, or paragraphs for each of the following:
   a. Desired outcomes for the situation and the realism for these desires.
   b. Alternative solutions.
   c. Awareness, realizations, and the like.
9. Look at the list written in step 6, and list any unused or unrealized inner resources you have that could help address the current situation.
10. Review all you wrote, and write a summary statement about the experience.

This deepening of the experience can take a considerable amount of time to complete, and leaders may want to do this as an extended session, or have parts of it completed as homework. Some intensity and support is lost when done outside the group, but some learning and insight can still occur.

# Chapter 9

# Member Focused Drawing Activities

## Introduction and Literature

There are few studies on drawing in groups. Most studies are with individuals, or large numbers of subjects not in a group setting, such as the 133 subjects in a study on drawing and pain (Ohnmeiss, Vanharanta, & Elkholm, 1999). These subjects in large studies are not in therapy groups. Only one study was found where group members participated in a drawing activity. Nowicka-Saver (2007) reported on the results for three of 38 women with lupus (SLE) who participated in a group session. The analyses concluded that the drawings were a rich source for understanding patients' perceptions of their condition, and the psychological dimensions for living with it.

Numerous studies point to the efficacy of drawing with individuals as means for expressing thoughts, feelings, and ideas about their issues, conditions, or concerns (Gonzalez-Rivera & Bauermeister, 2007; Guillemein, 2004; Hopperstad, 2008;

Lev-Wiesel & Liraz, 2007; Ohnmeiss, Vanharanta, Estlander, & Jansen, 2000). These studies were conducted in many countries: Puerto Rico, Sweden, Finland, Norway, Israel, England, and the United States, and with all ages and variety of conditions, all of which emphasizes the multicultural applications for drawing. What is missing and very much needed are studies on drawing as an activity in group therapy where the focus is not on interpreting the drawing product, but is used as a means to facilitate members' expressions, present them with new personal awareness and understanding, demonstrate and highlight similarities among group members, and to overcome resistance in a nonthreatening and supportive manner.

The use of drawing described here does not require specialized training, such as art therapists receive, nor are the products interpreted by the group leader. Drawing is used as a means for individual expression for current experiencing by group members, and if any deeper or past concerns or issues are tapped, the individual him- or herself identifies these. The group leader is the facilitator only for this exploration, and does not act as an interpreter for the drawings.

## Guidelines

The basic guidelines for exercises are presented in chapter 3. Presented here are some topics and examples relative to drawing activities; gather materials, and prepare expansion and enhancement topics.

### *Gather Materials*

Drawing materials for these exercises are very simple and modest. It is recommended that you secure the following materials to have readily available at all times.

- Several sizes of drawing paper, 8½" × 11" and larger. Look for pads of newsprint.

- Sets of crayons, felt markers, or colored pencils sufficient so that each member can have a set, or so that no more than two members have to share these.
- Pencils or pens for drawing.
- Unlined index cards, 3" × 5" and 5" × 8".
- Masking tape for mounting products on the wall or board.
- Other kinds of drawing paper if you desire.

### *Prepare Expansion and Enhancement Topics*

When you have a lot of experience under your belt, you will already have your topics ready to use in the group. But, until you gain this experience, it will be very helpful to develop your exploration and enhancement topics in advance, and to write them on an index card or something similar. The topics should relate to the purpose for the drawing exercise, members' triggered feelings, other associations and awareness that may emerge, and similarities among group members. These topics are usually presented in the form of open-ended questions such as the following.

What feelings did you experience as you completed your drawing? As you reported to the group?
What are you aware of as you look at your drawing?
Are there any associations with past events, people, or unfinished business that emerged for you?
What was easy or hard about the task?

Each of these can serve as a stimulus or guide without overly structuring the responses, and can permit members to have their own unique personal experiences.

## Benefits and Advantages for Drawing Activities

What are some benefits and advantages for drawing in the group setting? Discussed are uncontaminated expressions, focusing awareness, bypassing defenses, identifying important components, relieving tension, and helping to organize chaotic thoughts and feelings. Each benefit and advantage also has a sample exercise to illustrate the focus:

- Focuses awareness on important aspects of self that were nonconscious or unconscious,
- Bypasses some defenses, such as intellectualizing,
- Assists members in identifying important components or aspects of self, problems, situations, and so on,
- Can relieve tension, and give an opportunity for play and creativity,
- Helps to organize chaotic thoughts and feelings.

### *Uncontaminated Expressions*

Drawing can allow each member to express personal thoughts, feelings, ideas, and awareness at the same time, and these will not be contaminated by hearing what others have to say. Group members will have numerous and dynamic unspoken and unexamined thoughts, feelings, and ideas during group sessions. These are unspoken for a variety of reasons, but major reasons are the need to have only one person speak at any given time, and the time available in a group session. To these are added individual members' tendencies to minimize their experiencing, fear the potential for embarrassment for speaking about this experiencing, fear of offending, suppression to avoid conflict or other disagreements, a need to appear in control and competent, and many other such states. All expressive processes could facilitate expression, and drawing is one activity that group leaders will find useful.

In addition, some members may have limited vocabularies and do not have sufficient words to verbally express their thoughts, feelings, and ideas. They may try to express these, but can become frustrated or be shamed when their words are inadequate expressions for what they are thinking and feeling.

Drawing can provide another means for expressing these; allow complex and complicated thoughts, feelings, and ideas to be simplified and expressed; and can be reassuring and encouraging for the person that he/she can be understood in spite of the limited vocabulary. Following is a sample exercise for expression.

*Exercise 9.1—Express Feelings*
*Materials:* 5" × 8" unlined index cards, a set of crayons, colored pencils, or felt markers for each group member
*Procedure:*

1. Distribute materials
2. Ask group members to draw symbols for three to five feelings they think would be easy to express in the group.
3. Give time for members to share their symbols and feelings, but don't explore these unless the group member does so on his or her own. Give only empathic responses.
4. Turn the cards over and have members draw symbols for three to five feelings they think would be difficult to express in the group.
5. Repeat step 3, only this time try to get members to assess if the difficulty is of long standing such as wanting to be liked, or if there is something about the group, or if they are unaccustomed to expressing these feelings.

### *Focusing Awareness*

Each expressive process has the potential for focusing members' awareness, and a carefully selected drawing exercise can increase their awareness for important aspects of their selves. The act of drawing can reveal current experiencing which, in turn, provides associations in the present to past events, issues, and concerns that were not immediately apparent on the conscious level. For example, completing the life satisfaction exercise described later in this chapter could enable members to identify current areas of concern that had not yet risen to the level of awareness, to become more aware of positive lifestyle behaviors and relationships, and to increase awareness of how their past continues to influence them in unanticipated and unexpected ways. The following exercise demonstrates how to get group members to become more aware of their immediate reactions.

*Exercise 9.2—Immediate Awareness*

*Materials:* Paper and crayons, colored pencils, or felt markers, and a suitable surface for drawing.

*Procedure:*

1. Distribute materials.
2. Ask group members to draw symbols or representations for all the awareness they have at this moment for the self, other group members, and for the leader. The symbols are for their thoughts, feelings, sensations, and so on at this moment.
3. Allow 5 to 10 minutes for the drawings, and then ask members to share their symbols. This will give them an opportunity to explain the meanings.

### *Bypass Defenses*

Drawing tends to bypass defenses that prevent material from emerging into awareness. The act of concentration on what is needed to produce a product puts the energy that was used to suppress or deny into creating. Some people may be able to consciously lower their defenses, while most everyone can be unaware when they are mounting their defenses, and neither can be aware of what they are defending against. Becoming aware of how and when personal defenses are used can lead to an understanding of the material being defended, and these are major assets for constructive and productive therapy.

*Exercise 9.3—My Defenses*

*Materials:* Paper, at least two to three sheets per group member, and a set of crayons, colored pencils, or felt markers.

*Procedure:*

1. Find a suitable place for group members to draw, and distribute the materials.
2. Introduce the exercise by telling group members the following:

   *Everyone uses defenses at times, and the defense is to prevent the person from becoming hurt, either by others seeing something that they wish to keep hidden, or to keep yourself from knowing something about yourself that you fear may be hurtful or dangerous. Defenses are usually unconscious; that is, the person is unaware that he or she is using a defense. The exercise is intended to increase your awareness of when a defense is being used by you or by others. There will be two components: a drawing of what a defense looks like when used by another person, and what a defense you use looks like. The drawing can be representational, such as drawing a scene where you observed or used the defense, abstract or symbolic. Following are some common defenses, and you can select a defense for your drawings, or two separate defenses one for each drawing. Here are some examples of commonly used defenses, and there are others. (Note: the leader can either give each member a list like the following, or write it on a chalkboard or a piece of large paper for posting. The leader can also add to this list.)*

   - Intellectualization—analyzing or interpreting something to make it a content or factual discussion.
   - Deflection—such as changing the topic or focus.
   - Denial—refusal or inability to admit the existence of something that is painful or anxiety provoking, either internal or external.
   - Displacement—feelings toward one person that are transferred or placed onto another person.
   - Projection—putting onto another person something that you don't want to accept about yourself, and then acting toward the person as if he or she had the characteristic that was projected.

3. Members are to prepare two drawings, one of an observed defense that someone else used, and one for that member's defense. Have members title both drawings.
4. Give a time frame to complete the drawings, and remind members that they must complete their drawings about 5 minutes before the time expires.
5. Reconvene the group in a circle and have members share their drawings. Explore the experience by asking about feelings while drawing, when seeing others' drawings, and when displaying their personal drawings.
6. Summarize what emerged during the drawings and reports, and ask members to discuss what types of awareness emerged for them.

### *Identify Important Components*

It seems to be usual and common for people to try and get away from discomfort, especially mental discomfort that produces feelings of shame, guilt, inadequacy, incompetence, or impotence. We worry and fret because solutions are not apparent; we fear the possible or real negative consequences for action or inaction, there can be confusion about personal needs and wishes, and a whole host of other reasons that the important components and aspects of self, situations, problems, and the like are not fully examined.

A drawing exercise can help to focus on these important components. Associations the person makes for him- or herself can clarify the following:

- Central figures for the concern or problem;
- Personal feelings about others that are involved;
- Barriers and constraints that may interfere or prevent solution or resolution;
- Presence or absence of hope for the situation or relationship;
- Possible decisions, alternatives, or solutions.

An exercise that could help clarify the most important components follows.

*Exercise 9.4—My Concern(s)*
*Materials:* Sheets of paper and a set of crayons, colored pencils, or felt markers; and a suitable surface for drawing.
*Procedure:*

1. Distribute materials and explain the objective of the exercise; to clarify personal concerns.
2. Ask group members to draw a picture that captures the essence of their most important problem, issue, or concern at this moment.
3. Drawings are shared while the leader listens to determine if the concern is clear, can be addressed in the group, or if further clarification is needed.
4. The second phase is to ask members what would be a satisfactory outcome for their concern, and if it can be accomplished in the group.

### *Relieve Tension*

Do not underestimate the positive aspects for relieving tension for individual members and for the group as a whole. Some measure of tension and discomfort can provide fertile ground for exploration of meaningful material. However, when there is too much tension, and too much is ambiguous, then members' energies are used to defend and protect the self. They sense danger all around and can shut down. No productive therapeutic work can be accomplished under these conditions.

A drawing exercise can be used just for play, or to focus on what in the group seems dangerous and causing the tension, or to increase members' awareness of the presence and effect on them for being tense. For example, they could do an exercise that asks them to draw what their thoughts, feelings, and bodies experience when they are tense. Another example follows.

*Exercise 9.5—Tension*

*Materials:* Sheets of paper; a set of colored pencils, crayons, or felt markers; and a suitable surface for drawing

*Procedure:*

1. Introduce the exercise by noting that body tension is often overlooked or minimized, and that the exercise is designed to bring awareness of tension in the body.
2. Ask group members to draw a symbol, figure, shape, or the like for what tension feels like in their bodies, noting where it is located by putting the symbol on the following parts of the page.
   a. Tension in the head, face, or neck, at the top quarter of the page;
   b. Tension in the shoulders, chest, arms , or stomach (above the waist) on the second quarter of the page;
   c. Tension in the abdomen, pelvis, lower back, etc., on the third quarter of the page;
   d. Tension in the legs and feet on the bottom quarter of the page.
3. Drawings are then shared in the group and checks made on the extent or intensity of felt tension, was the tension more or was it less during or after drawing, and did it increase or decrease when reporting.

### *Organize Chaotic Thoughts and Feelings*

Organizing chaotic thoughts and feelings can be of immense help to group members. Instead of staying mired in the chaos, shutting down, or avoiding the chaos, members could learn to deal with this for now and for the future. There is something important that can be learned about oneself through working with the chaos rather than ignoring it, or denying that it exists.

For example, it is expected that members will experience some chaotic thoughts and feelings at the beginning of the group. They are concerned about their safety, inclusion, and other such matters as well as the problem or concern that brings them to therapy. A simple drawing exercise that focuses on the major feelings, or concerns about the group can reduce the chaos and focus members on the more important aspects of what they are thinking and feeling at the time. Further, commonalties can be revealed fostering the emergence of universality in the group. An example of an exercise follows.

*Exercise 9.6—Organizing Internal Chaos*

*Materials:* A list of possible feelings such as the one that follows, sheets of paper, crayons, felt markers or colored pencils, and a suitable surface for drawing

*Procedure:*

1. Prepare a list of possible feelings members may be experience in advance, and make enough copies for each member.

   *Feelings*

   | | | | |
   |---|---|---|---|
   | Dread | Hopeless | Fear | Irritation |
   | Anger | Embarrassment | Guilt | Shame |
   | Anticipation | Excitement | Relief | Numb |
   | Despair | Lost | Happy | Sad |
   | Hopeful | Contentment | Restless | Inadequate |

2. Distribute the lists and drawing materials.
3. Introduce the exercise by telling members that they may be experiencing multiple feelings, with some more important than others. Ask them to read the list of feelings, add any that they are experiencing but are not on the list, and then to select a different color for each important feeling and draw a symbol for each of the feelings on the sheet of paper with the most intense feeling symbols at the top, and the least intense at the bottom.
4. After drawings are complete, members are asked to share their drawings, describe the symbol, and the intensity.

# Chapter 10

# Group Focused Drawing Activities

Chapter 9 presented some literature on the uses for drawing activities which focused on individual members. This chapter focuses on the needs and challenges of the group as a whole. Whereas the member focused activities emphasized guidance and exploration for individual member concerns, this chapter emphasizes the group's concerns and needs. Individual members will also benefit, and personal associations will be made, but these are not the primary focus for the activities that are presented here. Group focused drawing activities are developed from the literature on group needs and members during the stages of group development, fostering the emergence of some therapeutic factors, and addressing some group level challenges.

## Basic Guidelines

### *Drawing as an Adjunct to Other Activities*

Many other expressive processes, such as fairy tales, can use drawing as a means of expression. The drawing then becomes a focus on the essence of the experience that can help identify the most important components and associations, and will capture the essence of the personal experience for the individual group member. Members can then report these experiences, associations, ideas, and so on without unconscious contamination from the productions of other group members which can happen when listening to them. This can be especially true for children. Further, members who may think or fear that something they experience is trivial or unimportant, especially when compared to what other members may report, can concentrate on their personal experience without evaluating it as being of lesser or no importance. It is important for that particular person where, what appears on the surface to be minor conceals a deeper and more significant concern or issue.

### *Consider Barriers and Constraints*

Although there are many good and valid reasons to use a drawing exercise, there may also be some barriers and constraints. Do not fail to anticipate or recognize these as they can negatively affect members' feelings about the group, the amount and kind of learning and insight that can occur, and may even be harmful in some instances. The group leader is in the best position to identify these possible barriers and constraints. Examples include the following.

- Physical conditions that would prevent one or more members from drawing, such as a broken arm on the dominant side, or severe visual problems;
- Cognitive deficits that would interfere with following directions or gaining self-understanding;

- Insufficient time in the session to complete all portions of the exercise;
- Inappropriate or insufficient working space. While some accommodations can be made to provide a flat hard surface for drawing, having to make do could be frustrating and thereby negatively affect outcomes;
- Using a drawing exercise that is too complex for group members;
- Emotional vulnerability of one or more members to the material so that overly intense emotions will be generated by the activity;
- Group members feared shame and embarrassment about their drawing ability.

Some barriers or constraints can be worked around, but some signal that a drawing activity is contraindicated; such as when one or more members cannot physically draw, follow directions, or there is insufficient time to complete the exercise. On the other hand, if all members can participate, an exercise to relieve tension doesn't usually present barriers and constraints. The guiding principle is that the group leader gives some attention to consideration of potential barriers and constraints.

### *Select an Exercise*

Selection of a drawing exercise can be fairly easy as many are presented in this book and are readily available from other sources. Almost all presented here can be adapted or modified for the specific group's purpose, and to meet the abilities of group members. Other considerations for selection include the following:

- The focus should be narrow and specific. Too much complexity can be confusing and use the time and energy that should be focused on the purpose.
- The concepts illustrated should be easily understood by group members.

- Drawings need not be representative. Symbols, splashes of color, and other abstract expressions can be helpful for some clients.
- Group members' abilities should fit the drawing requirements.
- All materials should be readily available for every session.
- The drawing activity should be relatively brief as the most important tasks are reporting, and the exploration and enhancement phases.

Group leaders may want to collect some exercises that they've experienced and found useful. These then become exercises that can be adapted for various purposes and audiences. It is helpful to remember that the drawing itself is the stimulus for members' personal material and associations, and that is its main purpose and value. Almost any drawing can be the stimulus so you don't have to spend an inordinate amount of time searching for the exercise that will be just right.

Activities for some of the following are presented below:

- Assist introductions in the first session;
- Relieve tension;
- Clarify members' wants, needs, desires, and wishes;
- Identify barriers and constraints for the group, such as resistance;
- Teach members how to give and receive constructive feedback;
- Practice problem solving and decision making;
- Provide a means for expressing difficult, unpleasant, or unacceptable feelings;
- Foster the emergence of therapeutic factors such as universality, encouraging hope, catharsis, and identifying unresolved family of origin issues and other unfinished business.

*Introductions* can be facilitated with a short drawing exercise where group members are asked to present something nonthreatening about themselves. The anxiety and uncertainty that members can experience can make them resistant to revealing anything they consider to be potentially embarrassing or that will lead to rejection and exclusion. There can be apprehension about letting oneself be seen by others because these are strangers, or even when the other group members are known to each other. Some group members will be unsure about what personal information to disclose, some members may not be articulate, some can be wary and cautious, and other such states where an exercise could be facilitative. Two examples for a focus for introductory drawing exercises are as follows:

*Exercise 10.1—Saying Hello*
*Materials:* 5" × 8" index cards, and a set of crayons, or colored pencils, or felt markers for each person.
*Procedure:* Ask members to use the crayons and draw a symbol for each of the following:

- Favorite pastime
- Valued possession
- Favorite color
- Favorite season of the year.

*Exercise 10.2—My Accomplishments*
*Materials:* 5" × 8" index cards, and a set of crayons, or colored pencils, or felt markers for each person.
*Procedure:*
Ask members to introduce themselves by drawing a symbol for each of the following:

- Greatest achievement
- A talent and how it is used
- An aspiration, and how they are working on it.

*Relieving tension* could be of value to the group, especially when that tension is retarding group progress. Tension is a result of fear, and each member can fear something different, but the outcomes are the same. For example, it doesn't matter if one member fears being shamed, another fears offending, another fears being attacked, someone else fears being rejected, and another person fears appearing stupid. They are all tense, fearing the worst. The group leader may not be familiar with the individual fears, but is very aware of the tension. A short drawing exercise could help relieve some of the tension so that the group could move forward. If the tension occurs during the beginning stage of group development, the drawing exercise should be something light and nonthreatening, such as the introduction exercises presented earlier in this chapter.

*Clarifying wants, needs, desires, and wishes* can assist members in making realistic choices and decisions, becoming aware of illogical and unrealistic thoughts and expectations, obtaining a clearer focus or achievable goal, and in identifying self-imposed and external imposed barriers and constraints. Lack of knowledge, chaotic circumstances, insufficient self-understanding, and other such states can make it difficult for group members to have a clear sense of what they want, need, desire, and wish for, and the extent to which these are reasonable, achievable, and will lead to the desired outcome(s).

When members have a clearer understanding of needs, wishes, desires, and wants they can be more motivated to have a realistic action plan, to relinquish unrealistic fantasies and expectations, to make needed changes, and to gain self-confidence. They begin to explore avenues that serve as alternatives to achieve the goals, to learn strategies to work around or overcome barriers and constraints, and to understand how they are contributing to not getting what they want, need, wish for, or desire, that is both realistic and achievable.

Giving up the fantasies will be the most difficult task, and this can take considerable effort. Common fantasies include the following examples:

- The other person must or will change.
- Unlimited wealth, success, and the like.
- Attention or admiration will be theirs without effort.
- All others will perceive them as unique and special.
- Effortless winning of others' approval and acceptance.
- Others will read their minds and give them what they want or need at all times.
- They will be powerful enough to make others bow to their will, to change others, to tell others what they need to do or be, and this will be carried out without dissent.
- They will never have to suffer or worry, and will be happy all of the time.
- They can do what they want to without negative consequences.

*Barriers and constraints* exist for the individual members and for the group as a whole, and a drawing exercise can highlight what these can be. This could be a nonthreatening way to make resistance visible, to heighten awareness of its existence and possible reasons for this, and to suggest ways to moderate or eliminate it. A further positive outcome could be an understanding for personal resistance and its role and contributions to forming and maintaining meaningful relationships.

It is generally not helpful to directly attack resistance as this can solidify defenses or leave the person unnecessarily vulnerable to overwhelming emotions or memories. It is much more helpful when the person him- or herself chooses to explore the resistance and make a decision to let go of it. These are some of the reasons why it is best to let resistance alone, and to use some nonthreatening means to highlight it. Word choice can make a difference also as some members can perceive resistance as wrong, feel guilty or shamed instead of being open to exploring the personal function the resistance is serving. When introducing an exercise to highlight barriers and constraints, use phrases such as the following.

- What in the group, or in yourself, feels like it's getting in the way of your participation, or disclosure, or feeling safe, or the like?
- What feedback do you want to give or receive that is absent?
- What does this group feel like to you?
- Describe, or use a symbol to depict, the space between you and other group members.

*Exercise 10.3—Wishes for the Group*
*Materials:* crayons or a set of colored pencils or felt markers, paper.
*Procedure:*

1. Introduce the exercise by telling group members that it could be helpful to get each member's perception of the group.
2. Ask members to select a different color for each and to draw symbols for each of the following:
   The most important wish they have for the group;
   What seems to be a constraint or barrier in the group;
   What they want or need from other group members;
   An overall feeling about the group.
3. When members have finished their drawings, they present them to the group and the leader asks each to respond to the presentation.
4. After all sharing and responding is complete, ask members to title their drawings and report these to the group.

*Constructive feedback* is very helpful to group members and the group's progress, and members' growth and development are facilitated by such feedback. It is most likely that group members will have to overcome fears of both receiving and giving feedback, and will need to be taught how to make their feedback constructive. Drawing exercises could be facilitative for focusing feedback, verbalizing fears about offending and rejection, show commonalties among members, and as a means for giving constructive feedback that can be accepted and used.

Basic guidelines that can assist members are the following:

1. Focus on observable behavior and don't infer the receiver's motives for the acts.
2. Select words carefully so that the feedback is not blaming or critical.
3. Do not use evaluative language or inferences, such as good, bad, right, or wrong.
4. Try not to imply what the receiver should or ought to be or do.
5. Refrain from giving advice.
6. The giver is encouraged to verbalize his or her feelings at the moment.
7. Note the impact of the feedback on the receiver.
8. Give a modest amount of feedback at any one time. Limit it to what the receiver can take in and use, not what the sender thinks needs to be said.

Drawing exercises can facilitate the focus for feedback and, at the same time, reduce the potentially threatening nature of the feedback since all group members will be participating, no one member is singled out to receive feedback or is put on the hot seat, and the group leader structures and directs the exercise to focus on important aspects of the self. For example, group members could be asked to draw a symbol for a characteristic they have observed about every member. Another facilitative exercise could be to have group members draw symbols, or select a color for the apprehensions or fears they have about giving or receiving feedback.

*Problem solving and decision making* can usually be accomplished by having members set goals, determine steps to reach the goals, identify constraints, and develop an action plan. However, there are times when members are so confused and frustrated that they cannot see their way clearly to work through these procedures. This is where drawing exercises could be of assistance.

For example, a drawing exercise could help members realize that their wishes and fantasies are getting in the way of their problem solving or interfering with making decisions. They are not using their resources or competencies, they are insisting that others change to suit them, or that magic will change circumstances so that they can prevail. The exercise could clarify their unrealistic expectations thus, clearing the way for them to work through a constructive and productive procedure.

Drawing exercises can also suggest alternatives to address problems or other options for decisions. The resources of the group can be used in this way for each group member to address his or her problem, or could be used for each group member to propose alternatives for one member's problem or decision. Projecting outcomes and consequences can suggest new strategies, or even a combination of the proposed alternatives and options. This use of drawing is another way of collaborative brainstorming that permits each member to create ideas and to share them. We're so used to talking that we forget that there are other means to derive and communicate our thoughts, feelings, and ideas.

*Exercise 10.4—Desired Outcomes*

*Materials:* Crayons, colored pencils, or felt markers, paper for drawing.

*Procedure:*

1. Ask members to close their eyes and go into the future and see the desired outcome. Stay with the picture for a while, noticing as many details as possible, and their feelings.
2. Give a few minutes for the pictures to emerge, and then tell members to open their eyes and draw what they saw.
3. The group leader should respond empathically during the sharing period, but don't explore or point out the illogic or unreasonableness of the desired outcome.
4. After sharing is completed, ask members to rate the possibility of the desired outcome, and its reasonableness. This is shared among members.

5. The final step is to have members describe what steps they could take to get the desired outcome, or to change their longing to a realistic outcome.

*Expression of feelings* can be expedited with drawing exercises because these don't require words that members don't have, or are unable to verbalize, seem threatening or dangerous for various reasons, are unacceptable, appear to be potentially shaming, or are abstract, complex, and difficult to describe with words. There are numerous reasons why group members could be assisted in expressing their feelings, and drawing could be one way to facilitate this.

There are also some group situations where drawing could aid emotional expression:

- Members who tend to intellectualize, story-tell, or monopolize would not be able to hide behind words.
- Members who are avoiding expressing their feelings because these are troubling or intense would have an opportunity to express them.
- If there is conflict, or denial of conflict, an exercise could aid in expressing emotions that accompany the conflict without having to directly address the threatening conflict.

### *Foster the Emergence of Some Therapeutic Factors*

*Universality* can be reassuring to members that they are not alone, isolated, or weird. The commonalties among group members promote disclosure, caring, and concern, and can lead to group cohesion. Thus, it is very important for a group leader to give some attention to this therapeutic factor and take every opportunity to highlight similarities among group members in attitudes, experiences, feelings, and so on. Doing so could help this therapeutic factor to emerge and be recognized.

*Exercise 10.5—Similarities*

*Materials:* Paper, a set of crayons, colored pencils, or felt markers, and a suitable surface for drawing.

*Procedure:*

1. Distribute the materials and ask members to draw a symbol or something that depicts each of the following: a value, a cherished material object, and a favorite activity. The value, object, and activity should be something that they think would make them connect to another group member if it were held in common. For example, if another member also read mysteries, the person would feel connected to that member.
2. After drawing, reconvene in the group circle and report on the drawings. The leader should point out similarities among the drawings.
3. Ask members if they identified any other similarities as they listened to each member present his or her drawing.

*Encouraging hope* can also be facilitative, and the group leader can assist in its emergence and encourage members to be realistic. Unrealistic hope is a fantasy, and failure to achieve what was hoped for can be depressing and lead to self-defeating thoughts and feelings. However, it is hope that promotes persistence in the face of adversity and motivates change.

Hope seems to be an individual perspective, and what is hopeful for one person may not be so for another. Further, it could be that some members are so focused on their misery, issues, problems, or concerns that they have not been able to see hope in their lives, nor do they have a clear idea of their personal signs of hope. A drawing exercise that focuses on identifying signs in indices of hope would be very helpful.

A further note, hope can grow among group members as they observe hopefulness in other members. Seeing others get better, resolve problems, make progress, and feel more secure and confident can serve as models for group members that they too can experience these. This is an example of hope that is realistic and reasonable.

*Exercise 10.6—Hopefulness*

*Materials:* Paper and a set of crayons, colored pencils, or felt markers.

*Procedure:*

1. Find a suitable surface for drawing and distribute the materials.
2. Introduce the exercise by telling members something similar to what was presented in the previous paragraphs, and ask them to draw a symbol of what hopefulness would feel or be like for them right now.
3. Reconvene in the group circle and share the drawings. Explore the meanings of hopefulness for members, and discuss how some or all of this can be obtained in the group. The leader should be careful to note which are realistic, and which may be fantasy. For example, having another person change is fantasy. Learning to cope with what is, can be realistic.

*Catharsis* is another therapeutic factor, and the expression of feelings that were suppressed, repressed, or denied; or becoming aware of having difficult or unacceptable feelings can be of immense help to group members. This can be especially true when the emotional venting is met with reactions of understanding, care, and concern for the person instead of the feelings being soothed, rationalized, minimized, or criticized as being irrational or wrong by others in the group, such as what can happen in other settings like the family.

However, catharsis is most helpful in the group when it is accompanied by the interpersonal learning described by Yalom and Leszcz (2005). The catharsis then is not just emotional venting because the person can learn something unknown, or something of which he or she was unaware that is valuable for self-understanding and growth. The group leader facilitates the catharsis and the feedback that promotes the interpersonal learning. One way feedback can be encouraged is by asking group members to tell the member experiencing catharsis their personal feelings experienced while listening to him or her. A drawing exercise could be used for each, expressive of strong, intense feelings and reactions to the catharsis.

*Exercise 10.7—Catharsis*

*Materials:* Paper and a set of crayons, colored pencils, or felt markers.

*Procedure:*

1. Find a suitable drawing surface, and distribute the materials.
2. Describe catharsis noting that it is more than just emotional venting. Ask members to draw a picture from their experiences that depicts catharsis where they learned something about themselves in the feedback they received in the interaction. For example, something upsetting happened at work, the person brought it to the group, vented, and the feedback he or she received increased the person's awareness of being in a toxic situation where nothing he or she did or said would make a positive difference, and that continuing to let it be upsetting was hurting the group member not the other person, and nothing positive was being accomplished.

*Identifying unresolved* family of origin issues and other unfinished business that members have can be very helpful to their progress, but can also be difficult to accomplish. Drawing exercises can contribute to the uncovering by each member at the same time. When either of these is the purpose or goal for using a drawing exercise, the leader should be emotionally prepared for intense emotions or for unexpected material to be uncovered. Further, the group should have sufficient safety and trust established so that members will be more secure when disclosing painful material. It is important in this situation that members not have to be overly concerned about the leader's reactions to this material, but feel confident that the leader's response will be understanding, show caring and concern, and that other group members will not be rejecting. All of this suggests that the first stage of group, and groups that are focused on issues other than counseling or psychotherapy may not be appropriate for an exercise that focuses on this factor.

When a drawing exercise is used to accomplish the goal or purpose of identifying family of origin factors or unfinished business, the group leader should do the following:

- Ensure that all members have an opportunity to report their personal experiences.
- Gauge the emotional intensity aroused for each member.
- Resist deeper exploration for a member at this time, but note a need to return to it.
- Block critical or blaming comments by other group members.
- Give empathic responses to each member (this can be essential).
- Identify similarities in experiences or feelings among members.
- Reduce emotional intensity before the group ends so that group members do not leave with feelings that are overwhelming or difficult for them to manage. A check on emotional intensity and a short relaxation exercise can be helpful.

## Address Group Challenges

There are numerous group level challenges that can arise, and drawing can be a helpful strategy to bring these to the awareness of group members and to suggest solutions. Group level challenges are issues and concerns that seem to be problematic for all group members even when they differ in intensity and kind for separate group members. For example, resistance and conflict are present in all groups, but in some groups these become barriers and constraints because members repress, suppress, or deny they exist. They tend to minimize or ignore them, fearing the loss of control, harmony, or even destruction. However, these challenges continue to affect the effectiveness of the group. Use of a drawing activity can reduce some of the perceived threat of even being aware of these challenges. Examples of group level challenges include:

- Fear of intimacy
- Resistance
- Suppression of important feelings
- Conflict
- Fear of being seen by others, and thus being shamed
- Loss of control.

Exercises follow that are intended to address resistance and conflict. Using activities such as these can make it easier for members to discuss these threatening concepts.

*Exercise 10.8—Resistance*

*Materials:* Suitable surface for drawing, 5" × 8" index cards, a set of crayons, colored pencils, or felt markers for each group member.

*Procedure:*

1. Distribute the materials and ask members to sit back, close their eyes, and think of the concept, resistance. Think about what resistance feels like, what it looks like, which can be symbolic or representational, and its other characteristics.
2. Tell them to open their eyes and to draw what emerged as they thought about resistance.
3. When the drawing is complete, ask members to share their drawings.
4. Explore the feelings that emerged as the directions were given to think about resistance, when drawing the concept, and when sharing their drawings in the group.
5. If appropriate and the group has developed sufficient safety and trust, the leader can have a discussion about members' experiences of resistance in the group with a focus on their personal resistance.

*Exercise 10.9—Conflict*

*Materials:* Paper, and a set of crayons, colored pencils, or felt markers for each group member.

*Procedure:*

1. Distribute materials and ask group members to draw a picture that captures the essence of a personal conflict with another person or persons, either from the past or currently.
2. When drawing seems complete (the leader may have to set a specific time frame for drawing), reconvene in the circle, and ask members to describe their drawing.
3. As they describe their drawing ask them what feelings are they experiencing as they talk about their conflict.
4. Ask each how they handled, or are handling the conflict. Note if they describe ignoring it, minimizing the impact on them or on others, suppressing the conflict, or even denying that there is a conflict or the seriousness of the conflict.
5. Bring the discussion to what is happening in the group, and explore if members are handling conflicts in the group as they did the conflict that they drew.

# Chapter 11

# Writing Activities

Writing activities are a means for expressing and exploring thoughts, ideas, and feelings to elaborate, clarify, and understand them. While generally used as communication to others, writing activities are used in therapy primarily in communication with oneself to better understand what the client is thinking, feeling, imagining, and associating. These activities can provide a thread that links the present, the past, the nonconscious, and unconscious, and can provide access to previously unexplored parts of self. Writing can differ from other expressive activities in its ability to cover more material in less space and time, can be a personal and private way to engage in self-exploration but also benefits from being shared with others, and has various modes for implementation.

Chapters 11 to 14 address different writing activities: general writing, poetry, writing for a single session, and journaling. This chapter presents a variation for *Expressive Writing*, which has a specific format and procedure, autobiographical activity, expansion for life events, and connects the past to the future.

## Benefits from Writing Activities

Oatley and Djikic (2008) define writing as "thinking that uses paper and other media to externalize and manipulate symbolic expressions" (p. 9). Getting one's thinking written down can accomplish several goals:

1. It enables the writer to communicate these thoughts to others.
2. Organizes and orders the thoughts.
3. Helps to make meaning, and to make that meaning clear.
4. Expresses abstract and complex inner experiencing.
5. Reveals hidden connections and associations.
6. Allows the imagination to be expressed.
7. Encourages and promotes creativity.
8. Provides inspiration and hope to self and to others.
9. Clarifies complex situations, relationships, and events.
10. Provides a guide on how to do something; for example, what this book does.

Therapeutic benefits from writing can include some of the following:

- Enable the expression of inner experiencing that is perceived by the writer as dangerous or shameful to verbally express. Writing the words can seem less threatening, especially when the writing does not have to be revealed to others. Also, it can be threatening to think about hearing how others will respond when the inner experiencing is openly verbalized.
- Clarification of confusing thoughts and feelings can be expedited through writing. The act of trying to express the thoughts and feelings can provide a means to help sort through them, prioritize their importance, and reveal inconsistencies and irrationality.
- Writing can provide an opportunity to explore thoughts and feelings on one's own to see where these lead. The

independence and privacy afforded by writing can provide the space and time to engage in self-exploration uncontaminated by others' thoughts or presence.

- Writing can be a visible realization of creative thoughts and ideas helping them to emerge. The act of putting these ideas on paper or on the computer screen, the opportunity to review them, and the possibility of seeing different associations and alternatives can be realized through writing.
- Writing can provide a record of moods, and their associations can provide insight and understanding. Precipitating situations, events, and so on become clearer, and can provide suggestions for alternative approaches or responses.
- Writing can provide a means to focus on the positives in one's life and on personal strengths. It is much easier for many people to emphasize the negatives in their lives, and focusing the writing on the positive aspects of the self and of one's life can be affirming, encouraging, and inspiring.
- Writing can lessen defense mechanisms that may arise from verbal interactions. Since writing can be much less threatening, it is less necessary for the individual to be defensive about shaming incidences, thoughts, and the like. The self can be more receptive and open to considering flaws and inadequacies, thus providing more opportunities to create better ways to behave and to relate.
- Writing is a way to personalize analysis when in a group. There are times when it is difficult to personalize group material because of the complexity of the group, the dynamic movement, the confounding that can occur from others' stories and responses, and so on. Writing about one's personal experience is a way to sort through that person's thoughts, feelings, ideas, reactions, associations, and the like without the confounding that can occur when interacting with other members. While

that constructive response and feedback is valuable, it is sometimes more helpful for individual members to personalize their understanding and analyses prior to sharing these with the group.

- Writing can help one center and ground oneself in the present. Writing can be a means to bring the members into the here and now and support their emotional presence in the group. Outside concerns, past experiences, and the unconscious continue to affect present experiencing, but becoming centered and grounded in the present expedites the work of the group and that of the individual members.
- Writing can assist with planning for the future, such as writing action plans and anticipating barriers to these plans. When group members write these they increase their awareness of the possibilities, their potentials, and can even create possible alternatives and solutions.
- Writing can be used to convey thoughts, ideas, and feelings to others. This can be especially helpful when what is being discussed carries intense emotional content that can make it difficult to select the words to adequately express what is intended. Writing these thoughts provides opportunities to sort through the myriad of feelings, to select words and phrases that are accurate representatives of the feelings, and to lessen intensity of feelings by becoming more cognitive.

## How and Why Writing Can Help

Robinson (2000) proposed that "research shows that the majority of people who write regularly feel that it helps them cope with and work on traumatic experiences and is beneficial to their well-being" (p. 83). He discusses how the process of writing relates to beneficial outcomes. It would appear that both what is written and the process of writing have benefits. Robinson uses Wilma Bucci's model (1995) as a basis for understanding the process.

This model assumes that experiences are stored in the mind in symbolic and nonsymbolic forms and that only symbolic forms are available for verbal communication and thought, both written and oral. The nonsymbolic forms appear in images, emotions that seem to have no label, and other internal representations of experiencing. Language is one way to try to connect to the nonsymbolic form via referential activity by naming the experience or feeling, and to identify it (Bucci, 1995). There are four stages for this process: Activation, Referential 1, Referential 2, and Reformulation.

1. Activation: Nonsymbolic images or feelings are activated.
2. Referential 1: Internal images are formed that have referential meaning.
3. Referential 2: These images are put into words.
4. Reformulation: The words assist in reformulation of the nonspecific images or feelings into known images or feelings.

This process illustrates the possible benefits for writing, and both the outcome and the process contribute. Insight, understanding, and assimilation of experiences can be facilitated for therapeutic benefit. Layers of ambiguity, unawareness, and uncertainty can be stripped away so that meaning becomes clearer, and a burden can be lifted.

Writing activities can be especially helpful in a group because they allow all members to participate at the same time and they personalize the material. The group leader does not have to be as concerned about what other members are experiencing while working with one member. In addition, the use of journals and other writing as homework can enrich and deepen the group experiences for group members. The remainder of the chapter describes Pennebaker's Expressive Writing.

## Expressive Writing

Pennebaker (1997a) and Esterling, L'Abate, Murray, and Pennebaker (1999) studied the effects of disclosure writing, termed *Expressive Writing*, on health and found that there were many positive effects. The basic format for Expressive Writing asks participants to write for 15 minutes each day on a topic for 3 days. The topics could be the participant's choice, or specific topics such as cherished values, life goals, or a traumatic experience. Since Pennebaker began his studies others have conducted studies, and he notes that the many studies on Expressive Writing show the following effects on participants.

- Immediate and long term cognitive changes;
- Immediate and long term emotional changes, such as reduction of negative affect about a trauma (Park & Blumberg, 2002);
- Positive changes in participants' social and relational lives;
- Gradual and cumulative biological effects, such as better physical health.

Hundreds of studies have been conducted using Expressive Writing for a variety of conditions and subjects with mixed outcome results. The technique seems to produce positive outcomes in most cases, but also tends to show positive outcomes for narrowly focused and specific conditions. For example, in the study by Koopman et al. (2005) using Expressive Writing effects changes in pain, depression, and PTSD symptoms for survivors of intimate partner violence. They found that depressed women showed a significant drop in depression, but the main effects were not significant for changes in pain or PTSD. Sloan, Marx, and Epstein (2005) found that Expressive Sriting with high risk drug dependent patients at a primary care clinic who wrote about the same traumatic event over three sessions had significant reductions in physical and psychological symptoms in comparison with a control group writing about different or nontraumatic events over three sessions. Samples of other studies on conditions and subjects include the following:

- Rape (E. Brown & Heimberg, 2001);
- Sexual abuse (Batten, Follette, & Palm, 2002);
- Cancer (Sloan et. al., 2005);
- Rumination and depressive symptoms (Gortner, Rude, & Pennebaker, 2006);
- Prisoners and illness (Richards, Beal, Seagal, & Pennebaker, 2000);
- Coping with job loss by engineers (Spera, Buhrfiend, & Pennebaker, 1994);
- Young adult smokers (Ames et. al., 2008);
- Maternal psychological distress (Barry & Singer, 2001).

Chan and Horneffer (2006) compared an Expressive Writing group, a drawing group, and a control group on psychological symptoms before and after two 15 minute writing sessions. The Expressive Writing group had a more significant decrease in their symptoms than did members of the other two groups. The analysis did not identify specific symptoms that showed a decrease, just that there was a general overall lessening of emotional distress.

Another approach to using Expressive Writing is described by Reisman, Hansen, and Rastegas (2006) where resident physicians were introduced to Abraham Verghese's system (2001) for writing that focuses on integrating creative writing with clinical duties. This approach uses personal journals, parallel charts, and critical incidents reports with an emphasis on describing the event and one's personal reactions. The purposes are to encourage reflection and awareness, increase emotional engagement and empathy, and to deepen interactions with others. The process involved having participants write on a topic relative to their experiences and feelings as residents, and a sample orally presented and discussed by other residents.

The discussion focuses on the extent to which the writing aroused the reader's/listener's imagination. The writer listens to the discussion, but can only comment at the end. Reisman et al. (2006) reported than an unanticipated outcome was the development of group cohesiveness. The other outcomes as reflected in a qualitative analysis of themes in the writings, and a post group focus evaluation, were increased awareness of self and of others, an outlet for feelings such as insecurity and impotence, and a deeper understanding of the healing power of compassion.

Reisman et al.'s (2006) approach used the group as part of the process which seems to have enriched the experience and even to have promoted group factors, even though that was not a purpose for the group. What may have happened that could be useful for other group leaders are the following.

- Unacceptable and uncomfortable feelings were expressed, were accepted, and not criticized by others.
- Commonalties for these feelings became visible, thus promoting connections and universality.
- Reading aloud was nonjudgmental and intended as expansion and exploration.
- Real experiences were described and possible alternatives, options, and changes explored which promoted feelings of self-efficacy.
- There was an increased awareness both for self and for others, especially for those who were in a dependent state (e.g., patients).

There are many different approaches to uses for Expressive Writing, but all seem to produce positive benefits. The following set of exercises uses Expressive Writing, but group leaders must be aware that intense and negative feelings can be aroused. Because of this, these must be used with caution and the group leader must be prepared to deal with what emerges, and to even be available between sessions if members are having difficulty coping with the emerging feelings.

*Exercise 11.1—Group Expressive Writing*

*Materials:* A suitable surface for writing, pen or pencil, paper, or a bound journal.

*Procedure:* Introduce the exercise by telling group members that the activity could help them integrate and reduce the intensity of feelings about a distressful event from their lives. Describe the activity as being three sessions of 15 minutes of writing each session. What they write will be personal and private for them, and although you will collect the essays, you will not read them and will keep them under lock and key. At the end of the three sessions, you will destroy the essays or return them to the writer, their choice. Another option is to offer to keep them until the last group session, and make the decision then.

Tell members that they will write whatever they choose, without paying attention to grammar or other technical writing concerns. They can write sentence fragments, or just words or phrases, they do not have to write complete sentences.

1. Session 1 writing—Ask members to think of a distressing event from their past that has a distress rating of 5 or 6 on a 10-point scale, where 0 is no distress, and 10 is extreme distress. They are then to write about the event especially noting feelings about it. Allow 15 minutes for writing.
2. Next, ask members to review what they wrote, and using another sheet of paper make a list of the feelings that emerged as they wrote and as they thought about the event. Rate each feeling on the 10-point scale described in step 1.
3. Collect the essays and feelings, and keep these under lock and key.
4. Session 2 writing—Use the same procedure as described for session 1, where they write about the same event, list the current feelings, and give these a rating. Collect the essays and feelings.
5. Session 3 writing—Use the same procedure described for session 1 and have them write about the same event,

make a list of the feelings experienced now. Collect the essays and feelings.

a. Ask members if they want to report on how or if their feelings changed after three sessions of writing. Allow any member to opt out who wants to.
b. Ask members how they want you to handle the essays and lists you collected; keep, destroy, return.

*Exercise 11.2—An Autobiographical Activity—Session 1*
*Materials:* Sheets of paper or a journal, and writing instruments.
*Procedure:*

1. Introduce the exercise by telling group members that the next few sessions will focus on writing an autobiography. They have lived their lives to this point, and the purpose is to engage in self-examination by writing about their life experiences.
2. Instruct members to take one sheet of paper and list all of the words and phrases that apply to them to finish the lead, "Currently, I am." You can suggest that they look at their general feelings experienced, the relationships, their work or other such activities, leisure pursuits, hobbies, interests, and so on. Who are they at this moment in time.
3. Once that list is complete, ask them to take another sheet of paper and to write an essay on their Current Self. Allow 20 to 30 minutes to complete this portion. It may be that some will need to complete their essays outside the group session, and the leader can decide if this is appropriate for this group.
4. After the writing period is over, ask members to reconvene in the group circle and to share what the writing experience was like for them. Questions that can guide the sharing include:
   What seems focal in your life today?
   What kinds of awareness emerged?
   What seems missing or incomplete?

Were there any surprises?
What feelings emerged as you thought and wrote about your current life?

*Exercise 11.3—An Autobiographical Activity—Session 2*
*Materials:* See Exercise 11.2.
*Procedure:*

1. Introduce the exercise by telling members that this session will focus on their past life; its significant events, important people, meaningful and important activities, and the like.
2. Instruct them to take three sheets of paper and to make a list of events, people, activities, and so on for three life periods: one list for childhood, a list for early adolescence, 12 to 15, and a list for late adolescence/early adulthood, 16 to 21.
3. The next step is to select one of the lists and to write an essay about that life period. When time permits, they can write three essays, but if there is not enough time for reporting, limit the writing to one list, and use the other lists for discussion or reporting at another session.
4. Reconvene in the group and use the items in step 4 of the previous exercise to guide the exploration of the essays.

*Exercise 11.4 —An Autobiographical Activity—Session 3*
*Materials:* See Exercise 11.2.
*Procedure:*

1. Introduce the exercise by telling members that this will be an exploration of their desires and dreams for their future selves.
2. Use the same categories listed in exercise 11.2 and ask members to make a list of their desires and dreams for each of these. These should be separate lists.
3. Instruct members to review these lists, and select the one that seems most important to them at this point, and write an essay about their desires and dreams in that

category; for example, what they envision their relationships as being in the future. When the essay seems finished, ask members to reflect on steps needed to realize the desire/dream, what they are doing now that will help them realize this, such as attending school to get a degree in the desired profession, and how are they resisting moving in that direction.

4. The questions in item 4 of exercise 11.2 can also be used to guide the discussion.
5. The other lists can be used for future group discussions.

*Exercise 11.5—Life Events*

*Materials:* Sheets of paper and a pen or pencil for writing.

*Procedure:*

1. Ask group members to make a list of significant events in their lives that occurred during childhood, adolescence, or as adults. They should have only one list for one period in their lives.
2. Have members review and reflect on their lists and select one event to explore. Depending on the available time, more events can be explored with the following process.
3. Write the event at the top of a clean sheet of paper, and then list all of the people involved, the feelings the person had at that time, and the feelings that are carried forward to the current time.
4. Next, write a paragraph, or more, that describes the event, the impact on the person, and the lingering effects of the event on them today.
5. Ask members to share either the event, or the feelings aroused then and now. They don't have to share all of what they wrote as some may have written a considerable amount.
6. Ask members to report on what the writing experience was like for them, difficulties, new awareness, and so on.

# CHAPTER 12

# POETRY, CINQUAINS, AND HAIKU

## Poetry

Blake (2002) describes poetry therapy as providing opportunities for clients to sort through, clarify, and communicate their thoughts. Poetry used in therapy can also have the following purposes:

- Extract meaning (Campo, 2003);
- Discover multiple realities (Frank, 2004; Greenhalgh & Taylor, 1997);
- Preserve details of an experience (Campo, 2003);
- Create useful, credible, and trustworthy truths (J. Shapiro, 2004);
- Use metaphor and imagery to access the nonconscious and unconscious (Kociatkiewicz & Kostera, 1999).

Although poetry therapy has evolved to include other forms of writing, this discussion focuses on the usual and classical understanding about what poetry is, and how it can be used in groups as expressions of members' thoughts, feelings, and ideas. This use of poetry considers that it is a means of capturing, distilling, and expressing the complexity and multiplicity of experiencing in words that do not have to follow a preordained and technical format, which is usually the case in essays. This format allows a freedom to access imperfectly formed thoughts and ideas, the use of metaphors and images to illustrate abstractions and layers of feelings, and to express these as streams of consciousness. Just as with all other expressive processes described in this book, meanings for their poetry lie within the person.

The literature has numerous references for individual use and experiences with writing poetry, but there are fewer references for group uses, especially within a group session. Most references seem to involve members writing outside the group and bringing their products to the group. Described here will be some within group exercises that have a focus on understanding members' thoughts, feelings, and ideas, and their associations for these as produced in the group session.

The first set of exercises involves reading a poem that has images and metaphors relevant to the material that emerged in the group in previous sessions. Used this way, the images and metaphors in the selected poem can expand the expression and understanding of the material, allow members to make deeper personal associations, and in some cases, can enhance universality. For example, suppose the group leader knows or suspects that there is unresolved grief among all or most group members. Selecting a poem that speaks of loss, abandonment, and past relationships could assist members to better access the thoughts and feelings around their unresolved grief. There are many possibilities and many poems available that tap into various themes or subjects that group members could use. Exercise 12.1 presents a basic format to use when reading a poem to the group, and one example of a written response that will be shared with the group.

*Exercise 12.1—Reading a Poem*

*Materials:* A preselected poem, paper and writing instruments for each group member.

*Procedure:*

1. Preselect a poem designed to present images, thoughts, feelings, and metaphors about group members' experiencing, needs, or wishes.
2. Distribute the materials to group members.
3. Read the poem aloud to the group, using emphasis and inflection.
4. After reading, ask members to write about their experiencing as they listened. The experiencing can include images, feelings, thoughts, associations, and so on. Complete sentences do not have to be used.
5. These written responses can be read aloud to the group, or members can present some of the experiencing.
6. Expansion and enhancement can focus on current life experiences, concerns, and problems; associations with people or events from the past; or with new kinds of awareness that were triggered.

Other formats for responses could be drawing, movement, collage construction, or other analyses, and there are other forms for written responses. The leader should decide in advance what format to use to make sure that any needed materials are available. The format should be appropriate for the age and competence of group members, and sufficient time be made available for adequate reporting, expansion, and enhancement. Examples for other types of written responses and for other formats include the following.

### *Written Responses to Hearing a Poem*

- List images, feelings, or thoughts that came to mind as you listened.
- Make a list of any personal associations you have with the poem, or parts of the poem.

- Write a brief paragraph about your experiencing as you heard the poem.

### *Other Response Formats*

- Draw an image, scene, or abstraction that captures the essence of your experiencing as you listened.
- Explore metaphors.
- Assume a body position that illustrates your feelings that the poem elicited.
- Construct a collage of personal images and aroused feelings.
- Relate images, etc., to personal past experiences.
- Act out the personal material that was aroused.

Another way to use poetry is to have group members write poems. These can be about topics that are of relevance to the group as a whole or to individual members. There are numerous poem formats, and the group leader can select one to present as a guide since many group members may never have tried to create a poem. It is recommended that the poem format be a simple and uncomplicated one because of session time constraints. These member poems could tell a story, express a multitude of feelings, describe an event and the member's place in it, present wishes and dreams, or illustrate a meaningful relationship that is either intact or lost to the person. There are many possibilities for subjects for poems.

*Exercise 12.2—Bring a Poem*

The final suggestion is to have group members bring in a poem that expresses a thought, feeling, or idea they find meaningful. These are then read to the group, and reactions solicited.

## Cinquains and Haiku

There are two other poem formats that could be especially helpful for exploring symbols, metaphors, and personal perceptions:

cinquain and haiku. Although both are brief and deceptively simple, both forms can reveal meaning and understanding. Each is described and illustrated with suggested uses.

*Cinquains* are simple five line poems. One version begins with a one word title that is a noun. The second line has a two word phrase related to the title, the third line has three adjectives to describe the topic, the fourth line has a four word phrase related to the topic, and the fifth line is a synonym for the title. An example follows.

Empathy (One word noun)
Understand feelings (Two word phrase)
Emotional, accordant, synchronous (Three adjectives)
Together but separate, independent (Four word phrase)
Identification (A synonym)

Another form for a cinquain has the same number of lines, but a different number of words. The first line names the subject in one word, the second line uses two words to describe it, the third line uses four words (double the number of words in line 2) to express feelings about the subject, the fourth line has two words that tell what the subject does, and the fifth line renames the subject. This format could be especially useful for exploring symbols from dreams and other sources, where the meanings may remain obscure to the person. This could also be used to have each member explore a symbol from their drawings, images that are experienced, ideas, and feelings. An example follows.

Conflict (One word topic)
Dissention, disagreement (Two word description)
Dread, discomfort, apprehension, excitement
(Four feelings)
Reveals perspectives (Two words, what it does)
Differences (Renames it)

This format can also use a two word subject. The sequence would then be four words to describe it, eight feelings, four words about what it does, and two words renaming it.

*Exercise 12.3—Construct a Cinquain*

*Materials:* The leader should prepare one or more examples of a cinquain on newsprint that can be posted where all members can see it. Other materials are sheets of paper and a pen or pencil.

*Procedure:*

1. Post the sample cinquain, distribute the materials, and explain the process for construction.
2. Ask members to construct a cinquain around the topic of their favorite color. Allow 10 to 15 minutes for construction.
3. Reconvene in the group circle and ask members to share their cinquains.
4. Explore the process by asking about feelings that emerged as they constructed their cinquains, and as they reported. Ask if the image became clearer during the construction.

A haiku is a Japanese poem form that has 17 syllables. The subject for the poem highlights something important for the writer, or a pairing of things in nature. It is a very abstract form of poetry that distills the essence. The 17 syllables are distributed in three lines; five, seven and five. Here's one I tried to compose.

Rabbit sits by tree (5 syllables)
Still, among the azaleas (7 syllables)
Every day, all day (5 syllables)

This is about a large wild rabbit who sat in my front yard in a group of azaleas. My husband and I observed that the rabbit just sat there all day long while the squirrels and birds moved around it. This went on for several weeks until one day we noticed that the rabbit was lying on the ground. The rabbit had died among the azaleas.

Poetry is a rich source for understanding the personal significance for images, metaphors, and seemingly unconnected thoughts and ideas. Some formats tell stories, explore feelings, express passion and love, and so on. Group leaders have many choices as to which format to use. It is advisable to use any form of poetry only as a stimulus for expression, and to not let it become the primary focus for the group.

Other meanings emerge or become clearer through a cinquain or haiku. While there may be numerous symbols and concepts available for exploration, discerning the meaning (or a meaning) for one can promote deeper understanding for others that are present in the same dream or other experience.

If you have not previously created cinquains or haiku, it is suggested that you first practice these for yourself before introducing them to the group.

*Exercise 12.4—Construct a Haiku*

*Materials:* The group leader should prepare a sample haiku in advance on newsprint that can be posted where all members can see it; paper and pencils or pen for writing.

*Procedure:*

1. Post the example, distribute materials, and describe the process for constructing a haiku, a poem of 17 syllables.
2. Ask members to construct a haiku about a current feeling they are experiencing or a previous feeling. Allow 10 to 15 minutes for this construction.
3. Reconvene the group and ask members to share their haiku.
4. Explore the feelings around the construction, reporting, and satisfaction with the outcome.

# Chapter 13
# Single Session Writing Activities

Writing activities conducted during a group session provide an opportunity for each member to work on his or her unique issue and reduce confounding or emotional contagion by hearing what others have to say. Writing activities can also assist in organizing members' thoughts and ideas, provide an additional means for expressing feelings, and can even tap material just below conscious awareness. Considerable learning, understanding, and insight are possible in just one session.

## Rationale

Session writing activities are conceptualized as stimuli to focus awareness on an important topic or issue for group members, provide an opportunity for individual input, and are completed within the time frame for the session. Thus, the group leader has to select writing exercises or activities that do not take much time to complete because most of the time has to be spent on members' reporting on their writing, and some exploration of what emerged. The writing portion is the stimulus for accessing group members' personal material in the form of thoughts, feelings, and ideas.

Another benefit for group members is that maybe, for the first time ever their writing is not evaluated. Misspelled words, verb-subject agreement, punctuation, and other grammatical concerns are not important, and the group leader has to make it clear that expression is the important concern rather than technical writing matters.

Below there are some sample exercises that can be accomplished in a single session for groups that have 10 or fewer members. If the group is larger than 10, the reporting phase may be facilitated by breaking the large group into smaller groups of five or less, and asking them to share their products in the smaller group. In this event, the group leader will also need to reconvene the large group and have the small groups each report on what emerged for those group members. They could be asked to report on the theme, commonalities, feelings, and the like. Refer to the basic guidelines in chapter 7 on management of a large group.

### *Session Writing—Past Reflections*

The first set of four exercises could form the focus for four sessions. These are not all intended to be completed in one session; do one exercise per session.

*Exercise 13.1—Childhood Event*

*Materials:* A suitable surface for writing, a pen or pencil, and paper.

*Procedure:* Introduce the exercise by telling members that the group is going to explore childhood events.

1. Ask them to think of a significant event or memory they have that occurred when they were 12 or younger, and to write as full a description as they can of the event or

memory. If they can only remember a portion, then just write what they can remember. Ask them to record all the feelings, actions, people present, and other thoughts they remember at the time. Allow about 15 minutes for this writing.

2. Approximately 3 minutes before the time is up, tell them that they have 3 minutes to finish.
3. Have all members report on what they wrote. They can summarize or give a brief description of what they wrote. The leader needs to allow enough time for every member to report, so do not deepen the experience of a member or explore what emerged at this time. If time permits, you can return to do some exploration. In any event, if it is significant for the member, he or she will bring it up again in another session.
4. Ask members what feelings emerged as they wrote about the event or memory, and what feelings they have now.

*Exercise 13.2—A Teen Event or Memory*
*Materials:* Same as for the previous exercise.
*Procedure:* Same as for the previous exercise.

*Exercise 13.3—An Adult Personal Event or Memory*
*Materials:* Same as above.
*Procedure:* Same as above.

*Exercise 13.4—An Adult Work Related Event or Memory*
*Materials:* Same as above.
*Procedure:* Same as above.

***Session Writing—Free Associations***

The next set is free associations. While five topics are suggested, group leaders can use the procedures to focus the group on what they are avoiding, resisting, or other important issues for the particular group. The five topics are the group, life satisfactions, life dissatisfactions, a wish, and "my relationships." The materials and procedure will be the same as described for "The Group."

*Exercise 13.5—The Group*

*Materials:* A suitable writing surface, pen or pencil, and paper.

*Procedures:* Introduce the exercise by telling members that there are times when thoughts and feelings seem difficult to express. At other times, there are numerous thoughts and feelings being experienced so that it is difficult to sort through them. This exercise will demonstrate how to do free association to make sense of difficult thoughts and feelings, or when they seem too numerous.

1. Present the topic or issue that they are to write about (e.g., The group).
2. Ask members to list all of the thoughts, feelings, and ideas that come to mind when they think of the topic or issue, and to do so without stopping to evaluate or judge what comes to mind. Write as many of these as they can in the time given. Allow at least 5 minutes for writing, but some groups may need a little longer.
3. The next step is to review their lists and place a check by all of the thoughts, ideas, and feelings that are negative.
4. Next, place a check by all of them that are positive.
5. Count the number of positives, and the number of negatives. Make a note of the number of neutral thoughts, feelings, and ideas that remain.
6. Ask each member to report the number of positives and negatives. The leader should pay attention to members who seem to have the majority of positives, and those that have a majority of negatives. Do not comment on these at the time. You are compiling the responses for the group as a whole response. When the compiling is complete, the thoughts, feelings, and ideas members have about the topic or issue should either be predominately positive, negative, or neutral.

7. Lead a discussion about the outcomes, and solicit members' input on what is contributing to the perceptions and responses and, if negative, what can be done to make it more positive.

*Exercises 13.6–13.9*

Use the same materials and procedures in exercise 13.5 to explore each of the following:

*Exercise 13.6—Life Satisfactions*

*Exercise 13.7—Life Dissatisfactions*

*Exercise 13.8—A Wish*

*Exercise 13.9—My Relationships*

***Session Writing—Letters***

The next set is comprised of exercises that focus on the inner self of group members. These can be done as a way of taking inventory of how each member feels about him- or herself, to increase awareness of self-satisfactions with oneself, and to increase awareness of the need for self-care around a major part of oneself. It is suggested that an exercise focusing on one aspect of self be completed in a session. Thus, the six presented could be the focus for six sessions.

The set of exercises are letters to aspects of the inner self of the person. The aspects are cognitive, interpersonal, emotional, creative, inspirational, and physical. Each is presented separately as the focus because each aspect is different.

*Exercise 13.10—Letter to My Cognitive Self*

*Materials:* A suitable surface for writing, a pen or pencil, and paper—several sheets for each person. Post the following where members can see it:

The Cognitive Self

Thinking

Organizing
Clarity
Memory.

If members and the leader agree, the writing can be done on a computer.

*Procedure:* Introduce the exercise by telling group members that the focus will be on writing a letter to their inner selves, and the first letter will be to their cognitive self. The cognitive self is the mind, the mental life of the person.

1. Begin the letter with, "Dear Cognitive Self," and write what you are thinking, sensing, and feeling about each listed aspect of the cognitive self. Write about what you appreciate, wish were different, any regrets, and close with "thanks for being there."
2. Allow 15 to 20 minutes for letters to be composed. If members need more time, give them 1 to 2 minutes and tell them they can finish after the group.
3. Ask members to read their letters if they wish, or any part of them. Notice similarities among the letters, and link these for members.

*Exercise 13.11—The Interpersonal Self*

*Materials:* Same as above, except post the following:

The Interpersonal Self
Relations with family
Intimate relationships
Work relationships
Other relationships.

The interpersonal self is the way in which you relate to others, and your satisfaction with your relationships.

Follow the same procedures for the cognitive self, substituting the interpersonal self.

*Exercise 13.12—The Emotional Self*

*Materials:* Same as above, except post the following:

The Emotional Self
Feelings experienced
Feelings easily expressed
Feelings difficult to express
Feelings you are unable to access—never feel them.

The emotional self focuses on the extent to which you can access and express feelings, and if you are able to appropriately express your feelings.

Follow the same procedures for the cognitive self, substituting the emotional self.

*Exercise 13.13—The Creative Self*
*Materials:* Same as above except, post the following:

The Creative Self
Imaginative
New and novel endeavors, processes, and the like
Unique ways of being and perceiving.

The creative self emphasizes trying new and novel ways for different aspects of your life. Examples are cooking, gardening, fixing things, artistic endeavors, inventions, and the like.

Follow the same procedures for the cognitive self, substituting the creative self.

*Exercise 13.14—The Inspirational Self*
*Materials:* The same as above, except post the following:

The Inspirational Self
Altruistic acts
Hopes
Meditation, prayers, and the like
Transcendent.

The inspirational self is the part of you that extends beyond the physical and known. It connects you to the universe and to others.

Follow the same procedures for the cognitive self, but substitute the inspirational self.

*Exercise 13.15—The Physical Self*

*Materials:* The same as above, except post the following:

The Physical Self
Health habits
Health status
Medical conditions and concerns
Appearance.

The physical self refers to the body, both inner and outer, its care or neglect, and sensations. Other topics that may be addressed include medications, use of other drugs and alcohol, eating habits, sleep, and exercise.

Follow the same procedures for the cognitive self, substituting the inspirational self.

### *Session Writing—Dreams*

Dreams can be a rich source of information for group members because these can tap into the area that is below awareness in the person's current life, provide a focus for what appeared to be indefinite concerns, and bring feelings into awareness. What follows is not dream analysis as would be done in psychotherapy, but a brief activity that can trigger insight and awareness for group members.

*Exercise 13.16—A Dream*

*Materials:* A suitable surface for writing, pen or pencil, and two or more sheets of paper for each member.

*Procedure:* Introduce the exercise by telling group members that sometimes a dream has a message for the dreamer, and that this activity could help reveal the message.

1. Ask members to think of a dream or fragment of a dream, either recent or in the past, and to write a summary of the dream. Allow time to complete the summaries.
2. The next step is to have members read over the summaries, and list the feelings associated with the dream, either then or in the present.

3. Ask group members to make a list of the major components in the dream, such as people, actions, colors, whatever seems important to them.
4. The final step is to review the two lists, and associate the items with their current lives. It is helpful to have them write a statement about the associations.
5 Group members can share any part or all of what was written, but time must be available for every member to share something. Group leaders could just have members share the final statement about their associations.

Each of the following exercises can be completed in a single session, but the effects can be enduring and material that emerged during the exercise can reemerge in later sessions. It is recommended that only one of these be used in a session.

***Session Writing—Self-Boosters***

*Exercise 13.17—The Power of Lists*

*Materials:* 5" × 8" index cards, a pen or pencil, and a suitable writing surface.

*Procedure:*

1. Distribute the materials and introduce the exercise.

   *Oftentimes some people tend to focus more on their characteristics that they perceive as inadequate, or negative. There are also times when others can say or do something that triggers these undesirable thoughts about one's self, leading to experiencing uncomfortable feelings like guilt and shame, or seeking to repress and deny the thoughts for fear of triggering those feelings. This activity is designed to focus on your strengths, and to provide you with a reminder of these.*

2. Ask members to list 10 strengths they have such as, being well-organized and the like. Allow enough time for members to finish their lists.
3. Next, ask them to share their lists with the group, or to share as much or as little as they desire.

4. After the sharing phase, explore the lists by asking the following questions:
   - What feelings did you experience as you created your list?
   - What feelings emerged as you presented these strengths to the group?
   - Are there strength similarities among group members?
   - Is there a strength you have that is underused? How could you capitalize more on this strength?
5. Tell group members to keep their cards in a safe place, and to review them periodically, such as weekly. Tell them that this strength list can be used when they begin to have self-doubts, feel inadequate, or are chastised for something. The list can help bring thoughts and feelings back to their strengths.

*Exercise 13.18—Life Enhancers*

*Materials:* A sample list of life enhancers on newsprint, 5" × 8"index cards, and a pen or pencil.

*Procedure:*

1. Prepare the sample list of personal life enhancers. These are the things, events, and the like that bring pleasure, make you smile, and can help you savor your life. These are usually cost-free or inexpensive. Following is an example:

   Kittens playing
   A child smiling at me
   Snow gently falling
   A snow covered landscape
   A fire in the fireplace
   A drink of water on a hot day
   Flying a kite
   Reading an interesting book.

2. Introduce the exercise by presenting the prepared list and telling group members the information in step 1.

3. Ask them to make their personal lists of life enhancers.
4. When members finish their lists, ask them to share these in the group.
5. Explore the feelings aroused as they created their lists, as they shared their list in the group, and as they listened to others' lists.
6. Summarize what transpired and tell them that they have many life enhancers, and that their pleasure and positive mood can be increased by trying to ensure that they experience one or more of these every day.

*Exercise 13.19—Self-Boosters*

*Materials:* A large sheet of newsprint, 5" × 8" index cards, a pen or pencil, and a prepared sample.

*Procedure:*

1. The group leader should prepare a sample in advance, either on the large sheet of newsprint, or written on a white board, or something similar.

   *Sample*

   Finish the statement that begins with, I have
   Good work habits
   An optimistic attitude
   A sense of humor
   A capacity to feel deeply
   A thirst for knowledge and understanding.

2. Introduce the exercise to group members by telling them that it can be helpful to remind themselves of some positive attributes they possess. Show the sample, and ask them to make their personal lists on the card.
3. Once members have completed their lists, have them read the list out loud as if they are talking to someone in another room, that is, read it in a loud voice. They can even shout if they like.
4. After all lists are read out loud, explore the feelings experienced as they compiled their lists, and as they read

them. Be sure to ask if anyone had difficulty in thinking of a self-booster.

*Exercise 13.20—A Letter*

*Materials:* Two or more sheets of paper for each group member, and a pen or pencil.

*Procedure:*

1. Distribute the materials and introduce the exercise.

   *This activity is focused on self-care and your satisfaction with what you do to take care of your self. This particular exercise is focused on physical self-care, but you can use this process to explore your self-care for other aspects of your self. To begin, sit in silence and concentrate on your breathing. Slowly, allow yourself to become aware of what bodily sensations you have. Mentally scan your body from head to toe.*

2. Tell members to begin their letters with "Dear (their name)," and write about their current body experience, and its reaction to their positive and negative health habits, such as sleeping, eating, exercise, medication/drug use, and so on. Write what your body wants to tell you about how you care for it. If any part of your body is distressed, write what you think it is saying to you. Tune in to all of your body and write about what its message is.
3. When members seem to have completed their letters, ask them to review them, and then write a summary statement about their body. For example, what did they become aware of that is positive or negative? What may they have ignored about their physical self that needs attention?
4. Ask them to share their summaries or their letters. They can share as much or as little as they are ready to disclose.
5. Explore members' feelings about the activity.

# Chapter 14

# Journaling

The final type of writing activity to be presented is journaling. Journal writing is another form of expressive writing because it also uses this format for the exploration of one's self for better understanding, healing, and fostering growth. It has been shown to have both psychological and physical benefits (Lepole & Smyth, 2002). One of the main benefits for journal writing is that it can be used for expressing thoughts, feelings, and ideas where doing so interpersonally is not possible, or the circumstances are inappropriate to do so. Further, journaling permits expression of these elements that is free from the constraints of grammar, logic, sequencing, and the like that are needed when trying to express these to another person.

Much has been written about the benefits of journaling in the past few years, and the research on expressive writing as a brief form of journaling has shown that there is considerable evidence for its efficacy. The benefits of journaling seem to be considerable; for example, as a stress reliever, clarifying thoughts and ideas, expressing and sorting through feelings, identifying vague issues and concerns, and so on. Other benefits include enhancing creativity and releasing the flow of new ideas, an aid to coping with stressful events by using energy to express reactions instead of having to suppress them, and as a record of life events both positive and negative. People who use this modality report many positive benefits.

There are numerous studies on the effects of written emotional expression on physical and psychological health conditions (e.g., Smyth, 1998; Smyth, Stone, Hurewitz, & Kaeli, 1999; Spiegel, 1999; Walker, Nail, & Croyle, 1999). One study on emotional writing and psychological symptoms that compared writing and drawing about a stressful event found that the psychological symptoms were significantly decreased after two 15 minute sessions for the journaling group compared to the drawing and control groups. This was especially significant for the journal group participants who had measured higher psychological distress on the pretest. A sample of other studies on the moderation of psychological distress or traumatic events includes Lumley, Tojek, and Macklem (2002), Pennebaker (1999), Pizarro (2004), Sweig (2000), and Ullrich and Lutgendorf (2002).

Other uses for journal writing are in physician and nurse training to promote reflective thinking and to explore and integrate experiences with patients. Four examples of this use reflective writing as a class blog (Chretien, Goldman, & Faselis, 2008); reflective journals for learning for postregistration nursing students (Chirema, 2007); medical students (Wald, Reis, Monroe, & Borkan, 2010); and for medical students experiencing the death of patients (Doll, Kereakoglow, Radhika, & Hare, 2008).

Other professional training programs also use journal writing:

- Veterinary clinical pathology (Sharkey, Overmann, & Flash, 2007);
- Dental hygiene (Hanson & Alexander, 2010);
- Emergency psychiatry (Bhuvaneswar, Stern, & Beresin, 2009);

- Physiotherapy (Donaghy & Morss, 2007);
- Athletic training education (Mensch & Ennis, 2002);
- Animal science and dairy science (Haugh, 1996).

The group leader must be prepared for some resistance when asking members to keep journals over a period of time. There are people for whom journaling does not provide relief, but rather presents them with a burden and chore which counter any possible positive benefits. Further, some group members can resist journaling because of past experiences where their writing was criticized or evaluated as inadequate, or they think that their technical writing skills such as spelling and punctuation are inferior, or they do not want others in their world to see their writings and privacy is a real concern, or they just don't see any benefits in writing a journal. These are some reasons why journaling may not be acceptable for some group members, and the group leader needs to respect and accept these perceptions and to not insist that members participate even when the leader feels that participation would be beneficial. Before initiating this activity, it is helpful to judge the level of the resistance because it is not beneficial for the group when some members are participating and some are not.

Let's suppose that the group leader has some members who want to do journaling, some who are skeptical, and some who are adamant about not participating. Instead of forcing the activity as conceptualized, or dropping it entirely, the leader could try one of the following exercises as a way to ease members into journaling.

*Exercise 14.1—Building Pleasure*

*Materials:* A journal book or composition book. These are generally inexpensive and can be found at many craft stores for a dollar. The leader can purchase these for the group. Also needed is a pen or pencil for each member.

1. Introduce the activity by telling members that it is helpful for their mood to be able to focus on pleasurable and

personally rewarding things each day. The journals are to record the following each day between sessions.

- A pleasant sight, such as flowers blooming, children playing, a smile directed toward them, and the like.
- A pleasant sound, such as music, a car engine running smoothly, birds singing, and so on.
- A pleasant smell, such as food, perfume, fragrant flowers, lotion, soap.
- A pleasant taste, such as coffee, fruit, toothpaste, candy.

2. They are also free to record anything else that was pleasant for them.
3. The first phase or week would have them talk about their recorded items if they choose to, or how it felt to remember and record these.
4. The leader can gradually ask for more associations, such as feelings experienced for each recorded item, difficulties encountered, impact on their mood and functioning. Members could also be encouraged to write these in the journals as they record their experiences, but the leader should present this as an option.

*Exercise 14.2—Home Contents*

*Materials:* Same as in the previous exercise.

*Procedure:* Introduce the activity as in the previous exercise but substitute writing about something in their home. If there are homeless group members, substitute writing about something that gives them a feeling of home. Items could be a piece of furniture, an article of clothing, a book, magazine, food, or anything they choose.

1. Select one item each day and write about it addressing each of the following:
   - Describe the item's appearance, color, shape, and so on.
   - List the feelings triggered as members look at or write about the item.

- Write a short statement about what the item contributes to their life.

## Other Types of Journals

Journals are a record of thoughts, feelings, and ideas experienced daily, weekly, or intermittently. There is no set pattern of what to write or when, it's up to the individual. Some people like to write daily, others want to write when they have something to work out, convey, or to record. Used this way in group settings, it becomes homework where members are free to participate or not, to disclose what they wrote or not, or to reveal to the group the insights and learning they gleaned from journaling.

It can be very important that members have some place they can keep their journal private and free from intrusions. It can be very detrimental to a relationship to have one's private thoughts read by someone else without permission, and when you live with others, this is a real possibility. Curiosity can overcome even the most well-meaning person when they see a journal. If privacy and confidentiality of the journals cannot be maintained by the members, it may be best not to use this technique.

What can members write about and how should they express themselves? There is no simple or easy answer to these questions. The group leader can give a focus topic such as those listed at the end of this section, or allow members to choose what to write about, or if there is a particular goal or behavior change that is the focus for the group to write about that. The group leader can instruct members to write however they wish. They can write poems, prose, a stream of consciousness, words, phrases, or what occurs to them as they engage in the process of writing. No one is evaluating what they write, grammar and punctuation are of no consequence except for the writer, and the purpose is more to express something than how it is expressed. Encourage members not to engage in self-evaluation or editing, to just let the flow of thoughts, ideas, and feelings continue without the interruption of thinking about technical matters. Some possible topics or foci for journals include the following.

- Daily thoughts and ideas;
- Feelings experienced throughout the day, and their triggers;
- What's it like to practice mindfulness;
- Current worries and concerns;
- Hopes, dreams, wishes.

### *Visual Journaling*

A variation for journals is the visual journal where drawings, painting, and collage are added to the written words. There can be doodles, tracings, rubbings, and other images that are added to the thoughts, feelings, and ideas that are expressed in the journal. These enhancers also are expressions, and can be clues to what is just below the level of consciousness at that particular time. When reviewed at a later time, these entries can help the person to better understand past experiencing and its impact on him or her. The following exercise is for a sample visual journaling page:

*Exercise 14.3—A Sample Visual Journal Page Demonstration*

*Preparation by the Leader:* Prepare a variety of pages (8½" × 11" or 9" × 10") to be used as background for the visual journal pages using heavyweight paper such as Bristol or watercolor paper. These background pages can be painted or smudged with ink pads. Use a variety of colors. These are prepared in advance because they need time to dry before adding writing or other embellishments.

*Materials:* Scissors; magazines or catalogues for cutting out images; pens or pencils for writing; glue sticks; sheets of paper; permanent black ink felt markers in fine, medium, and broad points; and sets of crayons, felt markers, or colored pencils.

*Procedure:*

1. It is best that the group work around a table so that materials can be shared and easily accessed. Introduce

the exercise by telling members that this is a demonstration for a visual journal entry about their day. Ask them to reflect on their day from the time they woke up to the present.

2. Ask members to take a sheet of paper and a writing instrument, and jot down 5 to 7 items about their day such as the following:
   - Moments of pleasure or beauty;
   - Thoughts they had throughout the day;
   - Sounds/tastes/ sensations experienced;
   - Events;
   - People they encountered;
   - Feelings experienced.

   They can list all items in one category, or spread across categories. These lists will be used to form the written entry for the page later.
3. Next, ask them to select a prepared journal page, and to cut out images from the magazines or catalogues and paste them on the page, or draw images, doodle on the page, or use a combination of collage and drawing. Remind them to leave room for their written entry.
4. The next step is to write about the items listed in step 2. Use the permanent felt pens for writing because these will write over the paint or ink. Members can write as much or as little as they wish, sentences do not have to be complete, and there are no rules about punctuation. The task is to write about their day.
5. Once pages are complete, reconvene the group and ask members to share something about their pages and the feelings experienced as they constructed the page.

# Chapter 15
# Imagery

## Introduction

Creative activities incorporating imagery, mindfulness, and music can tap other dimensions of experiencing for group members. People learn in different ways and these modalities can be used to enhance and expand learning and understanding of oneself and of others. Although each of these, when used as a focus and emphasis for therapy, call for specialized training, there are activities that can be adapted for use by group leaders who do not have that training. However, it is recommended that group leaders have some formal training with the technique or modality prior to using it with a group, such as taking a workshop.

Imagery is a process for visualization of thoughts, feelings, ideas, wishes, dreams, or fantasies that may be conscious or unconscious. These visualizations can increase awareness and understanding, suggest possibilities and alternatives, make conscious the nonconscious and unconscious material, and can provide comfort and solace. Mindfulness is a technique that has its roots in meditation, but has been expanded to provide focus and concentration in all aspects of one's life. Its mantra is: Be here in the present. Further, there is considerable research as to the efficacy of mindfulness for stress reduction, positive therapy outcomes, assistance with medical conditions, and other uses. Music therapy has been used for some time, and there is research to support its efficacy. Although what is presented in this chapter does not focus on music therapy, it does provide some activities involving music that can be used in groups.

## Imagery

A search of Psynet and other databases for research on the use of imagery in therapy revealed that the majority of studies were on medical conditions such as spasticity (Bovend'Eerdt, Dawes, Sackley, Izadi, & Wade, 2009), spinal cord injury, breast cancer (Cameron, Booth, Schlatter, Ziginskas, & Harman, 2007), and stroke and brain injury (Niemeir, Cifu, & Kishore, 2001). These and other such studies on medical conditions used prerecorded imagery exercises, or a therapist trained in imagery techniques. Serious conditions like PTSD, medical conditions, diagnosed anxiety disorders, and the like require specialized training in imagery for therapy, and this kind of training is beyond the scope of this book. What is presented here are the short and simple imagery activities that do not call for formal specialized training in the use of the technique, although readers are encouraged to participate in one or more workshops or classes on the technique. Such preparation can facilitate the use of simple and uncomplicated imagery techniques, and is useful in addition to the education and training in group therapy previously accomplished.

This chapter focuses on using imagery for the following therapeutic issues:

- Teaching relaxation—reduce stress and tension;
- Coping with negative emotions;
- Preparation for performances, such as tests;

- Coping with difficult situations, distress, and the like;
- Learning about one's self-perception.

## Guidelines

Focus on a single purpose for using imagery in the group. Group members may benefit in a variety of ways from the activity, but having more than one therapeutic purpose or goal makes it too complicated and less likely to accomplish any of the intended purposes. The purpose or goals should be clear, specific, and focused on one of the reasons given in the introduction.

Introduce the exercise by describing what will be done and what members are expected to do. Imagery activities can be described as a visualization where the leader provides verbal cues for what to do, what to attend to, and so on. Members supply their personal responses and associations, and are encouraged to just let these emerge and to not try to alter them. Permission is given to stop imaging at any time by opening their eyes or not to participate in the activity. There should be no penalty for declining to participate.

Group leaders may want to secure recorded activities, such as for progressive relaxation. Scripts are also available if the leader feels it important that group members receive the instructions direct from him or her. Most of the exercises presented in this book and in this chapter have a script the group leader can use. When reading or providing a script, be sure to do so with suitable pauses of sufficient time to allow members' images to emerge. What can appear as a long time to the leader can be experienced as a very short time to the group members.

Writing, drawing, or other expressive techniques are useful adjuncts for imagery. Writing or drawing their images allows group members to capture them before they become contaminated by thoughts, judgments, or evaluations, or by hearing what others experienced. Some group members may not need to write or draw, but using these techniques with the imaging can still be helpful. For example, I find that members' images of a place of peace seem to become more vivid and fixed when they draw after imaging.

## Imagery

This chapter begins a little differently than do other chapters by starting with an exercise to help set the frame for using imagery. The technique of imagery comes from behavioral therapy, particularly that of the multimodal therapy by Lazarus and Folkman (1984), and has many applications. Many of these will be presented and discussed later in the chapter. An exercise is introduced now the purpose of which is to provide group members with a refuge to retreat to when encountering distress or intense negative feelings. Imagery activities can trigger these feelings for some people, and other theories and therapies, such as Dialectical Behavioral Therapy, cognitive therapy, and eye movement desensitization reprocessing (EMDR) present such a refuge prior to members working with their serious issues and concerns. Although the activities in this chapter should not produce distress, the possibility does exist that some group member may experience this, and the following exercise can be helpful. It is also a good way to introduce group members to imagery.

*Exercise 15.1—A Haven*

*Materials:* None if imagery alone is used, but if drawing the image is a part of the exercise, the following materials will be needed: paper, a set of crayons, colored pencils, or felt markers for each group member.

1. Introduce the exercise by telling group members that they may want to have a respite from distress or intense negative feelings at times, and the image they produce from this exercise will be there for them to visit at any time. Tell them that the process will be as follows. You will ask them to close their eyes, and let the designated image emerge without trying to change or evaluate it as good or bad, right or wrong. If the image is disturbing,

opening their eyes brings them back to the room and stops the imaging. Determine if anyone wants to opt out of doing the exercise, and give them permission to do so.

2. Ask members to close their eyes and to become aware of their breathing. Note if their breath is deep and even, short and jerky, or if they are having difficulty breathing (e.g. a medical condition). Give 5 to10 seconds for this. Next, ask them to try to breathe deeply and evenly, and to notice how this makes them feel. Give another 5 to 10 seconds for this part.
3. Provide the following directions.

   *As you sit in silence, and your breathing becomes deeper and more even, allow an image of a place to emerge that gives you feelings of safety, peace, and serenity (allow 5 to 10 seconds at least for an image to emerge).*

   *Begin to notice details about your place of haven. It is a place where you can go at any time to be safe, peaceful, and serene. What do you see? What do you hear? What other sensations do you have?* (Allow 15 to 20 seconds or longer to fix the image in their minds.) *When you are ready, open your eyes and come back to the room.*

4. Ask each member to describe his or her image. Note similarities among members, but do not explore these or the images in detail. If you use drawing, ask members to first draw their images, and then present these to the group.
5. Have group members explore the following questions:
   - Was it easy or difficult to have an image emerge?
   - What feelings were triggered for you as you imaged? Talked about your image?
   - Was it difficult to try to make your breathing deep and even? Did this produce some calmness for you?
   - How do you feel now about your image?

This exercise was presented first because imagery can be frightening or distressful at times for some people, and having a safe haven image can be reassuring. This image provides group members with a means of support in the event of distress as they engage in other imagery activities, or in any of the other expressive activities described in the book.

## Reducing Tension and Anxiety

Marra (2004) describes anxiety as causing muscle tension and aches, reducing the effectiveness of one's ability to concentrate and pay attention, interfering with decision making, and lessening the person's capacity to experience joy, pleasure, and the like. Physical symptoms can be restlessness, irritability, fatigue, heart palpitations, breathing difficulties, and continual worry. Anxiety interferes with almost every aspect of one's life.

Teaching progressive relaxation to group members could be helpful to counter tension and anxiety. The script for relaxation is long, and readers are encouraged to locate a professional tape to use. However, there are brief relaxation activities that can produce enough relaxation for members to feel the difference, and that will help in producing images. One such activity follows:

*Exercise 15.2—Body Tension*
*Materials:* None.
*Procedure:*

1. Introduce the exercise by describing some of the effects of tension on the body and mind. Tell group members that you will guide them in a brief exercise that could reduce some of the tension. They can participate with their eyes closed or open. Mention that when eyes are closed it usually helps facilitate concentration on the body.
2. Survey group members as to the level of tension they currently feel rating it 0 (no tension), to 10 (extremely tense). Also ask them where the major tension is in their bodies.
3. Ask members to close their eyes and concentrate on their breathing, and note if it is jerky, short, coming

from their chest, or however it is at this moment. Allow 15 to 20 seconds.

4. Next, ask them to consciously try to deepen their breath and to breathe from their diaphragm (top of stomach). Tell them if they have difficulty to just keep concentrating on their breathing.
5. Guide members through the following sequence:

   *We're going to journey through your body from the top of your head to your toes. Along the way, become aware of any tension in that part of the body. You can consciously relax the tension by contracting or tightening the muscles, holding the contraction, and then release the contraction.*

   a. *We begin with the head. Notice if there is tension, tighten the muscles, hold it, and let go.*
      *(Provide at least 10 seconds between instructions to allow members to contract, hold, and let go)*
   b. *Next, we move to the neck. Notice if there is tension. If so, gently move your head from one side to the other to tighten those muscles and let go.*
   c. *Notice if there is tension in your shoulders. If so, hunch your shoulders up toward your ears, hold it, and then let go. You can do this several times if needed.*
   d. *Move to your arms and hands. If there is tension, make a fist as tightly as you can, hold and release. This should help release tension in the arms and hands.*
   e. *Notice if there is tension in your chest. Breathe deeply and evenly to release this tension.*
   f. *Move to noticing if there is tension in your stomach. To contract these muscles, pull your stomach in as far as you can, hold it, and then let go. You can do this several times.*
   g. *Notice if there is tension in your legs. Try to contract those muscles, hold it, and then release.*
   h. *We've reached the feet and toes. If you are able, flex your feet by stretching the leg horizontal, and flexing the toes to align with the heel. Feel the stretch, hold it, and then release.*

i. *Perform a body scan by starting at the top of your head and progressing through the body. Notice where you have tension, tighten those muscles, hold it, and then release the contraction.*

## Coping with Negative Emotions

Negative emotions such as anger, fear, and the like, also have negative effects on the body and mind. These can be triggered and become difficult to relinquish, or are so intrusive that the person cannot effectively function, or can be expressed in inappropriate ways so that relationships are impaired, and some group members may not know how to manage and contain them to reduce the negative effects. While it can be best that members learn to work through these emotions, or gain insight as to their causes, what can be helpful in the short term is to give them a coping skill that can be used immediately when they experience these emotions. The following set of exercises can help members develop distracting strategies as a coping skill that can be used when the negative emotions arise and linger.

It is recommended that group leaders use the entire set of imaging activities since members will be responsive to differing distractions. Complete each activity before moving to the next one.

*Exercise 15.3—Cope by Distracting Yourself*
*Materials:* None
*Procedure:* Introduce the activity by telling group members that it can be difficult sometimes to cope with negative emotions, and that they can become enmeshed or overwhelmed, find it difficult to relinquish the particular emotion, and that becoming mired can affect them and others who have to interact with them. What is presented is a set of four imaging exercises of distracting activities, and members will be taken through the entire set so they can better select the distracting image that best fits them.

*Activity A* Visual Distraction

*Procedure:*

1. Ask members to sit in silence and to concentrate on their breathing for a few seconds. Then, ask them to allow a pleasant image to emerge, a visual experience; for example, kittens romping, children at play, the beach, or anything that produces a feeling of pleasure. Tell them to note details of the image and surroundings.
2. Tell members that when they are ready, to open their eyes and return to the room.
3. Ask each member to share their image. After which, tell them that they can return to this image when they are distressed, or feel an intense negative emotion.

*Activity B* An Auditory Distraction

*Procedure:*

1. Ask members to sit in silence and concentrate on their breathing for a few seconds. Then, ask them to image a pleasant sound; a voice, music, birds singing, or whatever sound pleases them when they hear it.
2. Tell members that when they are ready to open their eyes, and then to share their images.
3. Tell them that the sound image can be used when distressed, or as a distraction from a negative emotion.

*Activity C* A Taste Distraction

*Procedure:*

1. Ask members to sit in silence and concentrate on their breathing for a few seconds. Then, ask them to image a pleasant taste, to become mindful of what it feels like on the tongue or in the mouth, the texture of the substance, and the feeling that it produces.
2. Tell members that when they are ready, to open their eyes, and then share their images.
3. After step 2 is completed, tell them that they can return to this image as a distraction whenever they are dis-

tressed, or use it as a distraction from experiencing negative emotions.

*Activity D* Positive Touch Sensation
*Procedure:*

1. Ask members to sit in silence and concentrate on their breathing for a few seconds. Then, ask them to image a positive touch sensation where they feel something on their skin. This could be something like a spray of refreshing water, a silk garment, rubbing on lotion, and the like. (It's probably best to not use an image or example of human touches since that can be upsetting to some group members who may have had negative experiences.)
2. Tell members that when they are ready, to open their eyes and share their images.
3. After step 2 is completed, tell them that they can return to this image to use as a coping strategy.

## Imagery for Performances

Performances, such as taking a test, speaking in public, asking for a raise, and other such situations can be very anxiety provoking, and even paralytic for some people. The fear can be so pervasive that the person cannot access the energy, information, or other resources needed to carry through with the task. While one exercise alone will not conquer this anxiety, an activity such as the following can show members that it is possible to reduce the anxiety or fear so that they can better perform whatever the task in question.

*Exercise 15.4—A Future Situation*
*Materials:* A suitable surface for writing, sheets of paper, a pen or pencil.
*Procedure:*

1. Distribute materials and introduce the exercise. Tell members that the activity you will guide them through

is a preparation for a future situation. They are free to choose the situation. Examples could be taking a test, giving a talk in public, or any situation that produces considerable anxiety for them.

2. Ask members to write a brief summary of the future situation. Give some time for them to finish, and ask if anyone wants to share their future situation.
3. Next, have them list the steps they will take to approach the situation beginning with waking that morning, and to be as specific as possible about what those steps will be.
4. After the lists are complete, ask them to review their lists and to write what feeling they think is associated with the step. For example, getting out of bed may have dread associated with it because of anticipation of the future event.
5. Next, ask them to write a statement or paragraph about what they could change that would allow them to behave differently. The change should be personal, not the situation or another person.
6. Have members put the writing instrument down, sit in silence, close their eyes, and concentrate on their breathing. Use the following script to guide the imaging.

   *As you sit in silence, allow the future situation to emerge with the change in yourself that will permit you to behave differently in the situation. As the situation emerges, become aware of your feelings, your actions, and how you imagine the situation will unfold. Stay with the action as long as you can, noting as many details as you can. When your imaging has stopped, open your eyes and come back to the room.*

7. Allow enough time for the images to unfold. When all members have opened their eyes, ask them to briefly write about the imaging.
8. Once that writing is complete, have members who wish to share the experience do so. Members should be free to not share if they choose.

## Coping with Difficult Situations or Distress

Some people find it difficult to cope with difficult situations or distress because they tend to "catch" others' feelings. Their psychological boundary strength is insufficient to prevent others' projections from being incorporated into their selves, accepted, and acted on. This is why they end up overly disturbed with intense emotions that do not disperse easily, they have their own feelings which are generally negative, and have now incorporated others' negative feelings on top of what they were already feeling. These are also the people who generally find it difficult to say no to others, or to not give in to others' demands.

Psychological boundary strength refers to having a clear understanding of where and how you are an individual person who is separate from others; that is, the boundary where you end and where others begin. The separation and individuation process described by Mahler (1975) is incomplete and the boundary strength is insufficient to keep others from projecting their negative emotions onto you. Growing in separation and individuation is a lifelong process, and when there are developmental delays, the person can have weak psychological boundaries. It takes time and effort to grow strong and resilient psychological boundary strength, and this is beyond the scope of the present book. What is presented here is a brief exercise that group members could use while they are working on developing and fortifying their psychological boundary strength. The imaging activity gives them some emotional insulation that can be employed to prevent taking in other's negative feelings, criticisms, or blame (Brown, 2009).

*Exercise 15.5—Boundary Fortification*

*Materials:* Paper or large index cards, a set of crayons, colored pencils, or felt markers for each group member.

*Procedure:*

1. Introduce the exercise by telling members that there are times when you feel disturbed or distressed in interactions with other people because you cannot prevent their feelings from overwhelming you, or you become

enmeshed in their feelings. You "catch" their feelings. You may even have termed this as being "too empathic," but what may be happening is that your psychological boundary strength is not sufficient to prevent this from happening. (The leader should be prepared to describe what catching means, and to give examples such as what is presented in the introduction to this exercise.) Explain that this exercise will give them a short term strategy to help prevent "catching others" feelings.

2. Ask members to sit in silence and concentrate on their breathing and to try and make it deep and even.
3. As they sit in silence, use the following script:

*Image a barrier between you and another person that will allow you to hear what they are saying, but will prevent you from catching their projected feelings. This barrier can be something like a door you close, a shade you pull down, a sliding steel wall that you close, a force field. It can be anything you choose, just image what barrier you could use to prevent yourself from becoming distressed, overwhelmed, or enmeshed in their feelings. Stay with the image and notice all the details you can. When you are ready, open your eyes, come back to the room, and draw your barrier.*

4. After the drawing is complete, ask members to share their drawings and note similarities between choices of barrier.
5. Tell members that they can image the barrier at any time, such as before they interact with someone who always seems to leave them disturbed, or when they are in an interaction and find that they are becoming distressed or disturbed.

## Self-Perception

This section will present an exercise to take inventory of members' self-perception in a way that can reveal their degree of satisfaction with different aspects of the self by comparing the current perception with the ideal they hold for themselves. Because humans are multifaceted, it is not unusual to find that some aspects of self are perceived positively, others may be perceived negatively, but almost everyone has some part of their self that they want to improve or change. The expansion and enhancement phase of the exercise can guide members in developing action plans for the desired changes.

*Exercise 15. 6—Self-Perceptions*

*Materials:* Two sheets of paper with the columns labeled as designated below for each member. (The space for each column can be larger); a set of crayons, colored pencils, or felt markers for each group member.

1. Current

| Physical | Cognitive | Emotional | Creative | Relational | Spiritual |
|---|---|---|---|---|---|

2. Ideal

| Physical | Cognitive | Emotional | Creative | Relational | Spiritual |
|---|---|---|---|---|---|

1. After distributing the materials, ask group members to sit back and close their eyes. Tell them you will present each aspect separately giving enough time for the image to emerge, and then ask them to open their eyes and draw. You will ask them to image six times, and to draw six times.
2. Present each aspect separately asking them to image that part of their current selves. Allow 30 to 40 seconds for the image to emerge. After each one, ask them to open their eyes and to draw the image that emerged.
   - Physical
   - Cognitive
   - Emotional
   - Creative
   - Relational
   - Spiritual.
3. After all six drawings are complete, ask group members to share their drawings. You can approach this by doing

all drawings for one aspect at a time, or have members present all six aspects of their self at one time.

4. Repeat steps 1 to 3, substituting ideal self.
5. Questions to guide self-exploration follow:
   - How are the symbols for the different aspects of your current and ideal self alike? Different?
   - Which aspect(s) of your current self is (are) most pleasing to you?
   - Are there any aspects that are displeasing to you?
   - Are there any aspects of your ideal self that are unrealistic to obtain, achieve, etc.?
   - Which are achievable?
   - Do you have an action plan to achieve the ideal aspect (s)?

## Addressing Group Concerns

When the group encounters a dilemma, or when members are suppressing feelings or conflict, it can be helpful to do an imagery exercise that focuses on the group as a whole. Such an activity can provide a way for group members to express difficult thoughts and feelings, and to clarify what they sense is happening in the group. It can be a safe way to express what they fear to say openly, and can allow the group leader to bring a difficult situation to the attention of the group. The following exercise could address unspoken group concerns.

*Exercise 15.7—Image of the Group*

*Materials:* None, unless the leader wants to have the group write or draw the image.

*Procedure:*

1. Ask members to sit in silence, concentrate on their breathing to try and relax, and to close their eyes. Tell them you are going to ask them to allow an image to emerge.

2. Begin by telling members how many sessions the group has met, and that they have discussed many topics during that time. Ask them to reflect on their experiences in the group, and to allow an image of the group to emerge. The image can be symbolic, abstract, or whatever comes up for them. Allow enough time for the imaging.
3. Tell them that when the imaging stops, to open their eyes and come back to the room.
4. Have a go around to let members share their images. Or, if they draw or write, provide enough time for this and then have them share their images.
5. Observe similarities, differences, and ask members what their associations are for the images, either their own, or that of others.
6. Try to summarize what the images are presenting about the group as a whole in the present and invite members to provide their input about your summary.

# Chapter 16

# Mindfulness and Music

## Mindfulness

Mindfulness occurs when you can stay focused on your thoughts, feelings, physical sensations, and actions in the present moment. In some ways, it is akin to meditation, but is more extending than meditation because it seeks to expand your awareness to both the inner and external experiencing. This section presents an overview of some literature that demonstrates the effectiveness of mindfulness, the benefits for using it as a group activity, and some exercises.

Kabat-Zinn is credited with conducting the research on the use of mindfulness with patients with chronic pain (Kabat-Zinn, Lipworth, & Burney, 1985). This pioneering research demonstrated a significant reduction (33%) in the pain rating index after 10 weeks of participation in mindfulness lessons, and also reductions in mood disturbances and symptomatology. Subsequent studies by Goleman (2003), Kabat-Zinn, Massion, et al.

(1992) Kabat-Zinn, Wheeler, et al. (1998), Segal, Williams, and Teasdale (2002), and Teasdale et al. (2000) provided additional evidence of mindfulness's efficacy for pain reduction.

Mindfulness has been shown to be effective in several studies of diverse illnesses and conditions. Evans et al. (2007) used a mindfulness-based intervention with patients with anxiety disorders and found that symptoms of anxiety and depression were reduced. Kingston, Dooley, Bates, Lawlor, and Malone (2007) used mindfulness with patients experiencing continuing symptoms after a depressive episode. They found that the depressive symptoms and rumination decreased, and this continued when measured a month later. Barnes, Brown, Krusmark, Campbell, and Rogge's (2007) studies on mindfulness and relationships linked mindfulness with positive relationships. Carlson and Garland (2005) studied the use of mindfulness with cancer patients who had sleep disturbance. The results showed a decrease in sleep disturbances and an increase in sleep quality. Prouix (2008) used mindfulness in the treatment of bulimia and found that subjects showed improvement in emotions, behavior, self-awareness, and acceptance.

Other research examples include the following:

- The elderly (Alexander, Langer, Newman, Chandler, & Davis, 1989);
- Gaining therapeutic insight (Kutz, Borysenko, & Benson, 1985);
- Cancer (Carlson, Speca, Patel, & Goodey, 2003; Speca, Carlson, Goodey, & Angen, 2000);
- Sleep disorders (Shapiro, Bootzin, Figueredo, Lopez, & Schwarta, 2003);
- Positive effects on quality of life (Teibel, Greenson, Brainard, & Rosenzweig, 2001);
- Stress reduction (Davidson, Scherer, & Goldsmith, 2003).

Mindfulness is also effective with children and adolescents. Saltzman (2008) used mindfulness training for eight consecutive weeks with a sample of fourth to seventh grade children and their parents. Outcomes included an increase in the ability to pay attention, and a decrease in anxiety. Biegel (2009) found that adolescents who had been diagnosed as depressed and anxious were able to experience reduced symptoms related to anxiety and depression, and increased self-esteem and quality of sleep.

An important use for mindfulness is seen in the incorporation of it as an integral part of Dialectical Behavioral Treatment (DBT). It is used to increase self-acceptance, becoming nonjudgmental about self and others, learning emotional regulation, and other therapeutic tasks in this system. Although the treatment system was initially developed to treat parasuicidal patients, it has been expanded as treatment for borderline personality disorder, mood, anxiety, addictive, eating, impulse-control, and other personality disorders (Marra, 2005).

The proposed uses in this chapter are for both the group leader and for group members. The group leader can increase his or her emotional presence and observational skills in the group. Members can benefit from learning how to expand their internal and external experiencing; quiet, calm, and focus their thoughts and feelings; and gain more self-acceptance.

Two principles from Tao that can be useful in mindfulness are the Principle of P'u, and the Principle of Wu Wei. The Principle of P'u is described as the state of the uncarved block, which Hoff (1983) terms the ability to attend to the simple and the quiet, the natural and the plain. This state promotes experiencing things and people without making judgments or evaluations. The Principle of Wu Wei refers to doing by not doing, allowing experiences to unfold and happen without trying to influence or change them. When applied to mindfulness, the two principles mean to attend to what is your internal and external experiencing without making judgments or evaluations; and to be content to allow your experiencing to unfold without trying to direct it in a particular pathway. These will be the major directions for the mindfulness exercises that are included.

It is recommended that the group leader practice mindfulness exercises before introducing them to the group. The first exercise is also a script that can be used when presenting mindfulness to group members. It is helpful for the group leader to practice the exercise for at least 15 minutes a day for 21 days so that it becomes effortless, and the leader has a richness of experiences to guide him or her.

*Exercise 16.1—Mindfulness Exercise*
*Materials:* A notebook or paper and pen to record your experiences.
*Procedure:*

1. Make a commitment to practice mindfulness a minimum of 15 minutes every day for a specified period of time, ex. 21 days.
2. Read the following script, and then follow it.

***Mindfulness Script***

*Find a place to practice where you will not be disturbed. Begin by sitting in a comfortable position. You can do the exercise with your eyes open or closed, whichever is most comfortable for you.*

- *Focus on your breathing, and try to make it even and deep.*
- *Become aware of your body and notice any physical sensations you are experiencing. Scan your body from the top of your head to your feet and note muscle tension, relaxed parts, tingles, and so on.*
- *Notice any smells you experience; pleasant, unpleasant. If you don't notice any, concentrate on your breath and how the air feels as you take it in, and let it out.*
- *Redirect your focus to your sense of hearing. Notice what sound you hear; near, far, loud, or quiet. If your thoughts emerge, just redirect these to the sounds.*

- *Attend once again to your breathing and notice if there are any changes.*
- *Let yourself become aware of what you are feeling at the moment, and note if there are changes.*
- *Try to sit in silence for the entire 15 minutes and just allow your feelings, thoughts, and ideas to emerge without following them, emphasizing them, or evaluating them.*

3. It can be helpful to write a brief summary of your experience each day.

It is not unusual for people to find it difficult to keep their thoughts from becoming central when they try to practice mindfulness. After all, there are usually tasks that have to be accomplished, planning and organizing for future tasks, concerns and worries, and so on that can be difficult to shut down and enter a state of mindfulness. It is helpful to be able to empty the mind, but that is difficult to do at times, especially when beginning the practice. However, if you persist, you will find this useful in all kinds of situations, such as trying to fall asleep at night. One way of keeping your thoughts and feelings from intruding, or taking over is to use the thought defusion strategy described by Hayes, Strosahl, and Wilson (1999). The following exercise demonstrates the strategy.

*Exercise 16.2—Passing Thoughts*
*Materials:* None.
*Procedure:* Find a place to work that is free from distractions and where you will not be disturbed.

1. Sit in silence with your eyes closed, and allow your breathing to become deep and even.
2. As you sit in silence, thoughts and feelings may arise. Picture each thought or feeling as one of the following:
   A bird flying by;
   A billboard sign you see as you ride by on a bicycle;
   Water swirling down a drain;
   Pollen, blown by the wind out of sight;

Any image where the thought or feeling is noticed but then disappears.

3. If you find that you are staying with a thought or feeling, return to your breathing, and try again to notice the thought or feeling as it is passing by you, but not lingering.

The next exercise uses mindfulness to cope with a distressing or negative feeling.

*Exercise 16.3—Managing Emotions*
*Materials:* None.
*Procedure:*

1. Find a place to practice where you will not be disturbed and that is free from distractions. You can either close your eyes or let them stay open.
2. Identify your current dominant feeling, such as anger, sadness, and the like.
3. Refrain from making a judgment about the feeling, such as it being good or bad, right or wrong. Perform a body scan and identify all sensations you are experiencing; for example, breathing hard, your heart racing, muscle tenseness, and so on.
4. Next, concentrate on one sensation at a time, and try to control your breathing. If muscles are tense, tighten these, hold, and then let go.
5. Identify where the feeling is located in your body and focus on each of the following characteristics.
   - What shape does the feeling have?
   - What is the weight? Heavy? Light? Moderate?
   - What is its color?
   - Is the feeling moving; such as pulsating, moving from place to place, or does it remain in one place?
6. Once you have completed the first set of questions in step 5, repeat it three times, and then note if there are any changes in the location, shape, weight, color, or

movement. It may be that the feeling has been reduced, subsided, or in some cases, it no longer exists.

## Music

Music therapy requires the leader to have specialized training. What is presented here are a few simple activities that use music as a stimulus to energize, calm, or to evoke emotions, but not as healing or for deep exploration of personal issues.

Babani (2010), in a qualitative study on musical triggered peak experiences, notes that "many individuals find that music activates insight, inspiration, emotional catharsis, and enhanced self-awareness" (p. 5804). Hays (2005) in a study on older adults found that meaning from the music experience was related to personal identity, self-expression, and feelings of well-being. Thus, music can activate many aspects of the self to promote understanding and increase awareness of experiencing.

Hodas (1994) proposes that music can influence the course of therapy by increasing morale, providing validation and change for belief systems, and promoting the therapeutic relationship. It is a way to tell a personal story, and deepen connections (Duffy, Somody, & Clifford, 2005; Hays & Minichiello, 2005). Silverman (2010) obtained the perceptions about five different modalities for music therapy from psychiatric inpatients who were severely and persistently mentally ill. Participants reported the individual music game as the most helpful, and the group musical game as the most enjoyable. The effects of music seem to be positive on a range of physical, neurophysiological, and psychological conditions.

Trained clinicians use music therapy with a variety of medical illnesses and conditions such as the following.

- Cancer (Boldt, 1996; Sabo & Michael, 1996; Williams et al. 2010);
- Organ transplant patients (Madson & Silverman, 2010);
- Premature infants (Gooding, 2010);

- Parkinson's disease (Batson, 2010);
- Cognitive rehabilitation (Thant & Abiru, 2010).

Research on treatment of emotional disturbances with music therapy has also shown to be effective. Examples of such studies include:

- Stress and anxiety (Hunter et al., 2010);
- Depression (Brandes et al., 2010; Castillo-Perez, Gomez-Perez, Caliullo, Perez-Campos, & Mayoral, 2010; Compass, Haaga, Keefe, Leitenberg, & Williams, 1998);
- Aggressive and oppositional children (Foulkrod & Davenport, 2010);
- Bereaved teenagers (McFerran, Melina, & O'Grady, 2010).

Burns (2001) describes studies that integrate music and imagery with the outcome of making the image "more vivid" (McKinney 1990; McKinney & Tims, 1995). A study by Band (1996) showed that the combination of music and imagery led participants to become more immersed in the image, and Auttner and Glueckauf (1983) proposed that music facilitated the emergence of images. The review of literature also shows that music is combined with movement (Luck, Saarikallio, Burger, Thompson, & Toiviainen, 2010); dramatherapy (Chipman, 2010); dance (Wengrower, 2010); art therapy (Crawford et al., 2010), and recreation therapy (Bauer, Victorson, Rosenbloom, Barocas, & Silver, 2010).

Since music can and does evoke emotions, images, memories, and the like, the group leader should have an understanding of the importance of selection of the pieces of music to be used in the group. In addition, it is also helpful to have a pretty comprehensive knowledge of all types and kinds of music such as classical, jazz, gospel, country, hip hop, rap, rock, tech rock, pop, and rhythm and blues to name a few. Trained music therapists will also know of specific selections and performances within types and kinds of music and be able to connect the renditions with the needs of the group members and the goal(s) for using music in the group. It's very complex to try and match music to the group's needs, and to decide what mode of presentation, such as listening or singing, to be used. While art talent is not essential to the use of techniques such as drawing or collage, it is difficult to see how music can be effectively used without some musical talent, knowledge and training.

The group leader may want to consult with a trained music therapist about how best to incorporate music into the group session, and on the selection of music. Following are some brief musical activities that can be used by almost any group leader.

*Exercise: 16.4—Music and Feelings*

*Materials:* A boom box or other device for playing prerecorded music; three musical selections to evoke energy, reminiscence, and calmness.

*Procedure:*

1. Introduce the activity by telling group members that you will play three musical selections, and after each, they are invited to report on the feelings evoked by the selection.
2. Play selection 1 for about 5 minutes, stop, and ask group members to report on their feelings.
3. Play selection 2 for about 5 minutes and repeat the process described in step 2.
4. Play selection 3 for about 5 minutes and repeat step 2.
5. Lead a discussion on the evoked feelings, and the feelings they are experiencing now.

*Exercise 16.5—What Am I Thinking and Feeling?*

*Materials:* A boom box or other device for playing prerecorded music; a musical selection that will be good as a background, paper and a set of crayons, colored pencils, or felt markers for each group member.

*Procedure:*

1. Introduce the activity by telling group members that you will play a musical selection, and they are to draw whatever they want as they listen. Tell them to try and just let the drawing emerge. They can begin drawing whenever they like, but you will be playing the selection for about 5 minutes.
2. Start the music, and observe what group members do. Do some begin with the music or shortly thereafter? Do some listen for a period of time and then begin drawing? What do you observe about their nonverbal behavior?
3. Stop the music and reconvene the group in the circle.
4. Have members display their drawings, and describe their experience of listening and drawing.
5. Ask them to explore how the music and drawing reflected their thoughts and feelings in the moment, and if there are any surprises in their products.

# CHAPTER 17

# MOVEMENT

## Dance and Exercise

### Introduction

This chapter focuses on releasing the wisdom, knowledge, creativity, and emotional life of the body. Within the physical self are connections to the other aspects of self that can be unavailable to the conscious. Some are nonconscious material just below the level of consciousness, while others are unconscious. Tuning into what one's body knows and understands brings meaning and relevance to much of what is experienced by other parts of the self. Or, this information can be used to reconnect to that part of one's self which may have become repressed or split off from conscious awareness. This can be very deep therapeutic work and is not the focus of this chapter because that use calls for well-trained therapists in the particular modality of body work as well as training in the therapeutic use of this work in groups. What is presented here are physical movement activities that group leaders can use that can enhance the therapeutic process without necessarily triggering deeper nonconscious or unconscious material. The activities presented here are primarily used for tension relief, to play and have fun, to focus on one's body and increase awareness of its present functioning, and to demonstrate access to one's creativity. Presented here are movement, dance, exercise, and drama/performance activities, such as improvisation and role-play.

## A Rationale: The Mind–Body Connection

The work and research on the mind–body connections provide a rationale for inclusion of physical activities in group therapy even when the primary focus and emphases are on other issues and concerns. Although the group leader may not be trained in a particular modality, such as dance therapy, there are occasions where a simple movement activity could be of benefit to the group and to members, and this is the intent of what is presented here.

Evidence for mind–body influences are derived from three sources (Goleman & Gurin, 1993):

- Physiological research on biological and biochemical connections between the brain and body. Exciting new findings are emerging through studies on neurobiology that is clarifying how and why these connections play an important role.
- Epidemiological studies that focus on the associations and connections between psychological factors and illnesses in the general population.
- Clinical studies to test the effectiveness of mind–body approaches to prevent, alleviate, or treat diseases and conditions.

A short sample exercise may help clarify what is meant by the mind–body connection.

*Exercise 17.1—Mind and Body*
*Materials:* A sheet of paper and a pen or pencil.
*Procedure:*

1. Find a place to work where you will not be disturbed and that has an appropriate writing surface available. Reflect or think about how you physically and mentally feel at this time.
2. Write a short descriptive response to each of the following:
   a. Your current mood;
   b. Your current mental/cognitive state;
   c. Your current body status (e.g. aches, tensions, arousal, etc.);
   d. Your feelings (e.g., sad, angry, pleased).
3. Next, list a description or response for each of the following for the previous 12 to 18 hours in your life. Write in as much detail as possible:
   a. Food and drink consumed;
   b. The quality of your sleep;
   c. Recreation/leisure;
   d. Exercise activities (e.g., walking, working out at the gym, etc.);
   e. Medications taken (e.g., prescribed, OTC, etc.);
   f. Vitamins and minerals taken;
   g. Physical and medical conditions (e.g., allergies, menopause, high or low blood pressure);
   h. Work or school related activities or situations.
4. Next, review your current status and your previous 12- to 18-hour activities. Reflect on how your previous activities are impacting your current mood, cognition, body, and feelings. The following questions can guide your reflection:
   a. Were you able to eat healthy foods?
   b. Did you obtain sufficient and good quality sleep?
   c. Was there an opportunity to exercise or move your body?

   d. How many pleasurable activities did you experience?
   e. If you have a condition or symptoms that require medication, how much did the medication control these?
   f. Did you feel stressed or overwhelmed, or were you relaxed and comfortable?
5. Finally, write a summary paragraph about the relationship of your body care in the previous 12 to 18 hours to your current physical, cognitive (mental), and emotional mood, and vice versa; that is, how were your previous mental or mood states influencing your mental state.

Taking time to reflect on your body and mind interrelationship, influences, and other connections can demonstrate the viability and strength of the relationship, and serve as a reminder of just how much can take place on the nonconscious and unconscious levels.

## General Guidelines

Any movement group activity has the potential to arouse intense feelings and the group leader should stay aware of this potential when planning and conducting such activities. Even ordinary physical activities such as walking across the room may trigger these feelings because of fears about being judged and evaluated, and the group setting produces a venue for observation by others that provides opportunities for judgments and evaluation by others. Members can fear that they will be found to be inadequate in some way and thus be shamed. Childhood memories of being taunted and teased about athletic ability or its lack, how one walks or one's appearance when moving, looking funny or weird when dancing, one's agility, and the like can easily be triggered by thought of a movement exercise in the group setting, and can be a source of resistance for movement activities. Further, if there is a history of body related trauma, such as rape, physical abuse, or multiple surgeries, fears and other emotions around the event(s) may be aroused even when the person may have deeply repressed such memories. The leader may not be aware of this history either because the type of group may not require this kind of information as part of screening or group assignment, because the member does not remember it or chooses not to reveal it, or other such reasons. However, these events do continue to exert their influences. Ensuring the safety of group members when group leaders may lack information about their past experiences or unresolved issues underlies the following guidelines.

Plan the activity based on group needs. It seems elementary to plan the activity based on group needs, but there may be times when you as the leader just want to do something spontaneously, or you think such an activity will be "good for the group." Those may be appropriate, but they are more likely to be your needs, and not those of group members. There should be a specific goal or purpose for the activity.

- Before using a movement activity, describe to members what they will be asked to do and the goal and purpose for the proposed activity. Introduce the activity in as much detail as possible so that members can give informed consent for their participation. Doing so will help prevent unanticipated distress, deep memories being accessed, intense feelings aroused that may be uncontrollable for the person, and other such negative outcomes.
- Use activities that are group focused and not just for a specific person or subgroup. Movement activities like other activities described in this book are intended for the entire group; leaders should take care that the chosen activity does not address what the leader feels a particular member or subgroup needs. They may benefit, but the focus should be on the entire group. This is also why I do not recommend that most activities be performed in dyads and triads. Members may work independently for some activities, but these are then shared and discussed in the whole group.

- Restrict or avoid movement activities that involve touching as this can be very scary and threatening for some group members even when they think they can handle it. It is almost impossible for a group member to know if touching others or being touched by others will trigger negative emotions based on past experiences, but that remains a definite possibility. Using activities that involve touch are risky and not recommended.
- Avoid activities that could trigger claustrophobic feelings, such as blindfolds. There are several trust exercises that call for one person in a dyad to depend on another person and one such exercise involves blindfolding a person and guiding him or her on a walk. In addition to such exercises not being recommended because they break the group up into dyads, there is the possibility that something like a blindfold could trigger claustrophobia, where the leader did know of that possibility, the member did not know having never experienced being blindfolded before, or for a whole host of other reasons. There are too many other exercises that could be used.
- Respect any and all member resistance and reluctance to participate. It is strongly recommended that group leaders respect any and all resistance and reluctance to participate in a movement activity. Holding a discussion about the feelings triggered by the thought of such an activity could be much more fruitful than pressing ahead with it.
- Provide clear and specific directions and check to ensure members' understanding. Most movement activities give all of the directions at the front end, and group members can get confused about what they are supposed to do. To cut down on this confusion, the group leader should ensure that the directions are clear, and to answer any questions members may have.
- Block comments by other group members about a member's appearance, agility, and the like. Keep the focus on the purpose for the activity. It is essential that any

comments be blocked that could be received as taunting, teasing, derogatory, or demeaning. The speaker may be trying to joke, but these are the type of comments that can hurt and cause narcissistic injury.

## Movement

Movement can be energizing as well as providing a means to tune into the body. Purposeful moving is described more fully in the sections on dance, exercise, and role-play. Movement here is simply to have group members participate in a movement of some sort, and then reflect and discuss what emerged for them as they moved. Topics that can be explored include feelings experienced, thoughts that emerged, awareness of bodily sensations especially pain and tension, and how they feel after the movement. Following is a short list of some movements that can be easily done in a session with reporting and exploration; most if not all members are capable of performing; are relatively non-threatening, and can be energizing. The group leader should, of course, ensure that all group members can participate in the particular movement before introducing it as an activity.

- Move around the room without talking, and make eye contact with every group member;
- Skip, jump, or hop around the room;
- Line up according to birthday, from January 1;
- Practice sports signals: touchdown, safe and out in baseball, walking in basketball, etc.

*Exercise 17.2—Speedy Introductions*
*Materials:* None.
*Procedure:*

1. Divide the group into dyads and label one dyad A, and the other dyad B. Have each dyad sit facing one another.
2. Instruct them to do the following:
   - Each person in Dyad A will talk to B for one minute, introducing him- or herself. At the end of the minute,

the leader calls time, and each A person will move one seat to the next B person, and repeat the introductions.
- This continues until every A has had an opportunity to introduce him- or herself to every B.
- The procedure is repeated so that every B now has an opportunity to introduce him- or herself to every A.
- The next step is to divide the As into dyads, and do the same for the Bs. They now speed introduce themselves to each other with all As introducing themselves to other As, and Bs doing the same.

3. Reconvene the group and explore what feelings emerged as they did the introductions, the listening, and the movement. What kind of information was shared in the introductions?
4. Ask members to identify any similarities among other group members as they were introduced.

## Dance

Dance is defined here as rhythmic movement usually accompanied by music. Dancing can be solitary, with a dance partner, or as a group activity, such as line dancing. Dance can tell a story, for example, ballet; convey nonverbal messages such as in many South American dance forms; tune into spiritual matters such as some Native American dances; and as a means of expressing emotions and other abstractions such as with modern dance performances. When used in therapy, dance can become an access to unknown and maybe unacceptable parts of one's self, repressed or denied memories, a release of energy, and an expression of creative and inspirational forces. When used for these reasons, dance activities are the primary focus for the group, they are used constantly in in every session or almost every session, and may have a sequential structure, and the group assumes less prominence for therapy. As noted before, dance as therapy requires specialized training and is not the focus in this presentation.

Literature on dance therapy has addressed uses for diverse conditions and issues:

- Body image (Langdon & Petracca, 2010; Swami & Tonee, 2009);
- Medically unexplained symptoms (Payne, 2009);
- Parkinson's disease (Hackney & Earhart, 2010);
- Emotionally focused couple therapy (Hazlett, 2010);
- Female perceptions of male strength (Hugill, Fink, Neave, & Seydel, 2009);
- Eating disorders (Burn, 1987);
- Schizophrenia (Xia & Tessa, 2009);
- The elderly (Alpert et al., 2009; Lima & Vieira, 2007).

Dance is included in this chapter for information, and because it can be used in a group for reasons other than those noted above. This presentation views dance as an activity that can be used as a movement activity where appropriate for the following purposes:

- To relieve tension and stress;
- As a means to express current feelings;
- To play and have fun;
- Bring attention to the physical self and focus on its current state.

*Exercise 17.3—Free-form Dancing*
*Materials:* Music and a music player.
*Procedure:*

1. Start the music and tell members to move around the room any way they want to. They can jump, skip, whirl around, do a dance step, and so on. Let them dance for 10 minutes.
2. Stop the music, ask members to return to the circle, and explore the experience of moving without direction or purpose. Ask for feelings experienced as they heard the directions, as they moved around the room, and now as they talk about it.

*Exercise 17.4—In Sync*

*Materials:* Music and a music player.

*Procedure:*

1. Pair off group members. While this is easier to do in pairs, triads can also be used.
2. The pairs are to try to synchronize their movements (dance) without talking. One will take the lead to begin the steps, and each should take a turn in changing the movement, all without talking.
3. Start the music and tell the pairs to begin moving. Allow 10 to 15 minutes for the dance, and observe how the pair performs, how much or how little in sync they are, and other body movements.
4. Stop the music and ask them to return to the circle. Explore the feelings aroused by the experience, especially noting the feelings aroused by not being able to talk. Ask them how they communicated without talking, if it was difficult to become synchronized, and the extent of satisfaction with their performance. The leader should note any observations as indicated in step 3.

*Exercise 17.5—Just Walking*

*Materials:* Musical selection that has a variety of tempos from slow to fast, and a music player.

*Procedure:*

1. Tell members that you are going to give them directions as they walk around the room, and ask that they become aware of the feelings aroused as you change the directions. (The leader can provide a demonstration of what the directions will be.)
2. Start the music and take them through the following sequence of walks. Try to change the walk to fit the tempo of the music.
   - Plod—Walk as if the legs are carrying a heavy weight, and each step seems to be an effort.

- Mosey—Walk as if you don't have a care in the world, have no time pressures, and are enjoying yourself.
- Stride—Walk fast and confidently.

3. Reconvene in the group, and explore the walking experience, with particular attention to feelings experienced with each kind of walk.

## Exercise

The use of exercise (physical movements) in a group usually calls for the group leader to have expertise and may even call for certification in the particular form used, such as yoga, in order to be most effective and to maintain appropriate boundaries. There can be many applications for an exercise focused group such as the following.

- Cancer survivors (Sherman, Heard, & Cavanagh, 2010);
- Veterans with comorbid psychiatric and medical conditions (Periman et al., 2010);
- Weight loss (Byom, 2010);
- Poststroke fatigue (Flinn & Stube, 2010);
- Chronic pain in elderly adults (Ersek, Turner, Cain, & Kemp, 2009);
- Depression (Kunic et al., 2008);
- Risk of coronary disease (Hardcastle, Taylor, Bailey, & Castle, 2008).

An exercise focused group is defined as one where the majority of time in a session is used for the exercise, and group discussion and interactions are less emphasized although this too is considered a vital component. These exercise focused groups can generally have the following sequence; introductions/check-in, warm-up, focused exercise for the session, cool down, and group discussion. This sequence requires that the leader be able to lead the exercise because having someone who is not a group member would be very disruptive to the process and may cause resistance to disclosure.

Another way to use exercise as a focus would be to have members perform the exercises outside the group session, and then the group sessions would focus on members' experiences as a stimulus for group discussions about sensations and feelings aroused, memories triggered, and other nonconscious and unconscious material. In some groups, the emphasis could be on the performance as an aid to the condition, such as that described by Kunic et al. (2008) for depression. Other groups may use members' outside exercise experiences to address other psychological concerns such as body image (Byom, 2010). Both medical and psychiatric conditions may be addressed with this use of exercise, and the leader need not be an expert in the particular exercise.

A third way to use exercise in the group would not have the exercise as a focus for the group session, call for members to perform exercises outside of the group, nor need the group leader be an expert in the particular group modality. This kind of application simply uses an easily explained and implemented brief exercise as a stimulus for group discussion where the majority of the time would be spent on that. As with most all movement activities, members would be instructed to perform the activity only to the point where they remain comfortable, and to not strain themselves beyond this point. Possible reasons for use of brief physical exercises in the group are to focus on the body, use sensations to access feelings, relieve tension and stress, to energize, and to affirm health enhancing behaviors.

*Exercise 17.6—Increase Energy*

**Note: Be sure to consider the physical state of members before initiating this activity.**

*Materials:* None. If music is used, then a recording and a player is needed.

*Procedure:*

1. Ask group members to stand and position themselves about 4 feet apart.
2. Introduce the activity by telling members that you are going to lead them in a short set of body movements

that are designed to increase energy. The movements are easy, and tell them that they are to only do what is comfortable for them.

3. Direct them through the following at a relaxed, easy pace:
    - Head—Stand and spread feel apart about 12 inches, stand straight with arms by the sides and knees slightly bent. Gently allow the head to move toward the right shoulder, hold for 2 to 3 seconds, bring the head back to center, and repeat for the left side. Do this slowly four to five times.
    - Shoulders—Assume the same position as before. Raise both shoulders up to the ears, hold for 2 to 3 seconds, and then relax. Do this four to five times.
    - Side stretches—Assume the same position as before. Slowly raise the right arm overhead, and lean toward the left, thus stretching the right side. Do the same for the left side. Repeat four to five times.
    - Legs—Begin in the same position. If group members have difficulty doing this move when standing, they can sit and do it. Instruct them to raise their right knee up toward the chest, wrap their hands around the knee, and pull it slightly toward the chest. Hold the position for 5 to 10 seconds. Repeat the process for the left knee. Repeat the entire process four to five times.
    - Thighs—Begin in the same position, hold arms out to side at shoulder height. Keeping the head up and eyes straight ahead, slowly bend forward at the waist and hold for 5 to 10 seconds. Bring body to upright position and repeat the bend four to five times.
    - Moving—Direct members to march around the room (music can be used). Allow up to 5 minutes for marching.
    - After the marching, repeat the stretching exercises with only two to three repetitions instead of four to five.

4. Reconvene, sit in the circle, and explore the experience with a focus on feelings before the routine, and feelings now as the group sits in the circle.

*Exercise: 17.7—To Relax*
*Materials:* None.
*Procedure:*

1. Ask members to rate their body tenseness at this time on a scale of 0 – not tense to 10 – extremely tense.
2. This set of exercises can be completed standing or seated. Use the following sequence of movements.
   - Tell members to open their mouths as wide as they can, yawn, and make a noise. Repeat for 30 seconds.
   - Next, tell them to stand if possible, and arch their backs while stretching their arms out to the side. Hold that position for 5 to 10 seconds, relax, and remain standing or seated, and repeat the move four to five times.
   - The next movement can be done seated or standing. Ask members to sit or stand straight, bring their shoulders back as far as possible, hold the position for 5 to 10 seconds, or as long as they can, and then relax. Repeat two to three times.
   - The final movement is in three parts:
     - Allow the arms to hang loosely at the side, either standing or sitting. Then, shake your fingers, hands, and arms for about 10 seconds.
     - Repeat the same procedure for each leg separately.
     - If seated, have members stand and shake their bodies for a few seconds. (This move is difficult to perform in a seated position.)
3. Ask members to again rate their body tension (0—no tension to 10—extremely tense). Explore the changes, if any, by asking where the tension was at the beginning, and where it is now. Ask if the tenseness or lack of tension make a difference in their mood, feelings, and the like.

# CHAPTER 18

# MOVEMENT

## Performance Activities

We now turn to a more controlled use of the body which also brings thoughts and feelings simultaneously into the experience, that of drama or performance activities. Benefits of drama/ performance activities include the following:

- Assists in breaking down social barriers between group members;
- Promotes empathic understanding;
- Reduces distancing and disassociation;
- Increases emotional expressiveness;
- Can be a means to demonstrate how to give and receive constructive feedback;
- Emphasizes the mind–body–emotional connections;
- Can help reconnect to unknown, disowned, or fragmented parts of self;
- Increase clarity of thinking.

Perhaps the best known form of drama is psychodrama created by Moreno (1964), which is very action oriented to promote insight, creativity, and explore personal problems. While there are some strategies used in psychodrama that can be used without training, this technique requires considerable and specialized training, and is presented here only as an example.

The main points for psychodrama are that spontaneity and creativity are encouraged; the work is done in the present regardless of when the condition, issue, or problem occurred; explores how connections are formed and maintained with others; what and how one is attracted or repelled by others; unrealized or unknown viewpoints are discovered; catharsis is promoted; and the group provides reality testing. Psychodrama has three phases: warm-up, action, and reporting and exploration. Procedures from psychodrama that have been translated to other theoretical approaches include role reversal, doubling where the auxiliary plays the protagonist's inner self, soliloquy, the empty chair, and the mirror technique .

There are several forms for drama therapy such as the following:

- Interactive storytelling (Park, 2005) involves the storyteller presenting lines from a well-known story or poem and group members responding by adding their own lines to the tale or poem.
- Dramatic play (Oon, 2010) has three elements or phases: play space, role-playing, and dramatic projection.
- Video interpretation (Horwitz, Kowalski, & Anderberg, 2010) involves group members being trained in body and voice expression, then acting in a drama with professional actors that is taped, the tape is viewed, and members interpret their own emotional expression in the performance.
- Narradrama (Dunne, 2010) is a blend of narrative therapy with drama therapy, and also uses other expressive arts such as music, poetry, and the visual arts.

- Story making drama and body mapping (Meyer, 2010).
- Improvisational theater (Veenstra, 2010).
- Cognitive behavior drama (Karnezi & Tierney, 2009) integrates principles and techniques from cognitive and behavioral therapies with drama.
- Psychodrama relapse prevention skills (Morris & Moore, 2009).

Drama therapy or dramatherapy encompasses numerous variations of performance, but only three will be presented here; role-play, improvisation, and simulation or games.

## Role-Play

Let's define role-play as assuming the role of another person as he or she is described, and participating in a prescribed scene to perform a situation or event. Benefits for this type of role-play include the following:

- Insight can be enhanced;
- Broader perspective gained;
- Deeper and more empathic understanding of self and of others;
- Ideas for alternatives and other possibilities generated;
- Practice new behaviors;
- Receive and give constructive feedback.

Insight can be enhanced via role-play because the participants have less intense emotional involvement and playing a role involves cognitive processes also. Further, when done in a group setting, there are also the variables and influences of being observed, possibly being evaluated, and concern about being found inadequate or becoming shamed that also combine to provide some distance. Insight is more possible because the person is able to see him- or herself in a more objective way.

The broader perspective can be provided by the feedback from the observing group members, leader, and other participants in the role-play. Others' perceptions have much less emotional involvement than the generator of the role-play, and that might give them other perspectives, and hearing these allows for a broader perspective to be adopted.

Playing another person's role can produce deeper and more empathic understanding of oneself and of others. Assuming a role requires that you think, feel, and act as you think the other person would, and that allows you to somewhat become as they are. Once you can get into the person, so to speak, you can better understand what that person is experiencing, which produces empathic understanding.

Stepping back and observing, hearing the feedback from others in the role-play and from the observers will likely produce ideas for alternatives and other possibilities. Some ideas and alternatives may come from others, but the person generating the role-play may now be able to see that there are other ways to perceive, manage, and act that may produce more satisfying outcomes.

Role-play is a wonderful opportunity to practice new behaviors and to receive feedback on how these are perceived by others, as well as how it feels and fits to assume new ways of behaving. Behavioral rehearsal is a valid technique that derives from behavioral therapy, and when there are others to participate, the experience is enriched as well as the individual being able to practice new behaviors in a safe environment.

The group can provide opportunities to give and receive feedback, and participating in a role-play gives opportunities to practice how to make the feedback constructive. Usually the role-play has some sensitivity, especially for the person generating the topic or scene for it, and group members are aware of this sensitivity, and can seek to provide important feedback but to also have it presented in such a way as to not hurt, insult, or offend.

## Guidelines For Role-Play

The following guidelines are for role-play in a group setting where three or more members participate. Guidelines for dyads are presented later.

1. Relationships among members and safety and trust must be built and established prior to initiation of any role-play activities in the group.
2. The leader should determine the focus, goal, or problem that the role-play is intended to address, and this should be at the group level so as to be immediately relevant for all group members. Examples of group level problems include shared difficulties in being appropriately assertive, conflict behavior, and confrontation.
3. Introduce the activity and get members' cooperation to participate. Have them write about or draw a situation or event that captures the essence of the focus for the role-play; that is, all members can have a personal involvement in the subject for the role-play.
4. After the writing or drawing, have members share their products, but do not explore or elaborate on these at this time.
5. Ask one member to volunteer to have his or her scene as the role-play. The member who volunteers becomes the director for the role-play.
6. The director selects the players, who do not have to play gender specific roles, and briefs them on the scene. The group leader is briefing observers at the same time. Observers are expected to report on their feelings, thoughts, and what verbal and nonverbal behaviors they saw during the role-play.
7. The action scene takes place.
8. The group leader then debriefs the director, the performers, and the audience, usually in that order. Sample debriefing questions are as follows for each:
    - The director: Ask about the accuracy of the performance; did the performers capture the essence of the director's situation or event. Explore the feelings aroused as the director watched the performance. Finally, ask if the director has any new thoughts, ideas, or insights.

- Performers: Ask each performer to report on what it was like for them to play the role? Was it difficult or easy? Did they find that they shifted back into being their selves? What were the feelings that emerged as they played the role? (Note: these can be reflective of the feelings of the other person(s) in the situation and may be new information for the director.)
- Audience/observers: Ask them to report on the feelings, thoughts, and ideas that emerged as they observed.

*Exercise 18.1—A Negative Confrontation*
*Materials for Drawing:* paper and a set of crayons, colored pencils, or felt markers for each member.
*Materials for Writing:* paper and a pen or pencil.
*Procedure:*

1. Distribute the materials and ask group members to think of a negative confrontation they experienced, either as the giver or receiver of the confrontation. They will be asked to draw or write about it first, and then one or more will be invited to role-play the situation. A negative confrontation is defined as one where intense, uncomfortable emotions were aroused or displayed, where there was not a consensual resolution, or where they left the interaction feeling dissatisfied or worse than when they began.
2. Once they have thought about the experience, members are to either draw or write a description.
3. When the writing or drawing is complete, reconvene the group and have members share their experiences. Do not explore at this time.
4. Ask if a member wants to volunteer to have his or her situation role-played.
5. Follow the guidelines for role-play for the action and exploration phases.
6. As a summary, ask the member whose situation was role-played if he or she gained any additional awareness

or understanding of the situation, and if there were additional steps that could have been taken to reduce the negative effects on either or both participants.

7. If time permits, ask for another volunteer and repeat the procedure.

## Simulations and Games

Other forms of role-play can be called simulations and games, and the new research that is emerging has revealed positive outcomes for neuroeconomic games. For example, Singer and Fehr (2005) found the Trust game to produce a greater understanding of the other's perspective that was also observed for changes in brain activity. There was increased activation in the parts of the brain that have associations with reward, and these patterns of activation were different when playing with a group than when playing on the computer. Other new and exciting data are emerging to support the notion of experiential learning in groups as a viable means for increasing skills and awareness.

Following is a sample of a simulation/game activity for a large group, 10 or more participants. The room should be large enough for small groups to work independently. The leader should select the topic for the creed in advance. Examples of a topic or focus for the creed include the following:

- Spiritual, spiritual practices, or a spiritual person;
- A positive work environment;
- Hope; positive attitude;
- Caring and compassion;
- Tolerance, respect.

A Sample Creed

*AUTHENTICITY*

***I believe*** *that authenticity is a valuable attribute that promotes deeper and more satisfying relationships*

***Someone who is*** *authentic can be trusted in what he or she says, and is congruent in his or her actions.*

***You get and maintain*** *authenticity when you have developed your self, have confidence that you are adequate and capable, and have reduced self-absorption.*

***When you are not*** *authentic, you can create ambiguity and uncertainty, promote distrust, and are demonstrating a lack of respect for your self and for others.*

***Authenticity*** *includes all aspects of life, valued relationships, and a commitment to oneself.*

***We accept that*** *becoming authentic is a process of developing oneself, is likely to be misunderstood and unrecognized by others, but is an essential component for initiating and maintaining enduring and satisfying relationships.*

*Exercise 18.2—Creation of a Creed*

*Goals or Purposes:* To demonstrate consensus building, and clarify beliefs about the topic.

*Materials:* Paper and pencils for writing, large sheets of paper for each subgroup to write its creed: write a list of the tasks on a posted large sheet of paper or a whiteboard.

*Tasks:* formulate a written creed arrived at by consensus, draft a position statement about the creed, and select a representative to deliver the statement and creed: and the following outline of statements that are included in a creed on another large sheet of paper to be posted:

*Creed Outline*

I believe ________________ is

Someone who is ___________

You get and maintain _______ when you abide by the principles

When you are not ____ you're

_______ includes these aspects of one's life

*Procedure:* Explain that the task will be to develop a creed statement that presents the group's beliefs that they hold in common about the topic which is a public affirmation of those beliefs, and which members can and do follow.

1. Divide the group into small groups of participants, and place the groups in different places in the room. Groups do not have to be equal in size, but that is the ideal.
2. Distribute the materials, and tell them the topic for which they will provide a creed. All small groups should work on developing a creed for the same topic or concept, and a position statement, such as why this is important. Tell them the time frame for development, and that the representative will report the creed to the large group. Another requirement is that the creed be a consensus agreement, no voting is allowed.
3. Ask the groups to write their creed on the large paper which will be posted for all to see.
4. Allow sufficient time for the groups to work. Walk around and observe the actions and the process. Tell groups when there is about 5 minutes remaining to complete the task.
5. Have each group representative report the creed and the position statement to the large group. Allow questions to be asked about content, but do not engage in exploration at this time.
6. After each group has reported, ask what it was like to participate in the activity; what thoughts, ideas, and feelings emerged as they contemplated their perspectives for the topic or concept; and thoughts and feelings about the process used.
7. If time permits, lead a discussion about the impact of the creed(s), how they are similar or how they are different; if it is possible to live by the creed; and if group members have reservations or are they committed to what was developed.

# Chapter 19

# Collage

This chapter describes how collage can be used in and with group therapy, possible uses for flats (paper doll representations of self or pets), and other expressive activities that are difficult to categorize. Collage is just another creative format for expression that can be more appealing for people who are apprehensive about drawing. Being asked or expected to draw can raise many fears about personal adequacy and rejection by others. Collage is much less threatening and group leaders will face much less resistance.

Aimone (2000) defines collage as being any material that is attached to a surface, simple or complex, and constructed without boundaries or rules. Because collage is truly a combination of art and crafts, it is well suited for use in therapy groups where expression is more important than artistic talent, and where literally anything goes.

Effective use of collage begins with the group leader's understanding and practice in construction, especially if this is not something that is in the leader's repertoire. Although a workshop or class can facilitate the learning, these are unnecessary as there are many books and Internet accessible resources to use as guides. This chapter will describe collage constructions and uses for groups. The first part of the discussion focuses on the leader's development, and then presents possible uses.

## The Group Leader's Development

The group leader's development will be described in phases that assume the leader has little or no experience with using collage. The first phase is an introduction to collage, the second phase is practice, and the third phase is forming activities for the group.

During the introductory phase, go to museums or art galleries and look at artistic collages to get some notions about how these are constructed, materials used, and what is being depicted or expressed. You are most likely to find that anything and everything can be used in construction, and that there are many forms of expressions. There are numerous magazines available that are intended for nonartists, which you will find in the craft and scrapbook sections of a bookstore or library. These usually show numerous examples and descriptions are provided for many of the techniques used. In some ways you never have to leave the introductory phase because you can continue to gather new ideas and techniques on an ongoing basis.

The next phase is the practicing phase, and this can be fun and enlightening. It is essential for the group leader to become familiar with some of the techniques used for constructing collages, because these will be needed for phase 3, and may be needed as illustrations for group members. All suggested procedures and techniques are brief so as to keep the focus on the purpose of the group.

The following three practice exercises can also be used later in the group.

*Exercise 19.1—My Fave Five*
*Materials:* A 5" × 8" index card, glue stick, scissors, and a favorite magazine or sales catalogue.

*Procedure:*

1. Search the magazine for pictures that represent some of your favorite objects and activities: symbols that represent anything in your life that you enjoy. Cut out the pictures and symbols.
2. Try different arrangements of the selected elements on the index card. These don't have to be symmetrical or straight.
3. After you find an arrangement that suits you, carefully remove the elements, and use the glue stick to replace them on the card.
4. Title your collage.

*Variations:* Use sheets of paper or smaller index cards; have precut images that group members can select from; use torn paper to back the images and provide a frame.

*Exercise 19.2—Whatever*

*Materials:* A sheet of heavy, smooth unlined paper; white glue or a glue stick; a collection of paper or paint chips in one family of color, say all purples; and scissors. (Note: you need a variety of colors, but not much paper.)

*Procedure:*

1. Cut or tear the paper or paint chips into various sized triangles and mix them in a pile.
2. Select a handful of triangles and let them fall on the paper. Do this several times.
3. Note the arrangements as they fall, and when you find one that is appealing to you, note the placement of the triangles, and carefully remove them. Replace them in the arrangement after putting glue on the back of the triangles.
4. Title your collage.

*Variation:* Include triangles with words or images.

*Exercise 19.3—Black and White*

*Materials:* Newspapers, magazines, or other print publications in black and white, such as brochures and catalogues; a sheet of paper 8½" × 11" or larger; scissors; a glue stick; a black sheet of paper and a white sheet of paper; and a variety of small objects such as buttons, bottle caps, string, and the like.

*Procedure:*

1. Decide first on what shapes you want to use; for example, hearts, flowers, stars, or some other simple image. If you have something like a cookie cutter that you can trace around, this could be your shape.
2. Trace the shape on the newspaper or print publication that you decide to use, and either tear or cut out the shape. You will need three to four large shapes, or six to eight smaller ones. If you need more shapes after you start creating your collage, you can cut or tear more.
3. Carefully tear two 1½" × 11" strips each of the black and the white paper.
4. Glue the long strips to your paper, overlapping them slightly.
5. Arrange your shapes on the glued strips.
6. Distribute your objects on the shapes or strips, and glue them. If the object is large or bulky, you may need to use a *glue spot* to attach it.
7. Title your collage.

## Preparation for Use In Group

If or when you decide to use collages in a group, gather and prepare materials in advance. Cut out images and shapes so that members then only have to choose what they want to use. Try to have a variety of these in case more than one member wants the same shape or image. The value of using images is that these can serve as symbols, and many different images can symbolize the same thing. Following are some topics that could be the basis for collages.

- Dreams and wishes for the future;
- Greatest accomplishments;
- Biggest disappointment;
- Values and beliefs about oneself;
- Positive personal attributes;
- Any feeling word; *happiness, excitement, sadness*;
- Concepts such as conflict, intimacy, inadequacy.

Depending on the complexity of the collages and the time available in group sessions, some could be given as homework. Another alternative: If there is space and it is appropriate for the group, let members come to a session early to make their collages. Basic materials include the following:

- A variety of paper in different sizes and colors;
- Several pairs of scissors;
- Sets of colored pencils, crayons, and felt markers;
- Old magazines and catalogues;
- Pens, pencils, and permanent marker pens;
- Twigs;
- Paper clips in a variety of styles and colors;
- Glue sticks, white glue, transparent tape, and double stick tape;
- Cardstock or other heavy paper in a variety of colors, cardboard, canvas, or other suitable backgrounds for collage;
- A variety of objects such as string, yarn, button, safety pins, fabric scraps, embroidery thread, sequins, and so on;
- Index cards: 3" × 5" and 5" × 8" unlined are best but not critical.

It is also helpful to have printed sets of directions available, especially if the collage is for a special project. Otherwise, just let members create on their own.

## Focusing the Activity

As with all expressive activities, collages should have a purpose and goals that relate to the group and to members' needs. While these can be created just to relax and have fun, that too has a goal and purpose to reduce stress and tension. Possible goals and purposes include the following:

Reveal an unidentified strength;
Increase awareness of accomplishments;
Assist in expressions for thoughts, feelings, and ideas;
Clarify goals, wishes, and fantasies;
Develop a creative part of self;
Give expression to abstract concepts, such as hope;
Make sense of chaos, overwhelming stimuli, and complexity;
Reduce intellectualizing, hiding behind words, masking feelings;
Highlight commonalities among members, and forge connections;
Increased feelings of being understood, competent, and of life's successes;
Assist in making associations and linkages to important personal material.

After determining the goal and purpose, it becomes easier to select the topic for the collage activity. This, along with an introductory rationale, should be written and read to the group when the activity is presented. It is easier to write this in advance rather than trying to remember the important points, or to create it as you stand or sit before the group. The introductory rationale should include behavioral manifestations of a need, such as noticing that members tend to minimize their strengths; or that members avoid conflict, and that making a collage will enable each member to express her or his fears or other feelings about conflict.

The group leader needs to plan and select the activity so that there is sufficient time for construction and sharing. Exploration and expansion may be possible, but just creating and sharing can be sufficient at times. This is why it is important to select an activity that doesn't take the majority of session time to construct. If it becomes important or meaningful to have group members explore more complex issues through collage, this can be given as homework, or be completed in space outside the group. A guide for construction time is that it consumes about 25% of session time at the most. For example, if the session is 60 minutes, construction time would be no more than 15 minutes. Using precut images and the like can expedite construction. Practice by constructing a collage on a 3" × 5" index card this way, and you'll see that you can do a lot in 15 minutes.

Some members may feel rushed, but restricting the amount of time can sometimes reveal more meaningful material because it forces the use of free association and reduces defensiveness. The focus is more on production and less on resistance. Some collage topics that are relatively quick to construct include the following, especially when materials are prepared in advance of the session.

- Two to three closely held values
- A dream for the future
- My talents
- Enjoyment
- Hurt, sadness, grief
- Acceptance and positive regard
- Anger, conflict, disagreements.

*Exercise 19.4—Who Am I—My Physical Self?*

*Materials:* 3" × 5" unlined index cards; cut out pictures of food, medicines, recreational and exercise activities, sports, relaxation, pillows, mattresses, sleeping aids, images reflecting doctor visits, tooth brushes, toothpaste, dental images, and other physically relative images including some that are not ideal or healthy; blank sheets of paper; glue sticks; scissors; and pens or pencils. Construct samples of 3" × 5" collages to use as illustrations.

*Procedure:*

1. Distribute index cards, and arrange images on a table where members can sort through them, and can construct their collages.
2. Introduce the exercise by telling members to select images that depict their physical selves at this time, and glue them on the card to construct a collage. Images can be arranged in any formation on the card.
3. Give a time limit, such as 15 minutes.
4. Re-form the group circle and have members display and explain their cards.
5. Distribute pens or pencils and sheets of paper and ask members to write a brief paragraph about their "physical self at this time"; feelings aroused as they constructed their collages, and areas of satisfaction and dissatisfaction.
6. Re-form the group and have members report any awareness that emerged from either or both parts of the exercise, and/or other thoughts or feelings.

***Variations and Materials***

*Emotional self:* 3" × 5" or 5" × 8" index cards, paint chip samples in a variety of colors; images that could be symbols for feelings, such as tears or tombstones for sadness and grief; glue sticks; scissors; crayons or colored pencils or felt markers.

*Instructions:* Construct a collage that depicts your most easily expressed feelings, or those that are most difficult for you to express openly and directly.

*Inspirational self:* index cards, crayons, colored pencils, or felt markers; images of beaches, mountains, and other scenic wonders; images that appeal to you as inspirational and those that you think would appeal to others—it may be best to let members draw their own religious symbols as these can be very personal and unique for them; plain sheets of paper for drawing; scissors and glue sticks.

*Instructions:* Reflect on your inspirational self, and construct a collage that conveys your sense of your inspirational self.

*Creative self:* 8½" × 11" cardstock in white or a neutral color; newspapers, magazines, and other print publications; scissors; glue sticks, white glue; crayons, watercolors, or poster paints; two or more sample collages prepared in advance.

*Instructions:* Construct a collage that reflects your creative imaginative self. You may creative in ways other than art, and your collage can reflect this. Other avenues for creativity include writing, cooking, gardening, sewing, and other needle crafts, dance, music, acting, fixing broken objects, and so on. Think of your creativity as the part of you that produces new and novel products or processes.

Two suggestions for sample collages prepared in advance:

1. Tear long strips (12") of newspaper and glue to white cardstock leaving spaces between the strips. On another piece of newsprint, lightly draw a simple small house outline, color it with the crayons, watercolors, or poster paints, and let it dry. When it is dry, cut it out leaving 1" border, and glue it to another piece of cardstock and let it dry. Now, cut the house out around the lines, and glue to strips on the other piece of cardstock. Look in your drawers, purse, or pocket, and find things to put on the house or strips. These are the embellishments for your collage. Title your collage.
2. Draw or trace three large simple flower shapes on newspaper or other print material, color in the flower shapes, cut out with a border, glue to cardstock, and let dry. When dry, cut out the flower shapes and glue to a large piece of cardstock. Repeat the process for three medium, three small, and three very small flower shapes. Stack three piles of flower shapes so that each stack has a

medium, a small, and a very small flower shape. Fold each flower shape in half, crease and put a narrow strip of glue down the backside of the crease. Glue the stacked flowers and let dry. After drying, put a narrow strip of glue down the back of each medium flower and place these between the larger flower shapes on the cardstock. Use buttons, coins, or other small round objects for the center of the flowers.

## Additional Collage Exercises

*Exercise 19.5—Inside/Outside*

*Materials:* Large envelopes 5" × 9" or larger; images from magazines or catalogues (the leader can have collection of these cut in advance, or provide a variety of magazines and catalogues where members can find images), glue or other adhesive, pen or pencil; and a set of crayons, colored pencils, or felt markers.

*Procedure:*

1. Distribute the materials and ask members to construct a collage on the outside of the envelope that illustrates what they find easy to disclose to others, how they see themselves, and how they think others see them. They are to find images that illustrate what they find difficult to disclose and their internal selves and put these inside the envelope. They will not have to share what they put in the envelope.
2. Give a timeline for construction, and notify members when about 5 minutes are left.
3. Ask members to describe the outside of their envelopes, but do not do exploration at this time.
4. After all members have shared, lead a discussion on what the experience was like, feelings and thoughts, was it hard or easy to find descriptive images, and what summary statement would they make about the external collage.

*Exercise 19.6—Home*

*Materials:* Cardstock, cut out images, paper scraps, glue, scissors, and a set of crayons, colored pencils, or felt markers for each participant.

*Procedure:*

1. Distribute the materials and ask participants to make a collage about the place or building that gives them a feeling of home. The home can be past, present, or a wish. The home can be representational, abstract, or symbolic. It is whatever they choose to create.
2. Announce the timeframe for constructing the collages, and remind them of the remaining time available about 5 minutes before you call time.
3. Return to the group circle and ask participants to describe their collages. Don't explore at this time unless there is considerable emotions aroused in the participant. All participants must have sufficient time to report on their collages.
4. Next, ask them to describe their feelings as they thought about "home," as they constructed the collage, as they displayed their collage to the group, and as they listened to others talk about their "home."

# CHAPTER 20

# MÉLANGE

## Artist Trading Cards, Flats, Scrapbooking

### Artist Trading Cards (ATCs)

ATCs are little works of art that are always 2½" × 3½" (the usual size of a playing card), and are traded or given away, never sold. They can be drawings, paintings, collages, mixed media, or even constructed of clay. These small working surfaces can provide numerous opportunities for personal expression. There are several advantages to using this creative activity in the group:

- The surface for construction is small enough so that it isn't intimidating or threatening, thereby reducing resistance to the activity.
- Personal expression is encouraged, and one does not have to possess drawing or other artistic ability.
- These cards can be quickly and easily constructed in the group session leaving time for reporting, exploration, and enhancement.

- People are generally pleased with what they produce.
- Materials are not costly as the card background can be cut from scraps, cardboard inserts from clothing, old greeting cards; and other construction materials are available at no cost, or minimal cost. In addition, found and recycled materials are also used.
- A variety of concepts, issues, and concerns can be used as focal topics for an ATC.
- When these are constructed during a session, interaction among group members can be enhanced as they work.

Disadvantages include members' resistance because of fear of being seen as inadequate because of their artistic ability, materials are limited to those the leader chooses, and some members may not find what they need in order to depict their personal expression. I've had group members tell me that they literally spent hours looking for the right image when given an ATC construction as homework. In addition, some members may find it challenging to work in a group setting instead of being able to work independently, and the time allowed in a session can be very limiting for those who prefer to take time to think it through before beginning to work.

## Guidelines

The rationale and goal for using ATCs should be developed with consideration of the group members' needs, stage of group and of member development, and what issue or concern would be addressed. The rationale and goals are similar to those for other creative and inspirational activities described in this book.

The group leader should try the activity before initiating it in the group. This allows for creation of examples, and an understanding of what instructions and materials may be needed for the particular subject for the ATC. It is helpful for the group leader to collect and have on hand a variety of materials. Basic and inexpensive or no cost materials are:

Purchased ATCs, or cardstock cut to size, or other similar materials—old greeting cards, cardstock inserts in clothing;
White glue, glue sticks, double sided tape, and transparent tape;
Images cut from magazines, catalogues, and the like;
Makeup sponges for painting, or sponge painters;
Pages from old dictionaries, music, or newspaper;
Purchased patterned paper in a variety of sizes and colors;
Crayons, colored pencils, felt markers, stamp pads, and other painting materials;
Scissors.

Optional materials that are usually more costly are:

- Origami paper
- Specialty papers
- Die cut shapes
- Gel medium for glaze, transfer, or as an adhesive
- Glue dots adhesive for heavy objects
- Decoupage paste or medium
- Pastels and oil pastels
- Stencils and rub on transfers
- Stickers
- Small tags.

Note: These lists of materials are also used for scrapbook activities. Also needed are tables to spread materials on, and for constructing the ATCs.

The usual procedure is as follows:

1. Introduce the activity, distribute materials and answer questions.
2. Allow sufficient time for construction and announce the time frame.
3. Remind group members how much time is left 3 to 5 minutes before the construction time ends.
4. Reconvene in the group circle and ask members to share their constructions. Make sure that all members have shared *before* exploring.

5. Explore the constructions and the experience in more detail with general questions such as the following:
   - What thoughts and feelings emerged as you constructed the ATC? When you shared your ATC?
   - What was easy about the construction? Difficult?

***Sample Topics***

Following are some sample topics that can be expressed with an ATC. These are presented as constructions, although drawing, painting, stamping, and mixed media are also used. Collage is generally easier for most group members, and all of the following examples are collages. Examples are provided in three categories: challenges, therapeutic factors, and member states and characteristics. Each category is described and an activity presented.

- **Group challenges** are group level behaviors that are negatively affecting the progress of the group. Members may or may not be aware of how their separate behaviors are contributing to the challenges. Topics that could be explored by an ATC activity are resistance, conflict, fear of becoming intimate, and empathic responding. Resistance will be used as an illustration.

*Exercise 20.1—Resistance ATC*

*Materials:* Refer to the materials lists under the section on guidelines.

*Procedure:* Find a suitable place for the group to work where there are tables to display the materials and create the ATCs.

1. Introduce the activity by explaining what ATCs are, and showing some examples.
2. Ask group members to reflect on resistance and what it feels like, especially in group sessions. Tell them that the resistance could be their own personal resistance, or when they feel others' resistance.
3. Spread the materials out where they can be available to all group members. Give a time frame for constructing the collage.

4. Allow members to work and observe if they talk among themselves or tend to be silent, and other behaviors.
5. Follow the guidelines for calling time, reporting or sharing, and for exploration and enhancement.

   - **Therapeutic Factors** can be helpful to the group as a whole as well as for individuals, and some can be illustrated with ATCs. The group leader and members can better understand the individual perceptions for these factors as members display their depictions of the concepts. Factors that can be illustrated include hope, altruism, cohesion, universality, and existential factors.

*Exercise 20.2—Hope ATC*

*Materials:* Refer to the materials lists and find a suitable place to work.

*Procedure:*

1. Introduce the exercise by explaining ATCs, showing examples, and then display the materials.
2. Ask group members to reflect on their personal perceptions of hope, and what it feels like or would feel like at the present time. Another way to present the topic would be to ask them to think about what would constitute or be illustrative of hope for them at the present time.
3. Give the signal to begin the constructions, and note how much time will be given.
4. Follow item 4 in the previous exercise, and the guidelines for reporting and exploration.

   - **Member states and characteristics** refer to attributes and behaviors such as expressed or unexpressed emotions, moods, values; cognitive, emotional, physical, relational, creative, and inspirational aspects of oneself; and hopes, dreams, and wishes.

*Exercise: 20.3—Dreams and Wishes*

*Materials:* Refer to the materials lists in the guidelines, and find an appropriate place to work.

*Procedure:*

1. Introduce the topic by telling group members that the focus for the activity is on expressing one or more dreams or wishes they have for their personal future. Then ask them to create an ATC that illustrates this wish or dream.
2. Distribute the materials and give the working time frame, such as 20 minutes for the construction.
3. Observe members as they work, and notify them when 5 minutes are left for working.
4. Follow the guidelines for reporting and exploration.

## Flats

Flats originated from a book by Jeff Brown, illustrated by Tomi Ungerer (1964) and has spawned a host of variations. Essentially, flats are paper dolls that are drawn and decorated usually to resemble a person, and are taken or mailed to various sites where their pictures are taken. Stories can be created around their travels, or a photo or scrapbook compiled, or a book written to illustrate their adventures. Flats are appropriate for all age groups, and can be used for a variety of reasons that are explained later in this section. We begin our presentation with a personal story about my experiences with a flat—Flat Samantha.

> *The evening before I was to leave to attend a conference in Sarasota Fla., my youngest daughter unexpectedly brought me Flat Samantha to take with me on the trip. It seems that it was a class project for my granddaughter, Samantha, where the flat had to travel out of town, and have photos to document her travels. To no avail, I pointed out that we lived at most 10 minutes from three other cities. Flat Samantha was traveling with me to Florida.*
>
> *Most flats have clothes drawn on them but Flat Samantha wore jeans, a sweater, earrings, and had a silver pipe cleaner belt. Somewhere there was a naked teddy bear. (The belt is mentioned because someone we met said that they wanted a belt like that.)*

*I carefully packed Flat Samantha in a bag and put her with the materials I took on the plane, taking no chances that she might not arrive with my checked luggage.*

*Flat Samantha's first stop at the conference was the committee meeting where she was introduced, made a member of the committee, photographed with the committee, and photographed with individual committee members. Later, the committee chair showed her pictures to the organization's board which included them with the conference pictures on the website.*

*Word got around the conference and many attendees asked to see her. We had a short break one afternoon before the evening meeting, and another committee member and I went to lunch and a stroll, taking Flat Samantha with us. We stopped to buy her a necklace at a bead shop. Visualize four grown women carefully selecting four or five beads for flat's necklace. She was photographed with her new necklace, with a strolling model, and on a bench outside of a shop with a new friend who was waiting for his wife. Flat Samantha also visited the Barnum museum and was photographed with docents, paintings by masters such as Titian and Rembrandt, and with the rather extensive model of circus life. Everyone was happy to take a picture with Flat Samantha.*

You probably can tell from my tale that the flat and I had a wonderful experience. The responses, even from strangers, were very positive and this is what I hear happened with others who participated in an activity with a flat.

I mentioned before that flats were usually of people, but I know of at least one occasion when flats were of pet dogs. A colleague who heard my story about Flat Samantha decided to make flats of her pet dogs to send to her step-grandchildren who lived far away. The children took pictures with their flats (there was a different dog flat for each child), took pictures of the flats in different places, and e-mailed her stories about the flats. Communications and relationships were enhanced.

### *Constructing a Flat*

Templates for flats and other guidelines can be found at www.flatstanley.com. Here are two exercises using a flat. The first could be used with group members who are deficient in socializing skills, and the second with members who have difficulty verbalizing their thoughts, feelings, and ideas.

*Exercise 20.4—Connecting*

*Materials:* A template for flats, heavy cardstock, scissors, and a set of crayons, colored pencils, or felt markers.

*Procedure:*

1. Introduce the exercise as an activity to foster creativity and imagination. Tell group members what flats are and provide them with an example of a flat prepared in advance.
2. Distribute the materials and have members cut the dolls out, and draw facial features, and clothes.
3. Members then give their flats a name. Names are usually the owner's name with Flat as the first name, such as Flat Samantha.
4. Next, members are to take the flat to three different outside places, such as a mall, where there are people, and photograph the flat at the site. Other people can also be included.
5. At the next session, have members report on their experiences, and note how the flat facilitated initiating contact with other people, and how communications were enhanced. Ask members about their thoughts and feelings as they talked with strangers and took pictures.

*Exercise 20.5—Stories*

*Materials:* Same as in the previous exercise, with the addition of paper and pencil, or a computer and printer if available to members.

*Procedure:* Follow steps 1 and 2 in the previous exercise.

3. The next step is to take the flat to three places in their world, and write a short story (even as short as a page) about each place they stop. For example, if they take the flat to work, that would be one story. Places could be different rooms in their home, the car, the yard, wherever they go. The stories would be about what the flat experiences, such as what does the flat see; what thoughts, feelings, ideas, reactions, and the like does the flat have. Tell them to try and see the place from the flat's perspective. They are free to be as fanciful as they want.
4. At the next session, ask members to share a story and then explore what the experience was like to go to the various sites, and finally write a story.

## Scrapbooks

Scrapbooking has expanded and is no longer just gluing materials about an event, such as a prom, in a photo book. Although they are also still used in this way, there are numerous enhancements and extensions that provide a creative venue for scrapbooks. Many materials and techniques are incorporated into the display including photos, objects, writings, drawings, poems, and the like. Almost anything can be included in a scrapbook.

Using scrapbooking as a group activity usually means that members complete their work outside of the group session, and periodically bring the completed work to share with other group members. It is recommended that the group leader schedule these sharing sessions in advance. Another variation is to have an extended workshop session for members to work on their scrapbooks, and this would also be an opportunity to share materials.

Advantages for using scrapbooks include the following:

- Members can get in touch with forgotten memories, people, events, and so on.
- Feelings of creativity and inspiration can emerge and be encouraged and supported.

- More self-disclosure about important parts of oneself can occur as members display their work, and resistance and defensiveness can be reduced.
- Interactions and emergence of therapeutic factors, such as universality, can be fostered.
- Exploration of important issues and concerns can be less threatening and allowed to unfold.

Disadvantages are that:

- Scrapbooking is a longer term activity that cannot be completed in a session.
- Some members may not work well independently.
- Disquieting memories can be triggered.
- Some members may not have personal photos from their past.
- The cost of materials.

Following are some examples of topics for a scrapbook focus, and one example of an exercise.

- **Photos** to tell a story, recall past events and people, highlight life's milestones and celebrations, show personal growth and development.

*Exercise 20.6—The "Now" of My Life*

*Materials:* A scrapbook, camera, and materials listed for ATCs for each member. Each member will need a collection of photos that depict important people, activities, objects, and symbols of desires and wishes at the present time. If photos are not available, or they don't have the ones they want, they should take pictures for inclusion in their scrapbook. Members may be asked to supply their own materials.

*Procedure:*

1. Introduce the exercise by noting that sometimes we fail to take full notice of our lives in the present and that the exercise is designed to focus on the important things in

members' current lives without making any judgment. There are no rights or wrongs, good or bad, just what exists in the present.

2. Distribute the list of materials and give members a timeline for completion, such as 2 weeks. Tell them to either use existing photos, or to take photos if the desired or needed ones are not available, and to compile them in a scrapbook. They are free to be creative in making the pages for the scrapbook.
3. When members return, have them share their scrapbooks in the group. Focus the discussion on awareness of a variety of topics that has emerged as they thought about what to put in the scrapbook that depicted parts of their current lives, feelings experienced while creating and developing the scrapbook, and feelings as they talked about the scrapbook in the group.
4. Have each member give a summary statement about the totality of their current lives.

- **Collage** to express thoughts, feelings, and ideas about a concept, a concern, or to showcase skills or talent.

*Exercise 20.7—Inventory of My Relationship Attributes*

*Materials:* Group members will need the following: a scrapbook (5" × 7" or 6" × 6", or 8" × 8"); list of materials for ATCs, photos (if desired), images from magazines or catalogues; paper for writing; and a prepared list and description for each attribute. The leader should prepare the list of materials and the list and description of each attribute for each group member.

*Relating Attributes and Descriptions*

Caring: Conveys that the other person is valued and important.

Concern: The welfare of the other person is of importance.

Tolerance: The capacity to value differences of others from oneself, accepting of diverse opinions, values, and the like.

Respect: Regarding the other person as unique, separate, and worthwhile.

Nonjudgmental attitude: An acceptance of differences (opinion, values, worldview, physical, etc.) without putting a value judgment as to right or wrong, or as being good or bad.

Openness: Being receptive to others as they are, and willing to consider differing perspectives.

Genuineness: An ability to be real and authentic in interactions with others.

*Procedure:*

1. Introduce the exercise by providing descriptions and examples for each of the relationship attributes. Ask members to reflect on these as they apply to them personally.
2. Distribute the materials and tell members the time line for completion, such as 2 weeks.
3. Direct members to create seven collages, one for each attribute, and put them in the scrapbook. The collages should depict their personal attributes.
4. Have members show their scrapbooks when they return and talk about what the experience was like for them, such as feelings that emerged. Lead a discussion about the importance of these attributes in interpersonal relations, and where members see that growth is needed or possible.

- **Found** materials, objects, and recycled materials to be imaginative and creative.

*Exercise 20.8—Old, New, Different*

*Materials:* A scrapbook, adhesives, scissors, a set of crayons, colored pencils, or felt markers; other embellishments; two or more sample pages made by the leader using the found objects.

*Procedure:*

1. Ask each member to gather a collection of found materials, objects, and recycled materials to use to create a

scrapbook that illustrates something important for that member. The scrapbook should have six or more pages, and can be about anything the member chooses. Show the members the sample pages noting the materials used, how they formed new elements, and that recycled materials are being used in new ways.
2. Give the members a timeline for completion, such as 2 or 3 weeks.
3. When members return with the scrapbooks, have them share and explain in the group just as was done in step 1 with the samples.
4. Explore the process of creating the scrapbooks; what was difficult, what was easy, feelings that emerged, and any new insights or awareness that occurred.

- **Make a scrapbook instead of cards**: such as for sympathy, thanks, congratulations, when you want to say more and not only use words.

*Exercise 20.9—A Card Book*

*Materials:* Small scrapbooks, such as 4" × 4", with about 6 to 8 pages; materials used for constructing ATCs, a pen for writing.

*Procedure:*

1. Ask members to select a topic or celebration for the scrapbook, such as happy birthday, condolences, or I'm thinking of you.
2. Tell them to construct the collages for the scrapbook that illustrates the various thoughts, ideas, and emotions around the topic or celebration. For example, a card about thanks could include collages that illustrate caring, gratitude, appreciation, pleasure, thoughtfulness, and giving. The facing page is where the member writes about the thoughts, feelings, and ideas that accompany the expression of the collage. Give a timeline for construction of the scrapbook.

3. When members return with their scrapbook, ask them to talk about their card and the ease or difficulty of construction. Ask if they feel differently about the topic or concept the card scrapbook expresses.

## A Collection of Activities

There are numerous creative and inspirational activities that do not fit neatly into the chapters. This section presents several of these activities.

*Exercise 20.10—Self-Perception*
*Materials:* Index cards 5" × 8" and a pen or pencil for writing. Prepare the following list in advance on a large sheet of paper that will be posted where members can see:
A flower or plant
A poem or song
A color
A piece of furniture
A type of book, such as a biography, picture book, and so on
An animal.

*Procedure:*

1. Provide a suitable surface for writing, such as a table, large book, or other firm surface. Distribute the materials.
2. Introduce the exercise by telling members that sometimes it can be difficult to describe oneself, and this activity can provide an indirect way of giving a self-description.
3. Display the large sheet of paper described in the materials. Ask members to think about themselves in a different way, as the items on the list, and to write a self-identifier for each of the items on the list; for example, what kind of flower are they?
4. Give sufficient time to complete the lists, and remind them of the remaining time about 5 minutes before the time is called.

5. Reconvene the group and have each member read her or his descriptions to the group.
6. Ask members if they have descriptors for each other, and allow time to note and write these.

*Exercise 20.11—The Layers of My Self*

*Materials:* A 4" × 5" or 5½" blank notecard for each person, a collection of collage materials, scissors, glue, and a set of crayons, colored pencils, or felt markers for each participant.

*Procedure:*

1. Find a suitable place for working, and distribute the materials.
2. Introduce the exercise by telling the group members that most people have several layers of the self: a public self easily seen by others; the self revealed to acquaintances, peers, and other casual relationships; the intimate self revealed only to those you trust and feel close to; and the self that you know but mostly keep hidden. The card will be used to construct collages that depict the four layers. The first side is the public self, the inside surfaces will depict the selfs that are revealed in casual and intimate relationships, and the back of the card is the self that is mostly hidden.
3. Allow about 20 minutes for construction, and remind them of the time remaining about 5 minutes before the 20 minutes is complete.
4. Reconvene the group and have members share their collages without having to identify what layers 3 and 4 depict. They can just talk about these in general terms.
5. Ask members to talk about the feelings and thoughts that emerged as they thought about their layers, as they constructed the collage, and when reporting to the group.
6. Close by asking members to give a summary statement about their selves as depicted by the collage. For example, what title would they give their construction?

# CHAPTER 21

# APPLICATIONS

## Member Concerns

This chapter focuses on some concerns that members may have as they enter the group, and as they begin to understand what is expected of them in the group. The group leader can use creative activities to reduce some of the ambiguity and uncertainty about the group, expected member behavior and interactions, and can also use these for addressing difficult member behavior. Presented are activities to promote universality, foster inclusion, encourage emotional expression, and suggested strategies for difficult member behaviors.

### Universality

Promote universality among group members to provide personal connections, increase feelings of safety and trust, reduce feelings of isolation and alienation, and to encourage participation. Universality is identified as a therapeutic or curative factor in groups (Yalom & Leszcz, 2005). It is defined in different ways by various authors, such as the following.

- Perceived similarities to one another (Yalom & Leszcz, 2005);
- "Sharing similar feelings or problems" (Kivlighan & Holmes, 2004);
- Being with others who share the same problems (Posthuma, 2002);
- Others in the group have similar experiences and feelings (Gladding, 1999);
- Aloneness is supplanted by a sense that others in the group experience similar difficulties (Conyne, Crowell, & Newmeyer, 2008).

It seems as if the concept of universality is not consistently defined even though its importance is recognized. A classic example of the need to promote universality is in the beginning stage for the group. While introductions and commonalities of condition and issues can be easily facilitated, these are not sufficient to promote universality for all members. The concept of universality goes beyond the surface similarities, and it is the group leader's responsibility to help members seek out and identify similarities that are meaningful for them, the similarities that help them feel connected to another person. This is vital for the development of cohesion as the group becomes cohesive around perceived similarities. Following are two introductory exercises to emphasize group members' similarities which promote universality.

*Exercise 21.1—How Am I?*

*Materials:* 5" × 8" index cards, a set of crayons, colored pencils, or felt markers for each participant, and a pen or pencil. The group leader should prepare in advance an example of possible feelings on a large sheet of newsprint for display to the group. Possible feelings could include apprehension, dread, excitement, sadness, hopelessness, envy, anger, numbness, shame, incompetence, frustration, resentment, and so on. Also prepared in advance is a sample 5" × 8" index card with colors on it to fill up the card, such as triangles or squares of color, with the name of the feeling written in the color.

*Procedure:*

1. This is an exercise to use after members have introduced themselves. Distribute the materials and ask members to use the colors to label their current feelings as they begin the group experience. Note that many people will have several feelings, but that each feeling may have differing intensity.
2. Instruct them to select the colors that best identify the feelings they have at the current time, and to construct their card of feelings with the names of the feelings in the color chosen. They can refer to the sample card for clarification.
3. After the cards are constructed, ask group members to give their cards a title.
4. Have each member display and describe their cards, noting similarities in feelings identified, and color choices.
5. Explore the experience by asking them the following:
   - Was it easy or hard to identify their current feelings?
   - What was it like to sort through the different feelings, and select colors?
   - What feelings emerged as they completed the exercise? When they displayed their cards?
   - What similarities have they identified among group members?

## Inclusion

It can be easy for some people to feel excluded in a group, and it can be easy for the group to exclude one or more members. Cliques and subgrouping are two examples of the group excluding members. However, the group is unlikely to become cohesive unless all members feel included. The group leader has to maintain an awareness of members feeling isolated, alienated, or excluded; and the group's behavior that excludes one or more members, such as can happen with an identified patient, or the member who is scapegoated.

Helping members to feel included involves giving them attention, soliciting and valuing their input, listening and empathic responding, and respecting their differences while emphasizing their similarities with other group members. The last point is especially important because it can be easier for the group to highlight and focus on differences than it is to recognize meaningful similarities. Visible differences, such as age, or skin color, or accent, or disability, can produce feelings of being different, or the member having the characteristic(s) can be responded to in a different way than for other group members, or the member can be put on the spot by having questions asked about race/ethnicity, heritage or national origin, or other such questions that highlight their "difference."

In addition, there can be hidden or masked characteristics that can cause someone to feel different or excluded when the members or the leader make comments that touch that characteristic; and because the characteristic may not be obvious or visible, the affected group member can be put in a double bind where they can be unsure whether to become visible or to stay hidden. An example would be socioeconomic status that is not usually visible in the United States from dress, language usage, accent, and the like. A group member may have a hidden characteristic that is discussed without it being known that a member has that characteristic, and discussion such as this can produce feelings of exclusion for the member in question.

Use of a creative activity can assist with promoting inclusion when all members report on their products, the responses and comments each member provides are invited and directly responded to, and linking is used. This can be easier to accomplish for all group members through reporting, exploration, and expansion of their creative activity products. When the group expectation and climate are set so that every group member has an opportunity to present his or her product; express thoughts, ideas, and feelings; have comments and responses responded to directly and with respect; be invited to have input and other such actions, the outcome can be a general feeling of being included. Promoting feelings and actions of inclusion is necessary so that group members can feel the group to be welcoming and caring with opportunities for members to experience being a part of an experience that transcends the individual. An introductory exercise that may facilitate inclusion follows.

*Exercise 21.2—Meet and Greet*
*Materials:* None.
*Procedure:*

1. Divide members into dyads and have them move their chairs to face each other.
2. Instruct the smaller groups to introduce themselves to each other by disclosing something important about themselves, and a goal they have for the group experience. They are given 3 minutes to complete this phase, and then they move to face another person.
3. Repeat step 2 until all members have had an opportunity for introductions.
4. Reconvene in the group circle and explore what the experience was like with an emphasis on the feelings aroused, making sure that every member has a chance to report.
5. Ask members to share with the group the goals they have in common with other group members.

## Encourage Emotional Expression

Creative activities can teach group members how to gain greater awareness of their feelings, to understand their intense negative feelings so as to reduce the fear that can surround these, learn more appropriate ways to express their feelings and have this accepted by others, to identify gradations of feelings so that subtle and less intense ones are consciously experienced, and to manage and contain their feelings.

Awareness of what is felt can be taught and the group can be a safe place to focus on and practice immediate feelings. Some people recognize what they were feeling at a particular time only in retrospect. Others, because of family of origin and other experiences, learned to repress or suppress their feelings because of negative consequences, and now cannot access these. Even some people who have some awareness of what they are feeling can grow in their awareness. Creative activities can facilitate increased awareness with their stimulus procedures.

Intense negative feelings such as anger, fear, and shame can be scary when experienced and thus can be denied, repressed, displaced, or expressed in inappropriate ways. These feelings are also detrimental to having and sustaining positive and satisfying relationships when they are not understood by the person experiencing them, or expressed in ways that are destructive to their relationships. Developing an understanding of why these feelings emerge, their triggers, and what they are responding to either from the external event or from an internal state can produce considerable self-understanding. The outcome can be a reduced need to have these feelings in response to a perceived threat whether an internal or external threat. Group members can be taught about their feelings to help them better assess the validity of the perceived threat that produces the feeling(s).

Learning more appropriate ways to express feelings can be taught and learned in the group. Not just word choice which can be important, but also learning to consider the importance of staying in contact with the responses and reactions of those who hear and receive the impact of the expressed feelings. Appropriate expression of feelings incorporates the setting where speaking of what is being felt takes place, the target receiver or audience, the internal need or impetus to speak of the feelings(s), immediacy and control where the intensity may suggest a loss of control, and the motive or intent. The entire process of a creative activity promotes the learning needed for appropriate emotional expression.

There may be group members who have never learned to identify gradations of feelings, so they are only aware of when they experience the intense level. For example, some people are not aware of the gradations for anger: disquiet, irritation, annoyance, anger, rage; and in consequence, tend to only recognize when they are angry or enraged. Learning to tune in to, accept, and express or understand less intense feelings when they first occur can help prevent these from escalating and becoming troublesome to the person or to his or her relationships. Following is an exercise that focuses on feelings that may be difficult to express.

*Exercise 21.3—Difficult Feelings*

*Materials:* Two sheets of paper, and a set of crayons, colored pencils, or felt markers for each group member.

*Procedure:*

1. Distribute the materials, and introduce the exercise by telling group members that there are some feelings that are easy for them to express, and some that are difficult.
2. Instruct them to use the first sheet of paper and draw symbols for feelings that they find easy to express. Ask them to use one color for each symbol they draw. The symbols can be representative, abstractions, or just splashes of color. Whatever they choose to do is acceptable.
3. Instruct them to take the other sheet of paper and repeat step 2 for feelings they find difficult to express.
4. Have each group member show the drawings for feelings that are easy to express. After which, each will show the symbols for feelings that are difficult to express. The group leader should note similarities among symbols and colors chosen.
5. Lead a discussion on what members find difficult to express, and how facilitation of these can be accomplished in the group.

## Difficult Member Behaviors

Difficult member behaviors include monopolizing, story-telling, prolonged silence, the help rejecting complainer, and scapegoating. There are leader strategies to address these behaviors, such as redirecting, linking, and the like; but there can also be group activities that can be effective interventions. Examples of creative activities for three of these behaviors are presented.

### *Monopolizing*

Attention can be the goal for the monopolizer. While group members can be grateful in the beginning of the group to have a person who keeps the session moving, it is not long before this behavior becomes tiresome and annoying. Leaders can use strategies such as blocking and redirecting as interventions, but there are times when these strategies may not fully address the behavior, or do not work. A creative activity such as the following may be helpful.

*Exercise 21.4—Gifts*
*Materials:* 5" × 8" lined index cards, and a pen or pencil for writing. A suitable surface for writing would be helpful.
*Procedure:*

1. Distribute the materials and introduce the activity by telling members that each brings unique gifts to the group.
2. Ask them to list each member by name, and to identify one or more gifts that person brings to the group, such as willingness to share important feelings.
3. Allow sufficient time for writing, and then ask members to read the lists aloud.
4. Ask members to report on how they feel about the gifts that were identified about them.
5. Explore the feelings and reactions that members had while doing the exercise, and while receiving the feedback.

### *Storytelling*

Many group members will engage in storytelling because they want others to fully understand their situation. However, it is seldom necessary to have all of the details, and although other group members will ask questions as a way of showing interest or to keep that person talking so that they don't have to talk, the group leader should intervene as valuable group time is being consumed in providing details that do not contribute to understanding or growth. An activity such as the following can be an effective way to block the storytelling, and to engage all group members.

*Exercise 21.5—My Story*

*Materials:* Sheets of paper for drawing, a set of crayons, colored pencils, or felt markers for each person; and a suitable surface for drawing.

*Procedure:*

1. Distribute the materials and ask members to close their eyes.
2. Next, ask members to think about a personal story they would like to tell the group, or think it would be important to share, and to let the story come to mind and unfold.
3. Tell them that when they are ready, to open their eyes and draw a picture that captures the essence of their feelings about their story. Not the story itself, the feelings about it. The picture may be realistic or abstract.
4. Allow sufficient time for drawing. When members seem finished, reconvene the circle and have them share their drawings.
5. Explore what was learned about each member's story from the feelings picture.

### *Scapegoating*

Group leaders have to take immediate steps to intervene when a member is becoming an identified patient, or is scapegoated.

While the identified patient is receiving attention and is being listened to, that member is also in the position of being placed on the hot seat with too much attention that produces discomfort. Further, by having an identified patient, other group members are not working on their personal issues and concerns, but are putting their energies toward fixing the identified patient.

The scapegoated member can easily feel excluded as he or she becomes the repository for other group members' negative feelings, and has to carry these unless there is an intervention that helps group members acknowledge and express their own negative uncomfortable feelings. Scapegoating can also be a disguised and displaced attack such as what can happen when the group is fearful of or reluctant to challenge the leader, and directs the challenge to a group member. The leader has to intervene in a way that protects all group members without placing any group member in a scapegoat position.

*Exercise 21.6—My Current Feelings*

*Materials:* Sheet of paper, and a set of crayons, colored pencils, or felt markers, and a suitable surface for drawing.

*Procedure:*

1. Distribute materials and ask members to select colors and draw shapes for the feelings they are experiencing in the here and now. Tell them that they may be experiencing several feelings, some are major and some are minor and to draw these in proportion. That is the minor feelings would be smaller than the major ones. Tell them to select the color that best depicts the particular feeling.
2. Allow time for drawing, and reconvene the circle and have members share their drawings with a focus on what the feelings are, not on why they have the feeling that they do. Discourage exploration of why they are experiencing that particular feeling.
3. Notice if the majority of the feelings depicted are positive or negative, and how difficult or easy it is for members to express these feelings.

# Chapter 22
# Group Level Challenges

Chapter 21 discussed member behaviors that can lead to difficulties in the group. This chapter focuses on group level challenges where the entire group is affected by one or more member behaviors, or where the group as a whole is collaborating in behaviors that also affect the functioning of the group. Presented are group level resistance, difficult behaviors, conflict, and existential concerns.

## Group Level Resistance

Group level resistance is defined as what happens when the group as a whole is not addressing something important for the group. The focus is on an unspoken threat to the existence and functioning of the group, and can also be threatening to the members who fear destruction of the group and of its members.

Identification of group level resistance is not always easy as each group member exhibits the collective resistance in his or her personal resistance in a different way. For example, one member may talk a lot, another member deflects the discussion, one or more members remain silent and resist invitations to join the discussion, or someone introduces an out of group content laden topic and other members eagerly join in. Another variation can be the attention to an identified patient where members provide advice, suggestions, and their own stories in an effort to fix that member and keep the attention from the real resistance. Alternatively a member becomes scapegoated or conflict breaks out. The leader has to address these issues because they are important and may be urgent, but the group may have effectively prevented the leader from identifying and addressing the real group level resistance.

More troublesome and destructive to the group is when the collective resistance is used to hide a group secret, such as an intimate relationship between two members, or a subgroup breaking an explicit group contract such as drinking alcohol together. The group leader has to stay alert to the possibility that the group is colluding to protect a group secret.

Group level resistances occur as a reflection of the members' fears of personal and collective destruction or abandonment, and the leader has to understand that these fears need to be visible before they can be adequately addressed, they can also be so overwhelming and strong that direct efforts to make them visible may have the result of driving them further underground. This state of affairs can be very frustrating for the group leader as the group is stalled and direct methods, such as process commentary, may not be effective. The group may need a more subtle and tentative intervention that takes into account the paralyzing fear(s) they may have. This is where a creative activity such as the following may be helpful to break the stalemate.

*Exercise 22.1—The Group's Image*

*Materials:* This exercise can be done without materials, but may be more effective if the images are drawn. If drawing is used, the materials needed will be sheets of paper and a set of crayons, colored pencils, or felt markers for each group member.

*Procedure:*

1. Introduce the exercise by telling members that they will be asked to let an image of the group emerge and then draw it.
2. Ask them to sit back, get as comfortable as possible, close their eyes, and concentrate on their breathing to make it deep and even. Allow about a minute for this.
3. Ask members to allow an image of the group to emerge, to let it unfold, and to not edit or change it. Allow 30 to 60 seconds for the imaging.
4. Tell them to open their eyes and draw the image.
5. Have group members share their images.
6. Discuss the experience, focusing on the feelings they experienced as they imaged the group, and as they displayed their drawings.
7. Note the feelings conveyed by the images and drawings, and those reported by group members, and ask if this represents how they feel about the group. Note positive and negative feelings.

## Difficult Member Behaviors

Brown (2006) proposes that group member behaviors labeled as difficult are serving a purpose for the individual and for the group. Gans and Alonso (1998) focus on how the group leader and other group members contribute to the troubling behavior and how the role is needed by the group, which allows it to emerge. Rutan and Stone (2001) understand this behavior as ineffective communication where that person cannot adequately voice his or her needs, wishes, or desires.

Difficult member behaviors are described in many ways but the usual terms used are storytelling, monopolizing, silent/withdrawn, help rejecting complainer, questioning, giving advice, and the like. The reason these are termed difficult is that the focus is on one person, the behavior interferes with the group's progress, other members become frustrated with the member and can begin to scapegoat him or her, the members exhibiting the behavior are usually not directly working on their problems or issues, and the goal for the behavior is not known.

Difficult member behaviors that are interfering with the group's progress and process are not easily addressed by a direct focus because this could be shaming for the individual. Another consideration is that other group members may be colluding with the difficult behavior even though they may be openly expressing displeasure. Another aspect is that the group leader has to address the behavior without allowing that member or members to become scapegoated.

Difficult group behaviors are described in chapter 1 and below. These are collective group member behaviors that produce a group atmosphere that has the potential to be destructive, or is detrimental to the group's functioning, growth, and development. Examples include the following:

- The group seems stuck or mired where the discussion becomes circular, no problem solving or insight occurs, members are exasperated but cannot seem to change the pattern, and therapeutic work is not being accomplished.
- Conflict has emerged in the group and is being ignored, suppressed, or denied. Or, the members fear conflict so much that they will go to extraordinary means to keep it under wraps and pretend that they are harmonious (see the next section in this chapter).
- The group seems over- or underenergized. When overly energized, they skip from topic to topic none of which is adding to the work of the group, a lot of squirming and other nonverbal communication of discomfort occurs, but interventions do not seem to help them concentrate or focus. The underenergized group seems depressed or dead, but they resist exploration of their feelings.
- Many or even most group members either cannot or do not express their feelings, or they express them in inappropriate ways. Feelings seem to be considered dangerous and members avoid expressing them.

- Members are exhibiting resistance and defensiveness well beyond what is usually expected in the group. They are not making meaningful connections with each other, and are avoiding attempts to promote interactions and involvement.
- Members are extremely tentative and cautious in revealing their selves to the point where they do not disclose anything of importance. While safety and trust need to be established before meaningful connections and disclosures can appear, this wariness has continued to the point where the therapeutic work is thwarted.

*Exercise 22.2—Reframe Criticisms*
*Materials:* 5" × 8" index cards, and pens or pencils for writing.
*Procedure:*

1. Distribute the materials and ask members to write a list of behaviors and attitudes that could be unhelpful to the group and its progress, when displayed by one or more group members. Emphasize that it is very helpful if they can identify specific behaviors, and when they list an attitude, to try and behaviorally describe what conveys that attitude. They can fantasize these behaviors and attitudes, which do not have to be present in the current group.
2. The next step is to have members reflect on the behaviors and attitudes they listed, and see if there is an embedded strength. For example, if monopolizing is unhelpful, the strength may be that it gives members and the group a focus, albeit an irritating one. The leader can have other suggestions for embedded strengths. Try and help members find strengths in each.
3. Go around the group and have each member share one or more of the items on their lists, both the behavior or attitude, and the embedded strength. Ask if members had the same behaviors/attitudes and the same embedded strength. Note similarities whenever possible.
4. Ask members to reflect on feelings that emerged as they compiled their lists and found strengths, and the feelings they have now.

## Ignoring or Minimizing Conflict

The group is ignoring or minimizing conflict. While doing so is a group level resistance, it is also presented here as a separate group situation because of its importance both for the group's learning and for individual members' learning. The fear of destruction, pain, and dissolution of relationships can be addressed by demonstrating constructive conflict resolution in a manner that is nonthreatening such as creative activities can provide.

Some group members may fear conflict in the group because of their family of origin experiences where conflict led to unpleasant outcomes such as physical abuse. Other past experiences can also be a basis for fear of conflict emerging as those experiences led to rejection, loss, and grief. There are many reasons that members ignore or minimize conflict in the group, such as an imperfect understanding of the many levels of conflict ranging from a disagreement to a battle. While they may be able to manage and tolerate disagreement, they can also fear that any disagreement will escalate into a battle. Thus, they work hard to ensure that even the most minor disagreements are not allowed to emerge in the group, and may lack confidence in the leader's ability to keep them safe.

The group leader can also play a role in ignoring or minimizing conflict depending on his or her level of comfort with it, perceived expertise to be able to manage it if or when it does appear, and capacity to tolerate intense negative emotions. If a group leader's experiences and issues with conflict have not been adequately addressed, then the leader too can fear abandonment or destruction. The leader also has to have confidence that he or she can effectively manage conflict so that it becomes a strengthening and growth opportunity for group members. Using constructive conflict resolution procedures teaches and illustrates to members that conflict need not always be destructive for a person or destructive to the relationship. Conflict can produce intense emotions for those in the conflict, and for others who are present when the conflict emerges. A group leader has to have sufficient personal development to be able to contain, tolerate, and manage these intense emotions for all group members, even for those who do not openly express them.

Creative activities can provide a safe and secure means to introduce the subject, allay fears, and encourage and teach conflict resolution. It can be very upsetting and threatening to members if the leader makes a process comment about their ignoring or minimizing conflict. Usual immediate reactions to such a comment are feelings of shame for "not doing it right" or for disappointing the leader; a denial and hardening of resistance; a disavowal and challenge to the leader's competence; and other such reactions that can deflect attention to something other than the original ignoring or minimization of a conflict in the group. The group leader can use creative activities to approach the topic and action in a way that promotes acceptance rather than defensiveness and resistance, especially if members seem fearful of conflict emerging in the group. Activities listed below help to introduce the topic of conflict; provide an opportunity for members to express their thoughts, feelings, and ideas about conflict; and to teach a conflict resolution strategy.

*Exercise 22.3—Perceptions of Conflict*

*Materials:* Paper, pencils or pens for writing, two or more large sheets of newsprint paper with a heading of either positive or negative, felt markers for writing on the newsprint, and masking tape for posting the newsprint.

*Procedure:*

1. Distribute the paper and pens or pencils.
2. Introduce the activity by asking members to quickly list all of the associations they have for the word *conflict*. List all thoughts, ideas, and feelings that come to mind. Allow about 5 minutes for writing.
3. Next, give each member a different colored felt marker (this will allow them to quickly identify their listing), and ask them to write the items on their lists on the newsprint under either positive or negative. That is, all items on their lists will be either positive or negative.

4. Once all items are listed, review the positive associations, and then the negative ones. Note if there are the following:
   - Some associations appear more than once or appear many times, even if phrased differently.
   - Some associations appear on both positive and negative lists.
5. Ask members about feelings that emerged as they compiled their individual lists, and when they categorized them as negative or positive.
6. Have members comment on their perceptions of each item.
7. Summarize the overall perceptions of conflict for group members.

*Exercise 22.4—Perceptions of Conflict II*

*Materials:* Paper and a set of crayons, colored pencils, or felt markers for each member.

*Procedure:*

1. Distribute materials and introduce the activity by noting that there are several levels of conflict ranging from a disagreement to a battle. Tell them that you are going to give them four words for four levels of conflict, and they are to select one color and draw a symbol for that level word. They can use the same color for all four levels, or different colors for them. They should try to have different symbols for each level.
2. Slowly read the words, one at a time, giving members time to draw a symbol between words.
   - Disharmony: lack of harmony, discord;
   - Dissension: differences in opinion;
   - Strife: heated struggle; bitter dissention;
   - War: open, armed, prolonged conflict, sometimes with weapons.
3. Ask members to display and describe their symbols. Ask if there is a significance in the color chosen.

4. Lead a discussion on the feelings that emerged as they thought of and drew their symbols, as they reported, and as they listened to other members.
5. Explore members' perceptions of conflict with particular emphasis on any changes in perception from before the activity to the present.

*Exercise 22.5—Conflict Role-Play*
*Materials:* Paper and a pencil or pen for writing.
*Procedure:*

1. Describe the activity by telling members that first they are asked to write a short description of a personal conflict they experienced but not one with parents or a lover or a spouse. It can be one from the past, or a current conflict. Next, you will divide them into dyads or triads to share their conflicts, and the last step will be to have a role-play of a conflict. Pause and ask if there are any questions or any objections.
2. If there are no objections, ask members to write the description. Allow 5 minutes for this.
3. Next, divide the group into dyads or triads and tell them that they have 6 to 9 minutes to share their descriptions.
4. After each member has an opportunity to report on their conflict, ask if anyone is willing to have their conflict role-played. Use the following sequence for the role-play:
   - Ask the member who volunteered to have their conflict as a role-play to select the performers and to take them aside and give them enough information so that they understand what their role is. This person is the director of the role-play, but not a performer.
   - While the preparation for the role-play is going on, the group leader instructs the remaining group members to listen and observe, and to note what feelings they experience during the role-play.
   - Let the director choose where to conduct the role-play: in the circle or somewhere else in the room, to set the scene such as moving chairs.

- Allow the role-play to unfold until it feels finished or at a good stopping point.
- Ask the director about the accuracy of the performance.
- Ask each performer to report on the thoughts and feelings he or she experienced during the role-play.
- Ask the director how she or he feels about the conflict after seeing the performance, and any feelings experienced during the performance. This is also a good time to ask if there is any new awareness, understanding, or the like.
- Ask each observing group member for their comments, feelings, and thoughts during and after the role-play.

5. Lead a group discussion on effective ways to use conflict resolution skills and process.

## Existential Concerns

Existential concerns will constantly emerge in the group. These can be addressed in the group whether they are overtly and directly present, or are indirectly expressed. These concerns are present in the group in varying levels and intensities and, although not always openly addressed, have an influence on the members and the group. These are the life concerns and issues that have no final answers, are a part of the human condition, can only be answered for the time being, and will reemerge throughout life. Examples of these issues and concerns are as follows.

- Meaning and purpose for one's life
- Death
- Freedom and will
- Human suffering
- Existential anxiety
- Isolation and alienation.

While these can and do emerge at any time and may not be recognized as existential in nature, they do tend to be triggered by life crises and transitions, such as births, medical or emotional illnesses, and retirement. Existential concerns can raise anxieties that are difficult to express even when the individual understand the dilemma, and are usually expressed in indirect ways such as the following.

- Fear and terror of the unknown when changes are needed or are forthcoming;
- Having to cope with ambiguity and uncertainty;
- Lack or loss of being centered and grounded;
- Old answers do not fit new circumstances and new answers are not yet formulated;
- Feeling adrift and at the mercy of forces not under the person's control;
- A sense of loneliness, emptiness, of being out of sync with the world, or feeling alienated and so on;
- The unfairness and injustice of one's circumstances.

Since existential concerns are expected and common, although they may not be expressed as being existential, the group leader needs to be aware of when these are emerging as an important concern for many group members, and seek ways to help them be openly expressed, linking them to show universality. Use of a creative activity, such as fairy tales which have existential themes, could help members identify and express their concerns thus reducing some feelings of isolation, alienation, and anxiety.

*Exercise 22.6—Focus on Existential Group Themes*

*Procedure:* the group leader selects a fairy tale that has the existential theme that seems to be prevalent in the current group or session, and follows one of the processes described in chapter 4; drawing, writing, or the like. The list of existential themes provided in this section can be the guide for selection.

The group situations described to this point focused on general and expected behaviors, but a group leader can also encounter unexpected and even more difficult group situations, although it is hoped that these are infrequent. Some examples are described in the next chapter with suggestions for creative activities interventions.

# Chapter 23

# Group Dilemma Cases and Creative Activities

Four vignettes are presented in this chapter, each of which describes some possible group situations, all with adult group members. Read each vignette and imagine that you are the group leader who is encountering the situation. Try to put yourself in the group, accept that you tried interventions but these were not successful, and that the group continued this unproductive behavior. What would you do then? Some suggested creative activities interventions follow each example.

## Case Vignette I

*This group had been meeting once a week for the past 3 months. The group was becoming more cohesive, and members were beginning to engage in important self-disclosures. Sessions were interesting and lively, the leader encouraged interactions among members and they responded well. Everyone seemed satisfied and willing to participate, attendance was regular, and members came to sessions prepared to work.*

*During the 12th session, about midway through the number of scheduled sessions, Angela, an active group member, announced that she was leaving the group to go and take care of her mother who had a stroke. Angela and the group leader had met in advance, and had planned her announcement and how to manage the feelings around leaving the group.*

*After the announcement, group members expressed their shock, dismay, and feelings of loss. The group leader had anticipated this and guided the session so that Angela and group members could express their feelings, and take care of any unfinished business that might be present.*

*The next session continued the goodbye and grieving process for the group members, and several of them expressed regrets that Angela was no longer a part of the group. The group leader had also anticipated this possible reaction, and did not push the group to move on, feeling that they would do so when they were ready. Some personal concerns surfaced, but members seemed disinclined to deal with them, as these were quickly dropped when getting little response.*

*The group leader became concerned when the pattern of surfacing personal concerns and then dropping them continued for the next two sessions. The leader tried to respond, but the member who spoke of the concern would not or did not pursue the leads or guidance. Members rarely spoke, and seldom was there any interaction among members, except at the beginning of the sessions where they did talk about the weather, traffic, sports, and other such topics. Sessions lacked energy, nothing the leader did encouraged participation, and little or no therapeutic work was being done. The leader tried to analyze what was taking place in the group and considered whether or not the group was continuing the grieving process, had fears of intense uncontrollable emotions surfacing in the group, that members wanted to challenge her but were fearful of doing so, and that she was missing something important that the group needed. She tried introducing each of these, but the group remained unresponsive, denying the possible fears, and stating that they felt safe enough to express their feelings, or to challenge her.*

Following is a list of questions that can guide the group leader, after which he or she may want to use the decision making procedure described in chapter three.

1. What is the probable stage of group development for this group?
2. What is the theme of this, or of several sessions?
3. What feelings are experienced by the leader that can be clues to what group members are feeling; that is, the leader is acting as a container for the group's feelings?
4. What are the prominent group dynamics in this session?

***Possible Interventions***

Let's assume that these are well-functioning adults without disabilities. The leader may want to consider using a movement activity to energize the group; or a drawing activity to label and express current feelings; or an imagery activity where members image the group as a whole.

## Case Vignette II

*Marcia was dreading the upcoming meeting for the group she was leading, but was unable to pinpoint the source or reason for her feeling. She had just finally admitted to herself what she had been feeling for the last two sessions; that is, dread and reluctance, and that there had been some disquieting thoughts and feelings about the group prior to those sessions. Marcia reviewed her session notes, and the information she had about group members, but nothing jumped out at her as a possible reason for her dread. She did not feel this way about the other groups she led, and usually looked forward to the group sessions.*

*The dreaded session began for the group of eight young adults ages 25 to 35, three males and five females. They were attending the 12 session group because of relationship problems that they wanted to resolve, and this was the 8th session. The members were all working in productive jobs, reported that they were in reasonably good physical health, did not have any major past traumas such as abuse or rape, and seemed to be genuinely interested in what the group could offer them. Two members were divorced, three were in the process of separation for divorce, and three had never been married.*

*Marcia started the session in the usual way by asking if there was any unfinished business from the previous session; there was none, and if anyone had something urgent and important to bring to the group, again there was nothing. The group sat in silence for a few minutes, which began to feel like an eternity to Marcia. Just as she was going to intervene, John started talking about his problems with his ex-wife, and did so for most of the session. When he sounded like he would stop, another member would ask him a question, and he would provide an extended answer. Finally, the session ended. As Marcia wrote her session notes, she became aware of a pattern that had emerged during the last three sessions. It had gradually emerged, so that it would have been hard to detect earlier, but this last session really highlighted the pattern. She realized that the group allowed and encouraged storytelling by one or two people, and that her efforts to stop it and get them more focused was ignored. The group seemed to agree with her, but went right back to telling the story. There were also some long silences that members seemed content to endure, although someone always broke the silence. The stories were always a rehash of what the member had told before, there had been no movement that suggested progress or resolution, and other members just listened and probed for more details when they spoke at all. Marcia realized that what she was dreading was more of the same, and at being unable or ineffective so far at stopping this pattern.*

The leader has identified the pattern of behavior, and is well aware of her ineffectiveness to intervene and interrupt the pattern. The following questions could guide the leader to consider using the decision making procedure described in chapter 7.

1. Does the group have a collaborative secret?
2. Has one or more cliques formed?
3. What is the level of trust and safety in the group, and has this grown or decreased?
4. Am I functioning as the container for the group members' feelings?

***Possible Interventions***

Since this is a group of young adults with relationship concerns, it is reasonable to consider that relationships in the group are a part of what is taking place. There are numerous possibilities; for example, the leader may not know of a relationship that has developed between two group members, other group members may know, but everyone is keeping it from the leader. There are other possibilities, but let's assume that somehow the safety and trust is eroded and that this is what the leader will choose to address. Creative activities could include using the next three sessions to have members write for 10 to 15 minutes about their thoughts, feelings, and ideas about the group, but to not read these or share in any way. Just to write. Another creative activity could be to have members construct ATCs on the topics of safety and trust in relationships, and to display and report on these in the group. A third alternative could be to use mindfulness; a 5 minute mindfulness meditation period, and afterwards report on the perceptions and feelings experienced.

## Case Vignette III

*The group had started off with much promise and Duncan, the group leader, was pleased with the progress so far. He felt that members were gaining benefits from the group that would encourage them to stick to their plans to combat their abuse of alcohol. He wasn't naive, he didn't have unrealistic expectations: he had worked with many clients having this condition over the years, and knew that their challenges would not be easily overcome, and there was much hard work to be done. But, he was encouraged because of the behaviors in the group, and their reported behaviors outside the group that seemed to be verified by family members.*

*During the sixth session, Duncan noticed that several topics introduced by members did not seem finished. As soon as one member finished talking, a perfunctory response was provided by another member, but then that member or another one, went on to talk about something else. Duncan made a mental note to himself to pay attention to this, and bring it to the group's attention if it happened again. The next session was a repeat of the previous one, and Duncan did intervene with a group process comment. The members reflected on what they were doing, and possible reasons, but it was not long before they were back into the skittering pattern. The same happened during the next session where Duncan tried another group process comment. Members tried to be reflective about what they were doing, but continued the established pattern. There was no new material in what the members were talking about, and they really seemed to try to cooperate with Duncan's interventions.*

This group appears to be in stage 2 of group development with an inability to sustain its focus. They are resistant to interventions where they seem to comply with the leader's intervention but in reality do not comply, the discussion is circular, and they are agreeable to the leader about whatever he says. It is possible that there is conflict among the members or with the leader that is being suppressed. It is also possible that they are fearful of challenging the leader, fearing personal or group destruction. Because the condition is alcohol abuse, we could also consider that members have difficulty expressing feelings, and if they were to maintain the focus, they would have to openly speak of their feelings. Although there are several possibilities, the suggested interventions address expression of feelings because doing so could also tap the other possibilities.

***Possible Interventions***

Suggested interventions using creative activities include the activities in chapters 6 and 19 using drawing and collage with a focus on accessing and expressing feelings. The group leader may want to reflect on identifying the feelings that the majority or all group members find difficult to express, such as appreciation, happiness, anger, and fear.

## Case Vignette IV

*A conflict broke out between two male members when one accused the other of being bigoted, and the accused responded that his religion was not bigoted, the other man was "just plain wrong." The group leader, John, could tell that this topic was of immense importance to these two members as their nonverbal language seemed to signal "fight." He tried to defuse the situation and lower the intensity by intervening and using his conflict resolution skills that generally worked. However, while the men participated in the resolution process, neither budged from his initial position, and the group atmosphere remained very tense.*

*When John asked other group members about their experiences around the conflict, all reported that they had high levels of discomfort, a couple of members just wanted to agree to disagree and move on to something else, and several members reported that they wanted to leave and get away from the conflict. John felt that if he could not reduce the emotional intensity in the room, that there was a real possibility that one or more members might not return to the next session.*

*John decided to explore members' feelings and reactions around conflict, to provide an opportunity to both members in the conflict to gain insight, and to possibly reduce tension in the group. Members had many fears around conflict because they perceived it as destructive, allowed fears of danger to reemerge from their childhood experiences, and did not have expectations for positive outcomes from the conflict that was currently in the group. There were even some comments made that suggested a lack of confidence in John's ability to moderate the conflict. Members were fearful that the group would be destroyed. The more members talked, the more intense the atmosphere became on top of the already heightened intensity.*

*The conflicting group members said that they wanted the group to remain intact, and would just let the conflict go, and not try to resolve it. John knew that it was very likely that, if the conflict was suppressed, it would go underground but it would continue to negatively impact the group.*

The group leader has to intervene quickly and take charge of the group. Members are very fearful and some may even be panicking, and if the issue of conflict is not addressed it could effectively destroy the group. The group leader has the following tasks to perform, and they are listed in order of priority:

- Reduce emotional intensity so that members can leave the session able to handle their difficult feelings.
- Reduce fears that the group or individual members are in danger of being destroyed.
- Increase feelings of trust and safety in the group, and in the competence of the group leader to protect them from destruction or becoming abandoned.
- Demonstrate that there can be a constructive resolution of conflict.

Suggested interventions can begin with a breathing activity as described next.

*Exercise 23.1—Reduce Emotional Intensity*
*Materials:* None
*Procedure:*

1. The leader asks members to rate their emotional intensity at the present time using a scale of 0, little or no intensity, to 10, considerable or extreme intensity.

2. Introduce the exercise by telling members that one way to reduce emotional intensity and to become calmer is to do a breathing exercise, and that you will lead them through this.
3. Ask them to close their eyes, sit in silence for a moment, scan their body and note the tense areas such as their shoulders, and to become aware of their breathing pattern. Ask if they are breathing fast, slow, almost panting, or however their breath seems to them.
4. Tell them that once they are aware of their breathing pattern, to try and consciously make it deep and even. They may not succeed at first, but to keep trying to breathe deeply and evenly. Allow at least 5 minutes for breathing.
5. At the end of the allotted period, ask members to open their eyes and once more, to rate their emotional intensity. If the emotional intensity is 5 or higher, continue the breathing exercise until all members have less than a 5 rating.

Another activity that could be helpful is the relaxation one in chapter 17 on movement. An exercise that can also reduce intensity is one where members image taking a walk. It is essential that the emotional intensity be reduced before trying to address any of the other possible concerns.

# References

Abernathy, A. (2002). The power of metaphor for exploring cultural difference in a group. *Group*, 26(3), 219–231.

Acuff, F. (1993). *How to negotiate anything with anyone anywhere around the world*. New York: American Management Association.

*Aesop's fables*. (1993). Newmarket, England: Brimax Books.

Aimone, K. (2000). *Creative collage for crafters*. New York: Lark Books.

Alexander, C., Langer, E., Newman, R., Chandler, H., & Davis, J. (1989). Transcendental meditation, mindfulness, and longevity: An experimental study with the elderly. *Journal of Personality and Social Psychology, 57*(6), 950–964.

Alonso, A., & Rutan, J. S. (1993). Character change in group therapy. *International Journal of Group Psychotherapy, 43,* 439–451.

Alonso, A., & Rutan, J. S. (1996). Separation and individuation in the group leader. *International Journal of Group Psychotherapy, 46*, 149–162.

Alpert, P., Miller, S., Wallmann, H., Haney, R., Cross, C., Cherulia, T., Gilles, C., & Kodandapari, K. (2009). The effect of modified jazz dance on balance, cognition, and mood in older adults. *Journal of the American Academy of Nurse Practitioners, 21*(2), 108–115.

Ames, S. Patten, Werch, C., Echols, J., Schroeder, D., Stephens, S., Pennebaker, J., & Hurt, R. (2008). Expressive writing as a nicotine dependence treatment adjunct for young adult smokers. *Nicotine & Tobacco Research.*

Auttner, A., & Glueckauf, R. (1983). The facilitative effects of music on visual imagery. *Journal of Mental Imagery,* 105–120. Babani, A. (2010). Exploring peak experiences as elicited by music: A qualitative study. *Dissertation Abstracts International B., The Sciences and Engineering,* 5804.

Bales, R. (1950). *Interaction process analysis*. Reading, MA: Addison Wesley.

Bales, R. (1953). The equilibrium problem in small groups. In T. Parsons, R. Bales, & E. Shils (Eds.), *Working papers in the theory of action* (pp. 111–162). Glencoe, IL: Free Press.

Band, J. (1996). *The influence of selected music and structured vs. unstructured inductions on mental imagery* (Unpublished doctoral dissertation). University of South Carolina, Columbia.

Barnes, S., Brown, K., Krusmark, E., Campbell, W., & Rogge, R. (2007). The role of mindfulness in romantic relationship satisfactions and responses to relationship stress. *Journal of Marital and Family Therapy* , *33*(3), 482–500.

Barry, L., & Singer, G. (2001). Reducing material psychological distress after the NICU experience through journal writing. *Journal of Early Intervention, 24*, 287–297.

Batson, G. (2010). Feasibility of an intensive trial of modern dance for adults with Parkinson disease. *Complementary Health Practice Review, 15*(2), 65–83.

Batten, S., Follette, V., & Palm, K. (2002). Physical and psychological effects of written disclosure among sexual abuse survivors. *Behavior Therapy, 33*, 107–122.

Bauer, C., Victorson, D., Rosenbloom, S., Barocas, J., & Silver, R. (2010). Alleviating distress during antepartum hospitalization: A randomized controlled trial of music and recreation therapy. *Journal of Women's Health, 19*(3), 523–530.

Beck, J. (1995). *Cognitive therapy: Basics and beyond.* New York: Guilford.

Bettelheim, B. (1976). *The uses of enchantment: The meaning and importance of fairy tales.* New York: Knopf.

Bhuvaneswar, C., Stern, T., & Beresin, E. (2009). Using the technique of journal writing to learn emergency psychiatry. *Academic Psychiatry, 33*(1), 43–46.

Biechonski, J. (2005). The use of fairy tales in adult psychotherapy and hypnotherapy. In *Mental health and psychotherapy in Africa* [Original Chapter] (pp. 95–111). South Africa: UL Press of the University of Limpopo-Terfloop Campus.

Biegel, G. (2009). Mindfulness-based stress reduction for the treatment of adolescent psychiatric outpatients: A randomized clinical trial. *Journal of Consulting and Clinical Psychology, 77*(5), 855–866.

Binder, J., & Strupp, H. (1997). "Negative process": A recurrently discovered and underestimated facet of therapeutic process and outcome in the individual psychotherapy of adults. *Clinical Psychology: Science and Practice, 4*, 121–139.

Bion, W. (1961). *Experiences in groups.* New York: Basic Books.

Blake, M. (2002). Poetry therapy and infertility counseling. *Journal of Poetry Therapy, 15*(4 ).

Boisvert, C., & Faust, D. (2006). Practicing psychologists' knowledge of general psychotherapy research findings: Implications for science-practice relations. *Professional Psychology: Research and Practice, 37*, 708–715.

Boldt, S. (1996). The effects of music therapy on motivation, psychological well-being, physical comfort, and exercise endurance of bone marrow transplant patients. *Journal of Music Therapy, 33*, 164–188.

Bovend'Eerdt, T., Dawes, H., Sackley, C., Izadi, H., & Wade, D. (2009). Mental techniques during manual stretching in spasticity—A pilot randomized controlled trial. *Clinical Rehabilitation, 23*(2), 137–145.

Brandes, V., Terris, D., Fischer, C., Loerbroks, A., Jarczok, M., Marc, N., … Thayer, J. (2001). Receptive music therapy for the treatment of depression:

A proof-of-concept study and prospectus controlled clinical trial of efficacy. *Psychotherapy & Psychosomatics, 79*(5), 321–322.
Brinson, J., & Fisher, T. (1999). The Ho'oponopono groups: A conflict resolution model for school counselors. *Journal for Specialists in Group Work, 24*, 369–382.
Brown, E., & Heiniberg, R. (2001). Effects of writing about rape: Evaluating Pennebaker's paradigm with a severe trauma. *Journal of Traumatic Stress, 14*, 81–85.
Brown, J. (1964). *Flat Stanley*. New York: Harper & Row.
Brown, N. (1992). *Teaching group dynamics*. Westport, CT: Praeger.
Brown, N. (1996). *Expressive processes in group counseling*. Westport CT: Praeger.
Brown, N. (1998a). *Psychoeducational groups: Accelerated development*. Philadelphia, PA: Brunner-Routledge.
Brown, N. (1998b). *The destructive narcissistic pattern*. Westport CT: Praeger.
Brown, N. (2003a). Conceptualizing process. *International Journal of Group Psychotherapy. 53*(2), 225–243.
Brown, N. (2003b). *Psychoeducational groups: Process and practice*. New York: Brunner-Routledge.
Brown, N. (2006). Reconceptualizing difficult groups and difficult members. *Journal of Contemporary Psychotherapy, 36*(3), 145–150.
Brown, N. (2007). *Coping with infuriating, mean, critical people*. Westport, CT: Praeger.
Brown, N. (2009). *Becoming a group leader*. Upper Saddle River, NJ: Pearson Education.
Brun, B., Pedersen, E., & Runberg, M. (1993). *Symbols of the soul: Therapy and guidance through fairy tales*. London: Jessica Kingsley.
Bucci, W. (1995). The power of the narrative: A multiple code account. In J. Pennebaker (Ed.), *Emotions, disclosure and health* (pp. 93–123). Washington, DC: American Psychological Association.
Burn, H. (1987). The movement behavior of anorectics: The control issue. *American Journal of Dance Therapy, 10*, 54–76.
Burns, D. (2001). The effect of the Bonny method of guided imagery and music on the mood and life quality of cancer patients. *Journal of Music Therapy, 38*, 51–65.
Byom, T. (2010). A comparison of the effectiveness of three group treatments for weight loss. *Dissertation Abstracts International: Section B: The Sciences and Engineering*. 2070.
Cameron, L. Booth, R., Schlatter, M., Ziginskas, D., & Harman, J. (2007). Changes in emotion regulation and psychological adjustment following use of a group psy-social support program for women recently diagnosed with breast cancer. *Psycho-oncology, 16*(3), 171–180.
Campo, R. (2003) *The healing art: A doctor's black bag of poetry*. New York: Norton.
Carlson, L., Speca, M., Patel, K., & Goodey, E. (2003). Mindfulness-based stress reduction in relation to quality of life, mood, symptoms of stress, and immune parameters in breast and prostate cancer outpatients. *Psychosomatic Medicine, 65*(4), 571–581.
Carlson, L., & Garland, S. (2005). Impact of mindfulness-based stress reduction (MBSR) on sleep, mood, stress, and fatigue symptoms in cancer outpatients. *International Journal of Behavioral Medicine, 12*(4), 278–285.

Cashdan, S. (1999). *The witch must die: How fairy tales shape our lives.* New York: Basic.

Castillo-Perez, S., Gomez-Perez, V., Caliullo, M., Perez-Campos, E., & Mayoral, M. (2010). Effects of music therapy on depression compared with psychotherapy. *The Arts in Psychotherapy, 37*(5), 387–390.

Castonguay, L., Boswell, J., Constantino, M., Goldfried, M., & Hill, C. (2010). Training implications of harmful effects of psychological treatments. *American Psychologist, 65*(1), 34–49.

Castonguay, L., Schut, A., Aikins, D., Constantino, M., Laurenceau, J., Bologh, L., & Burns, D. (2004). Integrative cognitive therapy for depression: A preliminary investigation. *Journal of Psychotherapy Integration, 14*, 4–20.

Chan, K., & Horneffer, K. (2006). Emotional expression and psychological symptoms: A comparison of writing and drawing. *The Arts in Psychotherapy, 33*(1), 26–36.

Chen, M. Y., & Han. (2001). Cross-cultural group counseling with Asians, a stage specific interactive approach. *Journal for Specialists in Group Work, 25*, 369–382.

Chinen, A. (1996). Aging and adult spiritual development: A transpersonal view of the life through fairy tales. In B. W. Scotton, A. B. Chinen, & J. R. Battista (Eds.), *Textbook of transpersonal psychiatry and psychology* (pp. 155–166). New York: Basic.

Chipman, L. (2010). Expanding the frame: Self-portrait photography in dramatherapy with a young adult living with cancer. In P. Jones (Ed.), *Drama as therapy* (pp. 105–125). New York: Routledge.

Chirema, K. (2007). The use of reflective journal in the promotion of reflection and learning in post-registration nursing students. *Nurse Education Today,27*(3), 192–202.

Chretien, K., Goldman, E., & Faselis, C. (2008). The reflective writing class blog: Using technology to promote reflection and professional development. *Journal of General Internal Medicine, 23*(12), 2066–2077.

Colijn, S., Hoencamp, E., Snijders, H., Van Der Spek, M., & Duivenvoorden, H. (1991). A comparison of curative factors in different types of group psychotherapy. *International Journal of Group Psychotherapy, 41*, 365–378.

Colmant, S., & Mertya, R. (1999). Using the sweat lodge ceremony as group therapy for Javajo youth. *Journal for Specialists in Group Work, 24*, 55–73.

Compass, B., Haaga, D., Keefe, F., Leitenberg, H., & Williams, D. (1998). Sampling of empirically supported psychological treatments from health psychology: Smoking, chronic pain, cancer, and bulimia nervosa. *Journal of Consulting and Clinical Psychology, 66*, 89–112.

Conyne, R., Crowill, J., & Newmeyer, M. (2008). *Group techniques: How to use them more purposefully.* Upper Saddle River, NJ: Pearson Education.

Corey, G. (2009). *Theory and practice of counseling and psychotherapy* (8th ed.) Belmont, CA: Brooks/Cole.

Corsini, T., & Rosenberg, B. (1955). Mechanisms of group psychotherapy: Process and dynamics. *Journal of Abnormal and Social Psychology*, 51, 406–411.

Coulacoglu, C. (2000). The cross cultural and clinical values of fairy tales and the fairy tale test. *SIS Journal of Projective Psychology and Mental Health, 7*(1), 27–38.

Crawford, M., Killaspy, H., Kalaitzaki, E., Barrett, B., Byford, S., Patterson, S., … Waller, D. (2010). The MATISSE study: A randomized trial of

group art therapy for people with schizophrenia. *BMC Psychiatry, 10,* Article 65.
Crits-Christoph, P, Gibbons, M., Crits-Christoph, K., Narduci, J., Schamberger, M., & Gallop, R. (2006). Can therapists be trained to improve their alliances: A preliminary study of alliance-fostering psychotherapy. *Psychotherapy Research, 16,* 268–281.
Crits-Christopy, P., & Gibbons, M. (2002). Relational interpretations. In J. C. Norcross (Ed.), *Psychotherapy relationships that work: Therapist contributions and responsiveness to patients* (pp. 285–300). New York: Oxford University Press.
Crouch, E., Block, S., & Wanlass, J. (1994). Therapeutic factors: Interpersonal and interpersonal mechanisms. In A. Fuhriman & G. Burlingame (Eds.), *Handbook of group psychotherapy: An empirical and clinical synthesis* (pp. 269–316). New York: Wiley.
Davidson, R., Scherer, K., & Goldsmith H. (Eds.). (2003). *Handbook of affective sciences.* New York: Oxford University Press.
Deutch, M. (1949). A theory of cooperation and competition. *Human Relations, 2,* 199–231.
De Vos, G., & Altmann, A. (1999). *New tales for old: Folktales as literary fictions for young adults.* Englewood, CO: Libraries Unlimited.
Diana, N. (1998). Let me tell you a story … Using fairy tales and fables with the hard to treat client. *Journal of Poetry Therapy, 11*(3), 175–182.
Dieckmann, H. (1997). Fairy-tales in psychotherapy. *Journal of Analytical Psychology, 42*(2), 253–268.
Dies, R. R. (1997). Comments on issues raised by Slavson, Durkin, and Scheidlinger. *International Journal of Group Psychotherapy. 47.*
Dimidjian, W., & Hollon, S. (2010). How would we know if psychotherapy were harmful? *American Psychologist, 65*(1), 21–33.
Doll, K., Kereakoglow, S., Radhika, S., & Hare, J. (2008). Using students' journals about death experiences as a pedagogical tool. *Gerontology Geriatric Education, 29*(2), 124–138.
Donaghy, M., & Morss, K. (2007). An evaluation of a framework for facilitating and assessing physiotherapy students' reflection on practice. *Physiotherapy Theory and Practice, 23*(2), 83–94.
Duffy, T., Somody, C., & Clifford, S. (2005). Conversations with my father: Adapting a musical chronology and the emerging life song with older adults. *Journal of Creativity in Mental Health, 2*(4), 45–63.
Dunne, P. (2010). Narradrama with marginalized groups: Uncovering strengths, knowledges and possibilities. In E. Leveton (Ed.), *Healing collective trauma using sociodrama and drama therapy* (pp. 25–53). New York: Springer.
Edwards, R., White, M, Gray, J., & Fischbacher, C. (2001). Use of a journal club and letter writing exercise to teach critical appraisal to medical undergraduates. *Medical Education, 35*(7), 691–694.
Egan, G. (2006). *The skilled helper* (8th ed.). Pacific Grove CA: Brooks/Cole.
Ellis, A. (1997). The evolution of Albert Ellis and rational emotive behavior therapy. In J. K. Zeig (Ed.), *The evolution of psychotherapy: The third conference* (pp. 69–82). New York: Brunner/Mazel.
Ersek, M., Turner, J., Cain, K., & Kemp, C. (2009). Results of a randomized controlled trial to examine the efficacy of a chronic pain self-management group for older adults. *Pain, 138*(1), 29–40.

Esterling, B., L'Abate, L., Murray, E., & Pennebaker, J. (1999). Empirical foundations for writing in prevention and psychotherapy: Mental and physical health outcomes. *Clinical Psychology Review, 19*(1), 79–96.

Evans, S., Ferrando, S., Findler, M., Stowell, C., Smart, C., & Haglin, D. (2007). Mindfulness based cognitive therapy for generalized anxiety disorder. *Journal of Anxiety Disorders, 21*(2), 716–721.

Forsyth, D. (1999). *Group dynamics* (3rd ed.). Pacific Grove CA: Brooks/Cole.

Foulkrod, K., & Davenport, B. (2010). An examination of empirically informed practice within case reports of play therapy with aggressive and oppositional children. *International Journal of Play Therapy, 19*(3), 144–158.

Frank, A. (2004). After methods, the story: From incongruity to truth in qualitative research. *Qualitative Health Research, 14*, 430–440.

Fuhriman, A. (1997). Comments on issues raised by Slavson, Durkin and Scheidlinger. *International Journal of Group Psychotherapy, 47*, 169–174.

Fuhriman, A., & Burlingame, G. (Eds.). (1994). *Handbook of group psychotherapy: An empirical and clinical synthesis.* New York: Wiley.

Gans, J., & Alonso, A. (1998). Difficult patients: Their construction in group therapy. *International Journal of Group Psychotherapy, 48*(3), 311–326.

Gelso, C., & Hayes, J. (2007). *Countertransference and the therapist's inner experience: Perils and possibilities.* Mahwah, NJ: Erlbaum.

Gelso, C. J., Latts, M. G., Gomez, M., & Fassinger, R. (2002). Countertransference management and therapy outcomes: An initial evaluation. *Journal of Clinical Psychology, 58*, 861–867.

Gladding, S. (1999). *Group work: A counseling specialty* (4th ed.). Upper Saddle River, NJ: Merrill/Pretice Hall.

Golden, K. (1999). The therapeutic use of the fairy tale "The Buried Moon" to inspire hope in caregivers and their clients. *Journal of Poetry Therapy, 13*(2), 65–72.

Goleman, D. (2003). *Destructive emotions: How can we overcome them? A scientific dialogue with the Dalai Lama.* New York: Bantam.

Goleman, D., & Gurin, J. (Eds.). (1993). *Mind/body medicine: How to use your mind for better health.* Yonkers, NY: Consumer Reports.

Gonzalez-Rivera, M., & Bauermeister, J. (2007). Children's attitudes toward people with AIDS in Puerto Rico: Exploring stigma through drawings and stories. *Qualitative Health Research, 17*(2), 250–263.

Gooding, L. (2010). Using music therapy protocols in the treatment of premature infants: An introduction to current practices. *The Arts in Psychotherapy, 37*(3), 211–214.

Gortner, E., Rude, S., & Pennebaker, J. (2006). Benefits of expressive writing in lowering rumination and depressive symptoms. *Behavior Therapy, 37*(3), 292–303.

Greenhalgh, T., & Taylor, R. (1997). How to read a paper: Papers that go beyond numbers (Qualitative research). *British Medical Journal, 315*, 740–743.

Guillermein, M. (2004). Understanding illness: Using drawings as a research method. *Qualitative Health Research, 14*(2), 272–289.

Hackney, M., & Earhart, G. (2010). Recommendations for implementing tango classes for persons with Parkinson disease. *American Journal of Dance Therapy, 32*(1), 41–52.

Hafen, B., Karren, K., Frandsen, J., & Smith, N. (1996). *Mind/Body health.* New York: Guilford.

Haley-Banez, L., & Walden, S. (1999). Diversity in group work: Using optimal theory to understand group process and dynamics. *Journal of Specialists in Group Work*, 24, 405–522.

Haley-Banez, L., Brown, S., & Molina, B. (1999). Principles for diversity-competent group workers. *Journal for Specialists in Group Work, 24*, 7–14.

Hanson, K., & Alexander, S. (2010). The influence of technology on reflective learning in dental hygiene education. *Journal of Dental Education, 74*(6), 644–653.

Hardcastle, S., Taylor, A., Bailey, M., & Castle, R. (2008). A randomized controlled trial on the effectiveness of a primary health care based counseling intervention on physical activity, diet, and CHD risk. *Patient Education and Counseling, 70*(1), 31–39.

Haugh, M. (1996). How to incorporate and evaluate writing skills in animal science and dairy science courses. *Journal of Animal Science, 74*(11), 2835–2842.

Hays, S., Strosahl, K., & Wilson, K. (1999). *Acceptance and commitment therapy: An experiential approach to behavior change*. New York: Guilford Press.

Hays, T. (2005). Well-being in later life through music. *Australasian Journal of Aging, 24,* 28–32.

Hays, T., & Minichiello, V. (2005). The meaning of music in the lives of older people: A qualitative study. *Psychology of Music, 33,* 437–551.

Hazlett, S. (2010) Attunement, disruption and repair: The dance of self and other in emotionally focused couple therapy. In A. Gurman (Ed.), *Clinical casebook of couple therapy* (pp. 21–43). New York: Guilford.

Henderson, M., Scott, S., & Hotoph, M. (2007). Use of the clock drawing test in a hospice population. *Palliative Medicine, 21,* 559–565.

Hodas, G. (1994). Reversing narratives of failure through music and verse in therapy. *The Family Journal: Counseling and Therapy for Couples and Families, 2,* 199–207.

Hoff, B. (1982). *The Tao of Pooh*. New York: Penguin Books.

Hohr, H. (2000). Dynamic aspects of fairy tales: Social and emotional competence through fairy tales. *Scandinavia Psychoanalytic Review, 10*(1), 51–77.

Holton, C. (1995). Once upon a time served: Therapeutic application of fairy tales within a correctional environment. *International Journal of Offender Therapy and Comparative Criminology. 39*(3), 210–221.

Hopperstad, M. (2008). How children make meaning through drawing and play. *Visual Communication, 7,* 77–96.

Horvath, A., & Bedi, R. (2001). The alliance. In J. Norcross (Ed.), *Psychotherapy relationships that work: Therapist contributions and responsiveness to patients* (pp. 37–70). New York: Oxford University Press.

Horwitz, L. (2000). Narcissistic leadership in psychotherapy groups. *International Journal of Group Psychotherapy, 50*(2), 219–235.

Horwitz, B., Kowalski, J., & Anderberg, A. (2010). Theatre for, by and with fibromyalgia patients—Evaluation of emotional expression using video interpretation. *The Arts in Psychotherapy, 37*(1), 13–19.

Hugill, N., Fink, B., Neave, N., & Seydel, H. (2009). Men's physical strength is associated with women's perceptions of their dancing ability. *Personality and Individual Differences, 47*(5), 527–530.

Hunter, B., Bryan, C., Oliva, R., Sahler, O., Gaisser, E., Salipanto, D., & Arezina, C. (2010). Music therapy as an adjunctive treatment in the man-

agement of stress for patients being weaned from mechanical ventilation. *Journal of Music Therapy, 47*(3), 198–219.
Jacobs, E., Masson, R., & Harvill, R. (2009). *Group counseling* (6th ed.). Pacific Grove, CA: Brooks/Cole.
Johnson, D. (2003). *Reaching out* (8th ed.). Boston, MA: Allyn & Bacon.
Johnson, D., & Johnson, F. (2006). *Joining together* (8th ed.). Boston, MA: Allyn & Bacon.
Kabat-Zinn, J., Lipworth, L., & Burney, R. (1985). The clinical use of mindfulness meditation for the self-regulation of chronic pain. *Journal of Behavioral Medicine, 8*(2), 163–190.
Kabat-Zinn, J., Massion, A., Kristeller, J. Peterson, L., Fletcher, K., Lenderking, W., & Santorelli, L. (1992). Effectiveness of a meditation-based stress reduction program in the treatment of anxiety disorders. *American Journal of Psychiatry, 149*, 936–943.
Kabat-Zinn, J., Wheeler, E., Light, T., Skillings, A., Scharf, M., Cropley, T., … Hosmer, D. (1998). Influence of a mindfulness meditation-based stress reduction intervention on rates of skin clearing in patients with moderate to severe psoriasis undergoing phototherapy (UVB) and photochemotherapy (PUVA). *Psychosomatic Medicine, 60*(5), 625–632.
Karnezi, H., & Tierney, K. (2007). A novel intervention to address fears in children with Asperger syndrome: A pilot study of the cognitive behavior drama (CBD) model. *Behavior Changes, 26*(4), 271–282.
Kernberg, O. (1976). *Object relations theory and clinical psychoanalysis*. New York: Jason Aronson.
Kim, B., Omizo, M., & D'andrea, M. (1998). The effects of culturally constant group counseling on the self-esteem and internal locus of control orientation among Native American adolescents. *Journal for Specialists in Group Work, 23*, 145–163.
Kingston, T., Dooley, B., Bates, A., Lawlor, E., & Malone, K. (2007). Mindfulness based cognitive therapy for residual depressive symptoms. *Psychology and Psychotherapy , 80*, 193–203.
Kivlighan, D., Jr., Coleman, M., & Anderson, D. (2000). Process, outcome and methodology in group counseling research. In S. D. Brown & R. W. Lent (Eds.), *Handbook of counseling psychology* (3rd ed., pp. 767–796). New York: Wiley.
Kivlighan, D., Jr., & Goldfine, D. C. (1991). Endorsement of therapeutic factors as a function of group development and participant interpersonal attitudes. *Journal of Counseling Psychology, 38*, 150–158.
Kivlighan, D., Jr., & Holmes, S. (2004). The importance of therapeutic factors. In J. DeLucia-Waack, D. Gerrity, C. Kalodner, & M. Rina, (Eds.), *Handbook of group counseling and psychotherapy* (pp. 46–61). Thousand Oaks CA: Sage.
Kivlighan, D., Jr., & Mulligan (1988). Participant's perception of therapeutic factors in group counseling. The role of interpersonal style and stage of group development. *Small Group Behavior, 19*, 452–468.
Klein, M. (1952). The origins of transference. In R. E. Money-Kyrle (Ed.), *Envy and gratitude and other works 1946–1963* (pp. 48–56). New York: Delta.
Kociatkiewicz, J., & Kostera, M. (1999). The anthropology of empty spaces. *Qualitative Sociology, 22*, 37–50.

Kohut, H. (1977). *The restoration of the self.* Madison, CT: International Universities Press.

Koopman, C., Ismailji, T., Holmes, D., Classen, C., Palesh, O., & Wales, T. (2005). The effects of expressive writing on pain, depression, and posttraumatic stress disorder symptoms in survivors of intimate partner violence. *Journal of Health Psychology, 10,* 211–221.

Kunic, M., Veazey, C., Cully, J., Souchek, J., Graham, D., Hopko, D., … Stanley, M. (2008). COPD education and cognitive behavioral group treatment for clinically significant symptoms of depression and anxiety in COPD patients: A randomized controlled trial. *Psychological Medicine: A Journal of Research in Psychiatry and the Allied Sciences, 38*(3), 385–396.

Kutz, I., Borysenko, J., & Benson, H. (1985). Meditation and psychotherapy: A rationale for the integration of dynamic psychotherapy, the relaxation response, and mindfulness meditation. *American Journal of Psychiatry, 142*(1), 1–8.

Langdon, S., & Petracca, G. (2010). Tiny dancer: Body image and dancer identity in female modern dancers. *Body Image, 7*(4), 360–363.

Lazarus, R., & Folkman, S. (1984). *Stress, appraisal and coping.* New York: Springer.

Lazarus, A. (1989). *The practice of multimodal therapy.* Baltimore MD: John Hopkins University Press.

Lepore, S., & Smyth, J. (Eds.). (2002). *The writing cure.* Washington, DC: American Psychological Association.

Lev-Wiesel, R., & Liraz, R. (2007). Drawings vs. narratives: Drawing as a tool to encourage verbalization in children whose fathers are drug abusers. *Clinical Child Psychology and Psychiatry, 12,* 65–75.

Lewin, K. (1944). Dynamics of group action. *Educational Leadership, 1*(4), 195–200.

Lewin, K. (1951). *Field theory in social science.* New York: Harper.

Lewin, K., Lippitt, R., & White, R. (1939). Conduct, knowledge, and acceptance of new values. *Journal of Social Psychology, 10,* 271–299.

Lilienfeld, S. (2007). Psychological treatments that cause harm. *Perspectives on Psychological Science, 2,* 53–70.

Lima, M., & Vieira, A. (2007). Ballroom dancing as therapy for the elderly in Brazil. *American Journal of Dance Therapy, 29*(2), 129–142.

Linenhan, M. (1993). *Cognitive–behavioral therapy for borderline personality disorder.* New York: Guilford.

Luck, G., Saarikallio, S., Burger, B., Thompson, M., & Toiviainen, P. (2010), Effects of the Big Five and musical genre on music-induced movement. *Journal of Research in Personality, 44*(6), 714–720. doi: 10.1016/j.jrp.2010.10.001

Lumley, M., Tojek, T., & Macklem, D. (2002) The effects of written emotional disclosure among repressive and alexithymic people. In S. J. Lepore & J. Smyth (Eds.), *The writing cure: How expressive writing promotes health and emotional well-being* (pp. 119–134). Washington, DC: American Psychological Association.

MacKenzie, K. (1990). *Introduction to time-limited group therapy.* Washington, DC: American Psychiatric Press.

MacKenzie, K. R. (1997). *Time-managed group psychotherapy.* Washington, DC: American Psychiatric Press.

MacNair-Semands, R. R., & Lese, K. P. (2000) Interpersonal problems and the perception of therapeutic factors in group therapy. *Small Group Research, 31,* 158–174.

Madson, A., & Silverman, M. (2010). The effect of music therapy on relaxation, anxiety, pain perception & nausea in adult solid organ transplant patients. *Journal of Music Therapy, 47,* 220–232.

Mahler, M. (1975). On the current status of the infantile neurosis. *Journal of the American Psychoanalytic Association, 23*(2), 327–333.

Mahler, M., Pine, F., & Bergman, A. (1975). *The psychological birth of the human infant.* New York: Basic.

Marra, T. (2004). *Depressed and anxious: A dialectical behavior therapy workbook for overcoming depression and anxiety.* Oakland, CA: New Harbinger.

Marra, T. (2005). *Dialectical behavioral therapy in private practice.* Oakland CA: New Harbinger.

Marrow, A. (1969). *The practical theorist: The life and work of Kurt Lewin.* New York: Basic.

Martin, D., Garske, J., & Davis, M. (2000). Relation of the therapeutic alliance with outcome and other variables: A meta-analytic review. *Journal of Consulting and Clinical Psychology, 68,* 438–450.

McFerran, K., Melina, R., & O'Grady, L. (2010). Music therapy with bereaved teenagers: A mixed method perspective. *Death Studies, 34*(6), 541–565.

McKinney, C. (1990). The effect of music on imagery. *Journal of Music Therapy, 27,* 34–46.

McKinney, C., & Tims, F. (1995). Differential effects of selected classical music on the imagery of high versus low imagers: Two studies. *Journal of Music Therapy, 32,* 22–45.

Meichenbaum, D. (1977). *Cognitive-behavior modification: An integrative approach.* New York: Plenum.

Mensch, J., & Ennis, C. (2002). Pedagogic strategies perceived to enhance student learning in athletic training education. *Journal of Athletic Training, 37*(4), S199–S207.

Meyer, K. (2010). Drama therapy with adolescents living with HIV: Story making drama and body mapping. In P. Jones (Ed.), *Drama as therapy V2: Clinical work and research into practice* (pp. 126–151). New York: Routledge.

Moreland, R., & Levine, J. (1988). Group dynamics over time: Development and socialization in small groups. In J. McGrath (Ed.), *The social psychology of time* (pp. 151–181). Newbury Park, CA: Sage.

Moreno, J. L. (1964). *Psychodrama.* Vol. 1. Beacon, NY: Beacon.

Morris, C., & Moore, E. (2009). An evaluation of group work as an intervention to reduce the impact of substance misuse for offender patients in a high security hospital. *Journal of Forensic Psychiatric & Psychology, 20*(4), 559–576.

Newcomb, T. (1963). Stabilities underlying changes in interpersonal attraction. *Journal of Abnormal and Social Psychology. 66,* 376–386.

Niemier, J., Cifu, D., & Kishore, T. (2001). The lighthouse strategy: Improving the functional status of patients with unilateral neglect after stroke and brain injury using a visual imagery intervention. *Topics in Stroke Rehabilitation, 8*(2), 10–18.

Nowicka-Sauer, K. (2007). Patients' perspective: Lupus in patients' drawings. *Clinical Rheumatology, 26,* 523–1525.

Oatley, K., & Djikuc, M. (2008). Writing as thinking. *Review of General Psychology,12*(1), 9–27.
Ohnmeiss, D., Vanharanta, H., & Elkholm, J. (1999). Relationship of pain drawings to invasive tests assessing intervertebral disc pathology. *European Spine Journal, 8,* 126–131.
Ohnmeiss, D., Vanharanta, H., Estlander, A., & Jamsen, A. (2000). The relationship of disability (OSWESTRY) and pain drawings to functional testing. *European Spine Journal, 9,* 208–212.
Oon, P. (2010). Playing with Gladys: A case study integrating drama therapy in behavioral interventions for the treatment of selective mutism. *Clinical Child Psychology and Psychiatry, 15*(2), 215–230.
Park, C., & Blumberg, C. (2002). Disclosing trauma through writing: Testing the meaning making hypothesis. *Cognitive Therapy and Research, 26,* 597–616.
Payne, H. (2009). Pilot study to evaluate dance movement psychotherapy in patients with medically unexplained symptoms. *Journal of Body, Movement and Dance in Psychotherapy, 4*(2), 77–94.
Pennebaker, J. W. (1997a). *Opening up: The healing power of expressing emotion.* New York: Guilford.
Pennebaker, J. W. (1997b). Writing about emotional experiences as a therapeutic process. *Psychological Science, 8*, 162–166.
Pennebaker, J. (1999). Psychological factors influencing the reporting of physical symptoms. In A. A. Stone, J. S. Turkan, C. A. Bachrach, J. B. Jobe, H. S. Kurtzman, & V. S. Cain ( Eds.), *the science of self-report; Implications for research and practice* (pp. 299–316). Mahwah NJ: Erlbaum.
Periman, L., Cohen, J., Altiere, M., Brennan, J., Brown, S., Mainka, J., & Diroff, C. (2010). A multidimensional wellness group therapy program for veterans with comorbid psychiatric and medical conditions. *Professional Psychology: Research and Practice, 41*(2), 120–127.
Pizarro, J. (2004). The efficacy of art and writing therapy: Increasing positive mental health outcomes and participant retention after exposure to traumatic experience. *Art Therapy, 21*,5–12.
Posthuma, B. (2002). *Small groups in counseling and therapy.* Boston, MA: Allyn & Bacon.
Prouix, K. (2008). Experiences of women with bulimia nervosa in a mindfulness based eating disorder treatment group. *Eating Disorders, 16*(1), 52–72.
Reich, W. (1972). *Character analysis.* New York: Simon & Schuster. (Original work published 1945)
Reisman, A. Hansen, H., & Rastegas, A. (2006). The craft of writing: A physician-writer's workshop for resident physicians. *Journal of General Internal Medicine, 21*(10), 1109–1111.
Richards, J., Beal, W., Seagal, J., & Pennebaker, J. (2000). The effects of disclosure of traumatic events on illness behavior among psychiatric prison inmates. *Journal of Abnormal Psychology, 109*, 156–160.
Robinson, M. (2000). Writing well health & the power to make images. *Journal of Medical Ethics: Medical Humanities, 26*, 79–84.
Rogers, C. (1951). *Client-centered therapy.* Boston, MA: Houghton Mifflin.
Rogers, C. (1970). *On encounter groups.* New York: Harper & Row.
Rutan, S., & Stone, W. (2001). *Psychodynamic group psychotherapy* (3rd ed.). New York: Guilford.

Sabo, C., & Michael, S. (1996). The influence of personal message with music on anxiety reduction with university students. *Cancer Nursing, 19*, 283–289.

Saltzman, A. (2008). Mindfulness-based stress reduction for school age children. In *Acceptance and mindfulness treatments for children and adolescents: A practitioner's guide* (pp. 139–161). Oakland CA: New Harbinger.

Santiago-Rivera, A., Arrendondo, P., & Gallardo-Cooper, M. (2002). *Counseling Latinos and la familia: A practical guide.* Thousand Oaks, CA: Sage.

Schapiro, R., & Katz, C. (1978). Fairy tales, splitting and ego development. C*ontemporary Psychoanalysis*. 14. 591–602.

Schut, A., Castonguay, L., Flanagan, K., Yamasaki, A., Barber, J., Bedics, J., & Smith, T. (2005). Therapist interpretation, patient-therapist interpersonal process and outcome in psychodynamic psychotherapy for avoidant personality disorder. *Psychotherapy: Theory, Research, Practice, Training, 42*, 494–511.

Segal, Z., Williams, J., & Teasdale, J. (2002). *Mindfulness-based cognitive therapy for depression: A new approach to preventing relapse.* New York: Guilford.

Shapiro, J. (1978). *Methods of group psychotherapy and encounter: A tradition of innovation.* Itasca, IL: F. E. Peacock.

Shapiro, J. (2004). Commentary: Can poetry be data? Potential relationships between poetry and research. *Families, Systems & Health, 22*(2), 171–177.

Shapiro, S., Bootzin, R., Figueredo, A., Lopez, A., & Schwarta, G. (2003). The efficacy of mindfulness-based stress reduction in the treatment of sleep disturbance in women with breast cancer: An exploratory study. *Journal of Psychosomatic Research, 54*(1), 85–91.

Sharkey, L., Overmann, J., & Flash, P. (2007). Evolution of a course in veterinary clinical pathology: The application of case-based writing assignments to focus on skill development and facilitation of learning. *Journal of Veterinary Medical Education, 34*(4), 423–430.

Shaw, M. (1964). Communication networks. In L. Berkowitz (Ed.), *Advances in experimental social psychology* (Vol. 1, pp. 111–147). New York: Academic Press.

Shee, T. (1976). Primordial structures of feminine maturation as reflected in fairy tales: Contributions to the anthropology of sexuality. *Journal of Clinical Psychology Psychotherapy, 24*(1), 28–42. (In German)

Sherif, M. (1936). *The psychology of group norms.* New York: Harper.

Sherman, K., Heard, G., & Cavanagh, K. (2010). Psychological effects and mediators of a group multi-component program for breast cancer survivors. *Journal of Behavioral Medicine, 33*(5), 378–391.

Silverman, M. (2010). Applying levels of evidence to the psychiatric literature base. *The Arts in Psychotherapy, 37*(1), 1–7.

Singer, T., & Fehr, E. (2005). The neuroeconomics of mindreading and empathy. *American Economic Review, 95*(2), 340–345.

Sloan, D. M., Marx, B. P., & Epstein, E. M. (2005). Further examination of the exposure model underlying the efficacy of written emotional disclosure. *Journal of Consulting and Clinical Psychology, 72*, 165–175.

Smyth, J. (1998). Written emotional expression: Effect sizes, outcome types, and moderating variables. *Journal of Consulting and Clinical Psychology*, 174–184.

Smyth, J., Stone, A., Hurewitz, A., & Kaeli, A. (1999). Effects of writing about stressful experiences on symptom reduction in patients with asthma and rheumatoid arthritis. *Journal of the American Medical Association, 281*, 1304–1309.

Speca, M., Carlson, L., Goodey, E., & Angen, M. (2000). A randomized, wait-list controlled clinical trial: The effect of a mindfulness meditation-based stress reduction program on mood and symptoms of stress in cancer outpatients. *Psychosomatic Medicine, 62*(5), 613–622.

Spera, S., Buhrfiend, E., & Pennebaker, J. (1994). Expressive writing and coping with job loss. *Academy of Management Journal, 37*, 722–733.

Spiegel, D. (1999). Healing words: Emotional expression and disease outcome. *Journal of the American Medical Association*,1328 –1329.

Spierings, J. (2004). *Multicultural EMDR*. Hamden CT: EMDR Humantarian Assistance Programs.

Stevens-Guille, M., & Baersma, F. (1992). Fairy tales as a trance experience: Possible therapeutic uses. *American Journal of Clinical Hypnosis, 34*(4), 245–254.

Sue, D., & Sue, D. ( 2003). *Counseling the culturally different: Theory and practice* (4th ed.). New York: Wiley.

Swami, V., & Tonee, M. (2009). A comparison of actual weight discrepancy, body appreciation and media influences between street dancers and non-dancers. *Body Image, 6*(4), 304–307.

Sweig, T. (2000). Women healing women: Time-limited, psychoeducational group therapy for childhood sexual abuse survivors. *Art Therapy, 17*, 255–264.

Teasdale, J., Segal, Z., Williams, J., Ridgeway, V., Soulsby, J., & Lau, M. (2000). Prevention of relapse/recurrence in major depression by mindfulness-based cognitive therapy. *Journal of Consulting and Clinical Psychology, 68*, 615–623.

Teibel, D., Greenson, J., Brainard, G., & Rosenzweig, S. (2001). Mindfulness stress reduction and health-related quality of life in a heterogeneous patient population. *General Hospital Psychiatry, 23*(4), 183–192.

Thant, M., & Abiru, M. (2010) Rhymthic auditory stimulation in rehavilitation of movement disorders: A review of current research. *Music Perception, 27*(4), 263–269.

Thibaut, J., & Kelley, H. (1959). *The social psychology of groups*. New York: Wiley.

Torres-Rivera, E., Wilbur, M., Roberts-Wilbur, J., & Phan L. (1999). Group work with Latino clients.: A psychoeducational model. *Journal for Specialists in Group Work, 24*, 383–404.

Trotzer, J. (2011). Personhood of the leader. In R. K. Conyne (Ed.), *The Oxford handbook of group counseling* (pp. 287–306). New York: Oxford University Press.

Tschusckke, V., & Dies, R. (1994). Intensive analysis of therapeutic factors and outcome in long-term inpatient groups. *International Journal of Group Psychotherapy, 44*, 185–208.

Tuckman, B. (1965) Developmental sequence in small groups. *Psychological Bulletin*, *63*, 384–399.

Ullrich, P., & Lutgendorf, S. (2002) Journaling about stressful events: Effects of cognitive processing and emotional expression. *Annals Behavioral Medicine,24*, 244–250.

Veenstra, E. (2010). Improvisational theatre and psychotherapy: A new model. *Dissertation Abstracts International Section B: The Sciences and Engineering*, 7867.

Ventres, W., & Frankel, R. (1996). Ethnography: A stepwise approach for primary care researchers. *Family Medicine, 28*, 52–56.

Verghese, A. (2001) The physician as storyteller. *Annuals of Internal Medicine, 135*, 1012–1017.

Wald, H., Reis, S., Monroe, A., & Borkan, J. (2010). The loss of my elderly patient: Interactive reflective writing to support medical students' rites of passage. *Medical Teaching, 32*(4), e178–e184.

Walker, B., Nail, L., & Croyle, R. (1999). Does emotional expression make a difference in reactions to breast cancer. *Oncology Nursing Journal* , 1025–1032.

Wampold, B. (2006). The psychotherapist. In J. Norcross, L. Beulter, & R. Levant (Eds.), *Evidence-based practices in mental health: Debate and dialogues on fundamental questions* (pp. 200–208). Washington, DC: American Psychological Association.

Weber, R. (2006). *Principles of group psychotherapy.* New York: American Group Psychotherapy Association.

Wengrower, H. (2010). The dance of discovery: Research and innovation in dance/movement therapy. *Body, Movement and Dance in Psychotherapy, 5*(2), 203–205.

Whitaker, L. (1992) Healing the mother/daughter relationship through the therapeutic use of fairy tales, poetry and stories. *Journal of Poetry Therapy, 6*(1), 35–44.

Williams, P., Balabagno, A., Manahan, L., Piamjariyakul, U., Ranallo, L., Laurente, C., … Williams, A. (2010). Symptom monitoring and self-care practices among Filipino cancer patients. *Cancer Nursing, 33*(1), 37–46.

Xia, J., & Tessa, J. (2009). Dance therapy for people with schizophrenia. *Schizophrenia Bulletin, 35*(4), 675–676.

Yalom, I. (1995). *The theory and practice of group psychotherapy* (4th ed.). New York: Basic Books.

Yalom, I., & Leszcz. M. (2005). *The theory and practice of group psychotherapy* (5th ed.). New York: Basic. Books.

Zander, A. (1996). *Motives and goals in groups.* New Brunswick, NJ: Transaction. (Original work published 1971)

Zed, L. (2003). Helpful symbols in fairy tales: A storytelling group employing ancient wisdom to treat depression at midlife. *Dissertation Abstracts International: Section B: The Sciences and Engineering, 64*(6-B), 2949.